ONE HUNDRED YEARS
OF
MOTORCYCLES

Editorial consultant MASSIMO CLARKE

ONE HUNDRED YEARS OF MOTORCYCLES

DARIO AGRATI • CARLO CANZANO • MARIO COLOMBO • ERNST LEVERKUS •
GIOVANNI LURASCHI • ROBERTO PATRIGNANI • CARLO PERELLI •
FABRIZIO PIGNACCA • CLAUDIO PORROZZI • VIC WILLOUGHBY

PORTLAND HOUSE
NEW YORK

Copyright © 1986   Arnoldo Mondadori Editore S.p.A., Milan
English translation copyright © 1988   Arnoldo Mondadori Editore S.p.A., Milan

Translated by   Valerie Palmer
Produced by   ERVIN s.r.l., Rome
under the supervision of   ADRIANO ZANNINO
Editorial Assistant   SERENELLA GENOESE ZERBI
Editors   Maria Luisa Ficarra – Loredana Carossino
Production   Bruno Bazzoni

This 1988 edition published by Portland House, division of dilithium Press, Ltd., distributed by Crown Publishers, Inc., 225 Park Avenue South, New York 10003.

Contributors

Dario Agrati
journalist
Enduro – Six Days Trial – Motocross – Trials

Carlo Canzano
motorcycling correspondent, *La Gazzetta dello Sport*
New formulae and new champions

Massimo Clarke
journalist and technical writer
British engines between the wars – Postwar high-powered four-stroke engines – Italian engines of the fifties – Two-stroke horizontal cylinder engines of the sixties – Two classic British engines – European twin cylinders of the seventies – The development of two-stroke engines – Valve gear – The development of Japanese engines – Entries on French and Belgian manufacturers

Mario Colombo
journalist
The great recovery

Ernst Leverkus
journalist and contributor to periodicals in Germany and Switzerland; was for many years editor of *Das Motorrad*
Entries on German, Austrian, Swiss and Czech manufacturers

Giovanni Luraschi
historian
Origins

Roberto Patrignani
journalist and head of PR and publicity department, Agrati Garelli
Racing in the postwar years

Carlo Perelli
managing editor, *Motociclismo*
Entries on Italian, Spanish, American, Russian, Danish and Swedish manufacturers – Scooters

Fabrizio Pignacca
journalist and writer
From the first competitions to 1940

Claudio Porrozzi
editor, *La Moto*
Entries on Japanese manufacturers

Vic Willoughby
writer and journalist
Entries on British manufacturers

Colour illustrations

Nicola Arolse	24, 31, 33, 48, 78, 79
BMW	24, 41, 75
Honda	108
Kromos	11, 13, 14, 15, 28, 30, 34, 35, 36, 37, 38, 39, 40, 42, 43, 45, 51, 53, 55, 56, 63, 65, 66, 67, 69, 70, 73, 74, 76, 78, 82, 83, 84, 85, 86, 87, 88, 89, 90, 91, 92, 93, 94, 95, 96, 97, 98, 99, 100, 101, 102, 103, 104, 105, 106, 107, 108, 109, 110, 110, 111, 112, 113, 114, 115
Pierluigi Pinto	10, 17, 18, 19, 20, 21, 23, 25, 27, 29, 33, 57, 59, 60, 61, 63, 65, 69, 71, 72, 73, 77
Suzuki	79

Black and white drawings

DKW	99
Cavara	94, 95, 105
Daniela D'Alia, Valeria Matricardi	11, 12, 14, 16, 43, 49, 50, 53, 79
EMAP.	54, 85, 86, 94, 96, 98, 99
NSU	87, 88, 89
Roberto Rubini	15, 49, 50, 53, 59, 93
Zündapp	54

h g f e d c b a

ISBN 0-517-64757-5

Printed and bound in Italy by Arnoldo Mondadori Editore S.p.A., Verona

CONTENTS

Love it or loathe it, the motorcycle is the child of our century. Is it elegant, dynamic, versatile, magnificent? Dangerous, noisy, aggressive? Would you make sacrifices for this indispensable charger? Or do you think the world would be a far better place if it had never been invented? Hundreds of thousands of pages have been written in support of one or other viewpoint. Hardly a day goes by without the media exposing the motorcycle's good or bad points: the doctor who saved a mother and newborn baby, isolated by a landslide, by travelling to them on a trail bike; the bike-mounted thief who mugged a tourist or robbed a pensioner. It all goes to show that this very useful vehicle is also highly controversial. Something that is much loved often arouses antipathy and hatred too; this is the price of fame and familiarity.

Certainly, anyone watching the strange vehicle called a "velocipede" rattling its way along the road a hundred years ago could scarcely have imagined the popularity such a machine would later achieve. First with a wooden frame, then almost like a bicycle, then further removed from the velocipede with characteristics of its own – until each acquired an individual style.

What a far cry the modern motorcycle is from its hundred-year-old ancestors – and not just technically or in terms of reliability. Some people might still favour the authorities' decree in those early days that motorcyclists must be preceded by a man on foot, waving a red flag. But apart from the difficulty of finding anyone to do the job nowadays, modern traffic could never permit such a thing.

Psychoanalysts have gone to great lengths to explain the significance of the motorcyclist's dress and riding style by attributing it to the instinct to dominate, to repressed desires and such like. But motorcyclists are not interested in pseudoscientific speculation. What matters to them is the sheer practicality and freedom that only a two-wheeled motorized vehicle can give.

To move around easily in the chaotic traffic of our cities, now choked by millions of vehicles; to visit places off the beaten track safely, economically and with the glorious sensation of being immersed in the surrounding landscape – a motorbike makes all this possible. And there are certainly enough models to choose from, even if the majority are "multipurpose." It is simply a matter of deciding what you want, much as you would choose a friend. You may prefer a lively and aggressive motorbike or one that's calm and reassuring; flirtatious, elegant, loud; sober, traditional, straightforward. You may want an affectionate, understanding companion, or a more demanding one who will not easily forgive any lack of attention on your part.

The motorcycle can be all these and more, but will in any case always be at your command, faithful and reliable, if you will only treat it with the respect it deserves.

Avv. Francesco Zerbi
President, Italian Motorcycling Federation

ONE HUNDRED YEARS OF PROGRESS

ORIGINS

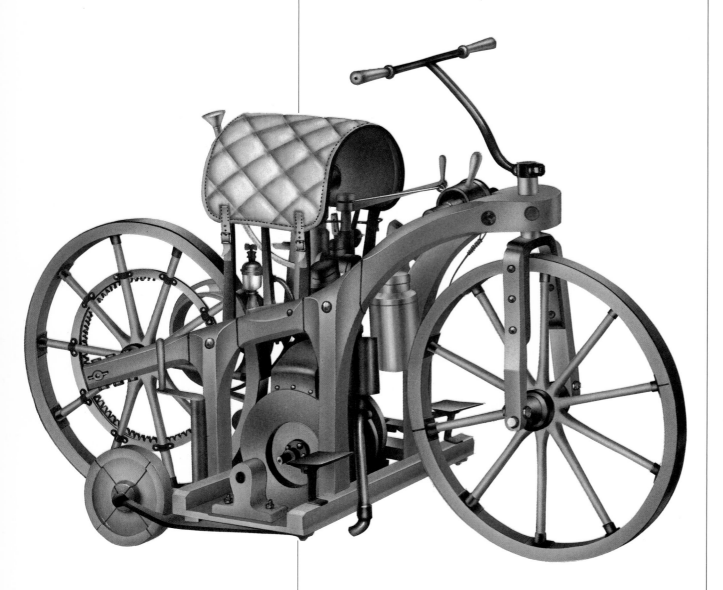

Gottlieb Daimler's "motorcycle," nicknamed boneshaker because of its total lack of suspension, served as a means of testing the 0.5 HP, 600 rpm engine which Daimler had developed in conjunction with Wilhelm Maybach.

The German Gottlieb Daimler is the official father of the motorcycle, because in 1885 he fitted a petrol-fuelled internal combustion engine to a two-wheeled vehicle entirely built of wood, to which he had added two lateral balancing wheels. The motorcycle was thus a hundred years old in 1985, but if you define a motorcycle as any vehicle with two wheels in line and a non-animal propulsion system, then the true father of this vehicle was the French engineer Perreaux. He patented the application of a steam engine of his own design to a Michaux bicycle in 1868. This vehicle at one time belonged to pioneer Grandseigne, and is still to be seen in perfect condition in a French museum.

Perreaux was in fact convinced that individual steam locomotion had a great future and wrote several very interesting pamphlets on the subject, whereas Daimler had no intention of producing a two-wheeled motorized vehicle. He merely wanted a means of road testing his engine, which was designed for an automobile, as he believed that the future lay not with two-wheeled but with three- and four-wheeled vehicles.

Thus it was in 1868 and then in 1885, that the seed was sown which was to yield such a harvest of two-wheeled vehicles, capable of offering independence and providing an alternative to collective transport.

The Daimler engine of 1885 was an improved version of an earlier model: it was an air-cooled vertical single cylinder (the air was forced upward along the body of the cylinder, which had no finning) with a displacement of

In 1869 the French engineer Perreaux fitted a steam engine to this velocipede by Michaux, which had two pedals on the front wheel.

Lucius Copeland's bicycle. The rear wheel had a much larger diameter than the front one, and it was driven by a single cylinder steam engine.

The German Hildebrand & Wolfmüller of 1894. The engine had two horizontal cylinders placed side by side along the cradle frame.

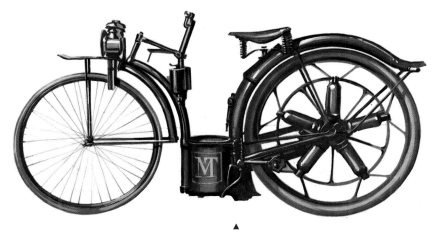

The Werner of 1898 had a 232 cc four-stroke engine fitted above the front wheel.

In 1893 the Frenchman Millet made a bicycle with a five cylinder radial engine fitted inside the rear wheel.

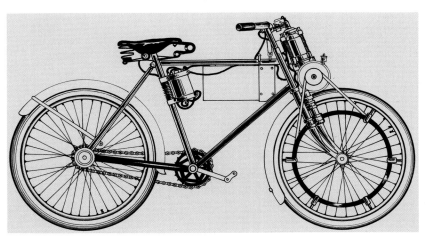

264cc, a power of 0.5 HP and a rotational speed of 600 rpm. It had surface carburetor fuel feed, ignition by incandescence, an automatic inlet valve (i.e. the valve was opened by the depression formed in the cylinder during the induction stroke) and mechanically controlled exhaust.

Compared with the engine – a superb piece of engineering – the wooden structure to which it was fitted was extremely crude, supporting the theory that it was designed only to test the efficiency of the engine. We should perhaps add that the Daimler vehicles on display in German museums are not the originals, which were unfortunately destroyed at the beginning of the twentieth century: they were reconstructed using existing parts and reproducing others from Daimler's original designs.

The British attribute the invention of the motorcycle to Edward Butler, who in 1884 took out a patent for a petrol-engined tricycle which was not in fact built until 1887, after Daimler's machine. Butler's engine was a

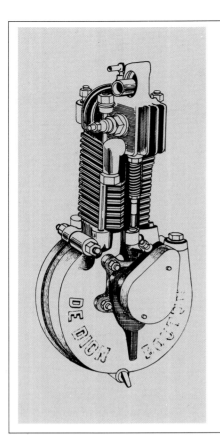

DeDion-Bouton

This De Dion-Bouton tricycle of 1895 with a 138 cc single cylinder engine, developed 0.5 HP at 1,800 rpm. The cylinder block was made of aluminum, while the cylinder head and cylinder itself were of cast iron. The inlet valve was automatic, while the exhaust valve was operated by a cam. It had electric ignition. Thanks to continual improvements, the power developed by this engine was greatly increased within the following few years.

1037 cc two-stroke twin-cylinder, with a rotary valve mechanism (which is not therefore a modern invention, as many people believe), electric spark ignition and water cooling. We should perhaps mention that the number of wheels was irrelevant to the classification of motor vehicles until the beginning of this century: a quadricycle could be either a motorcycle or an automobile, depending on the intention of its builder.

In 1938 it was claimed that the motorcycle had been invented by an Italian called Giuseppe Murnigotti, who in 1879 had written a paper on "two- and three-wheeled vehicles with gas engines." Murnigotti's vehicle was never built but had it been, it would probably have left the road at the first bend.

Many projects involving two-wheeled motorized vehicles were undertaken in the years after 1885, but none was developed commercially. A Frenchman called Millet made a tricycle with a five-cylinder radial engine in the front wheel (the first ever engine of this type) and also, in 1893, a bicycle with the same engine incorporated in the rear wheel. The American Lucius Copeland fitted highly efficient steam en-

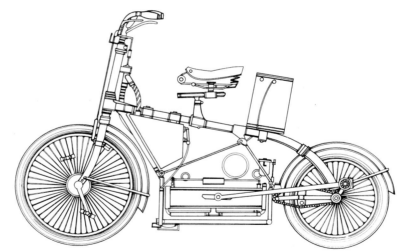

The first motorbike with four horizontally opposed cylinders was the Holden of 1896.

The low voltage ignition magneto developed by the German Robert Bosch was first used on the Rubb and Haab of 1895. This is the 1899 version, with two cylinders fitted one behind the other between the front downtube and the pedals.

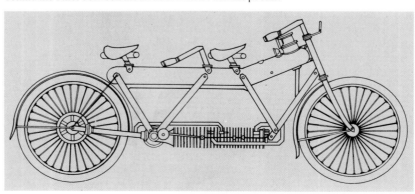

gines to bicycles from 1881 to 1890: a notable example was the 1886 model which had a cylinder weighing just one kilogram (2.2 lb); the boiler and cylinder combined weighed only nine kilograms (20 lb).

Professor Enrico Bernardi built a trailer motor in 1894: it could be fastened onto any pedal cycle, thereby transforming it in to a motor cycle. But Bernardi too was chiefly interested in automobiles, and his trailer was probably only a means of road testing the engine.

By the end of the last century, numerous engineers had caught onto the idea of motorcycles and in 1894 Hildebrand and Wolfmüller in Germany were the first to try series production. After a promising start – partly thanks to an advertising campaign throughout Europe and the establishment of a sales network (in Italy, for example, the Hildebrand was marketed by Turkheimer in Milan, who also pioneered the Otav engine) – the attempt failed due to a fundamental defect in the machine, which had direct transmission from the engine to the rear wheel by means of long connecting rods outside the engine, coupled to a crank that was an integral part of the rear wheel hub.

The motorcycle built by Colonel Henry Capel Holden failed for the same reason. The Holden, the first motorcycle to have a horizontally opposed four-cylinder engine, was produced from 1896 to 1902, first with an air and then with a water cooling system.

The tricycles built by De Dion-Bouton in France met with a very different fate. The first, which was produced in 1895, was an immediate success and matters were improved still further when the company decided to sell the engines separately as well, to whoever wanted them. The motorcycle had become an established means of transport thanks to the light, strong and thoroughly reliable De Dion-Bouton engines. Apart from anything else, this factory was the first to supply a complete service manual to accompany its vehicles and engines: no one had thought of doing such a thing before.

Another interesting machine from the end of the last century was the German Rubb & Haab of 1895, which was fitted with a low-voltage Bosch ignition magneto (the first to be used on a self-propelled vehicle). The engine had two cylinders, one behind the other, between the steering head and pedals, replacing the front downtube of the frame. The two cylinders, which might have appeared at first sight to be opposed, were in fact arranged "in file," the top of the rear cylinder forming the bottom of the front cylinder. The connecting rod of the rear cylinder, after reaching the piston, passed through it and was coupled to the piston of the front cylinder, with the result that the two pistons travelled back and forth together. In 1899 the two cylinders were arranged horizontally, replacing the bottom tube of the frame in a tandem arrangement, which had shafting with bevel gears at the ends.

After 1894, the idea of motorizing two-wheeled vehicles began to be taken seriously, not just by enterprising engineers but also by capitalists who were prepared to finance the most interesting projects.

Thanks to the example set by De Dion-Bouton, France had established a thriving motorcycle industry and could thus claim, at a

The Clement of 1902 was the first 4-cylinder racing bike. The 1,200 cc V-type engine enabled it to travel at over 110 km/h (68 mph).

The second Werner motorcycle had a 2.75 HP 262 cc four-stroke single-cylinder De Dion-Bouton engine installed in the conventional position (i.e. low down in the center of the frame).

later date, to have laid the foundations of international world motorcycle development. Equally serious enterprises grew up in Germany and in Britain (where the Locomotive Act, which had virtually prevented the development of road vehicles with mechanical traction, had been abolished in 1896). Despite numerous adventurers, the foundations of true motorcycle technology were laid in that period, with clear-cut principles that were independent of both pedal cycle and automobile technology. In Italy the motorcycle was still essentially a custom-built object, partly because the economic conditions of the population were such that very few people could afford one (even a bicycle was a luxury).

Toward the end of 1905 the motorcycle industry suffered a sudden crisis, caused by the number of speculators. The customers, who had been seduced by the publicity, often found themselves with unreliable machines on their hands, which did not live up to expectations and were virtually useless. Sales fell and many companies went bankrupt. The motorcycle survived only because the reputable companies refused to lose heart and managed to

regain the confidence of the public.

Around the year 1900 tricycles, which had dominated the market till then, began to disappear, outclassed by four-wheeled vehicles which offered far greater advantages without costing much more: it was in fact the manufacturers, like De Dion-Bouton, who made the decision to switch production to automobiles, absorbing the section of the market represented by tricycles.

The motorcycle industry at the end of the last century

In Britain, James Norton fitted a Clément engine to a bicycle frame in 1889, later replacing it by a single or twin cylinder Peugeot. The Norton company began using engines of its own design only in 1908, the 633 cc single-cylinder being the first step on the road that was to make it the world's top motorcycle producer.

The British Excelsior, which used Minerva engines built in Belgium, was constructed in 1897. In 1898 the Stevens brothers, who up till then had been manufacturing engines only, began producing complete motorcycles under the AJS trademark, derived

from the initials of one of them: Albert John.

In 1898, Ariel built quadricycles with a vertical single-cylinder engine, followed by motorcycles with Kerry engines.

The first Matchless was built in 1899 by Harry Albert and Charles Richard Collier, who fitted with an engine of their own design one of the bicycles which their father, H. H. Collier, had been producing since 1878.

Having introduced a tricycle with a Daimler engine built under license, in 1899 Peugeot of France designed their first motorcycle featuring a spring fork, which was quite exceptional for the period.

Still in France, in 1895 (or 1896, depending on the source) two Russian journalists who had moved to Paris, the brothers Michel and Eugène Werner, who were interested in cinematography, fitted an engine purchased to operate an Edison kinetoscope (the ancestor of the modern movie projector) to a bicycle, for publicity reasons. The experiment was a success because the engine proved an excellent propulsor for the bicycle, and the brothers, having given up journalism and the cinema, devoted themselves successfully to the production of

13

This Laurin and Klement bike with a twin cylinder V-type engine came out in 1904. The displacement was 691 cc and it had magneto ignition. The fuel tank was beneath the saddle.

This motocycle with a triple cylinder arrow engine was made by Alessandro Anzani at the beginning of the century.

This motor bicycle produced in 1898 by Figini & Lazzati was driven by a single-cylinder engine, delivering 0.75 HP.

The Carcano single-cylinder engine of 1899 could easily be fitted to any bicycle frame. It had belt drive and delivered 0.75 HP.

motorized bicycles. In 1901 they designed a tubular frame to hold the engine, which thus became an integral part of the bicycle. Before then, manufacturers had generally been content to fit an engine to a bicycle, perhaps reinforcing a few parts of the vehicle but without making any changes to its structure. To distinguish their machines from the motorized bicycles of the day, the Werners coined the term "motocyclette," which was subsequently adopted universally in nearly all languages to describe a new vehicle in which the frame and engine were fully integrated.

The Werners thus produced the first "true" motorcycle. The same idea had been developed in 1898 by Laurin & Klement of Mladá Boleslav in Bohemia, which was then part of the Austro-Hungarian Empire, but the Werners were responsible for its rapid diffusion throughout the world.

The French company René Gillet began motorcycle production in 1895. Another French firm, Clément, after producing tricycles and quadricycles, built its first motorcycle in 1902 and in the same year introduced a 1200 cc motorcycle which was undoubtedly the first four-cylinder racing model.

In Belgium – apart from Minerva, who built engines on their own – the Saroléa company passed from the production of bicycles to motorized tricycles in 1896, followed by motorcycles before the end of the century.

In Italy, manufacturers included Figini & Lazzati in Milan, Marchand (later Marchand Orio), which became one of the leading Italian companies of the early 1900s after moving from Milan to Piacenza, and Carcano of Milan where the Maserati brothers, who were to become famous in the automobile sector, worked as mechanics.

Other Italian pioneers at the end of the century included Rosselli, Prinetti & Stucchi, Trevisan, Storero, Quagliotti, Musso, Mantovani, Cappa and Garabello (who built an interesting single-cylinder machine) and many others. Sadly, most of these factories closed down before 1914.

The Bianchi company, founded in 1885 by Edoardo Bianchi in Milan as a bicycle factory, was much more successful. It built its first motorized tricycle in 1890 and the first motorcycle came out in 1897. In a few years, the company acquired nationwide standing as a producer of bicycles, motorcycles and automobiles.

Alessandro Anzani, who pioneered the motorcycle and aviation, is worthy of special mention. He was born in Milan and emigrated to France at the beginning of the century. A racer and a skilled engineer, he decided to start building his own engines in 1906 and in 1907 brought out a model with three cylinders in a fan shape (the first cylinder was tilted forward, the second was vertical and the third was tilted backward), which he fitted to a tubular frame.

Technical development

At the beginning of the 1900s the way motorcycle frames were built, with a few rare exceptions, still reflected the fact that they were derived from bicycles. People dared not yet abolish the pedals, with the result that the frames had to be quite tall and the front fork was still of the typical bicycle type, sometimes reinforced. But round about 1905, spring front forks began to be used. The frames were generally rigid but a few motorcycles – such as the 1903 Minerva and various American machines – had elastic rear suspension.

At the beginning of the century motorcycle engines were installed in every conceivable position, but toward the end of 1905 the arrangement first adopted by Minerva was established, with the engine sloping forward and fitted in front of or behind the oblique front tube of the frame (downtube), between the steering head and the pedals.

Dunlop tyres were the most widely used up to 1904. The British company's chief rival was Michelin in France, who in 1891 had invented a removable tyre that could be changed or repaired very easily – an almost desperate undertaking before then. And it was Michelin who in 1905 patented an "antidérapant" (nonskid) tyre with a tread. The most popular types had a 1.5 or 2 inch (2.5–5 cm) cross-section and at the beginning of the century were of the beading type (in which the ply was fixed to an invariable circumference, determined by steel bead wire inserted for the purpose). In 1904 the German company Continental patented the "clawed" tyre, so called because the base of the outer casing had a spur which slotted into a recess in the rim, to keep it in place. This was the most common variety of tyre after 1905. The rims normally had a diameter of 26 or 28 inches (66–71 cm).

The brakes were initially like those of bicycles, with a pad on the tyre shoe or wheel rim, or on the

In Belgium, Minerva, having established itself on the market selling engines, brought out its first motor bicycle in 1901, which could do over 30 km/h (19 mph). The four-stroke single-cylinder engine (with side valves) developed 1.25 HP.

belt transmission pulley. Then Bowden invented the horseshoe brake. However, ribbon brakes were also found and in 1905 a rudimentary disc brake was used on the British Imperial, although the idea was subsequently abandoned. Still in 1905, the Belgian four-cylinder FN was given an internally expanding (i.e. drum) brake on the rear wheel.

The first lamps for motorcycles appeared at the beginning of the century. They ran on oil or acetylene, were larger than those used previously for bicycles and had spring attachments to act as

shock absorbers.

The transmission generally consisted of a belt running from the engine to the rear wheel. To begin with the belts were of circular cross-section, made up of plaited strips of leather; then flat leather belts came into use, to be replaced in their turn by the more efficient V-section belts. Subsequently, rubberized fabric belts were fitted; these continued to be used until final drive gear chains were universally adopted. Bowden, who were already producing their covered wire flexible transmission, also began marketing

flexible oil tubes.

Up to 1905, engines throughout Europe were built on similar lines to those of De Dion-Bouton, which were the most popular because of their reliability, although there were a number of exceptions; these were mainly four-stroke, single-cylinder engines with an automatic inlet valve and a mechanically controlled exhaust valve. But controlled inlet valves also came into use from 1905. The power of the engines, which generally varied from 1.5 to 2 HP at the beginning of the century, was increased in 1905 to 3.5 HP for single-cylinders, rising to 4 or 5 HP for twin-cylinders, which were nearly all V-type.

DUNLOP CORD

Most of them were air-cooled, although a number had mixed cooling, with air for the cylinder and water for the cylinder head, and some were entirely water-cooled.

After the very primitive system of ignition by transported flame, ignition by incandescence using a small tube or platinum mantle became popular: however, electric spark ignition gained ground, thanks first to low-voltage and then to high-voltage magnetos, which were invented in 1901.

To begin with, motorcycle designers were also responsible for the electrical installations and spark plugs of their machines, but in 1902 Bosch started mass-producing ignition plugs for all types of engine. The first spark plugs had two types of seat, either flanged or threaded, but the flanged type soon disappeared.

Michelin

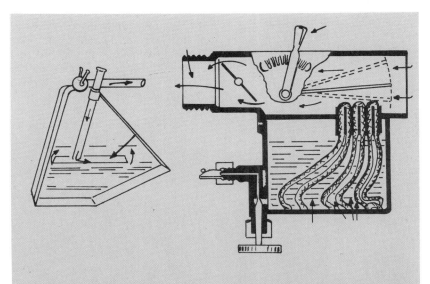

One of the biggest problems with the first motorcycle engines was how to mix the fuel with the air drawn into the cylinders to the correct concentration, and control power delivery properly. In other words, what was needed was an efficient carburetor. Before this problem was solved by fixed-spray and needle-valve carburetors, various devices were used, all of which proved unsatisfactory, such as "lapping" carburetors (left), which were sometimes built directly into the fuel tank (to which the air drawn in by the engine was sent), or "wick" carburetors (right), in which the fuel filtered upward from the float chamber to the inlet pipe along wicks which were lapped by the current of air at the top.

From the beginning of the century, Scott produced excellent two-stroke twin-cylinder engines which were highly progressive for the period. The cylinders were parallel and induction was controlled by a rotary valve. The earliest examples were air-cooled, but water cooling was soon used, first for the cylinder heads only and then for the cylinders as well. The two cranks projected to either side and the crankshaft, which turned on two bearings, had a big central flywheel.

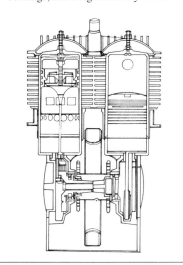

Up to 1905 surface carburetor fuel feed was used, although the much more efficient spray carburetors were already coming into use. The surface type of carburetor was in fact none other than the petrol tank to which a special current of air was sent which skimmed the surface of the fuel (or, in the "barbotage" system, was injected into the fuel, causing it to bubble), thus favouring evaporation: the petrol vapour was then sent to the cylinder along a pipe, together with fresh air, to be ignited by the electric spark or incandescent tube.

Other big motorcycle companies appeared at the beginning of the century. Royal Enfield was established in 1901, and shortly before the war designed a 298 cc experimental engine with a sliding sleeve valve mechanism which never went into production because no solution was found to the problem of cooling.

In 1902 Triumph fitted a Minerva engine to a bicycle frame, and three years later built their first bike with an original engine. Triumph increased their rate of production from five vehicles a week in 1905 to 3,000 a year in 1909 – a very high figure for the period. They built an excellent 547 cc single-cylinder in 1914, with semi-automatic lubrication, magneto ignition and Sturmey Archer three-speed gears.

The extraordinary Scott two-stroke twin-cylinder was built in 1908, when the plant had been in operation for a few years. The 333 cc engine block was air-cooled, while the cylinder heads were water-cooled: it had an open frame and chain primary and secondary drive (from the engine to the gearbox and from the gearbox to the rear wheel). The two-speed gears were operated by a rocker pedal, which was most unusual at a time when gears were generally operated by a hand lever. The Scott twin-cylinder, apparently the first two-stroke engine to use pistons without a deflector, was enormously successful in races. Because no other machine could compete with it, the British Motorcycle Federation made the absurd decision of stipulating that the Scotts should be entered in the class immediately above the one to which they were entitled to belong according to their displacement. In 1912, the displacement of Scott machines was increased to 532 cc: rotary-valve feed was adopted but operated by gears rather than a chain. In 1914, a much improved model was brought out and Scott announced that no modifications of any kind would be made thereafter.

In 1901 the JAP company was founded; by 1914 it had become one of the biggest engine producers in the world.

Zenith, established in 1904, achieved world fame in 1908 when it fitted its first Gradua variable-ratio transmission (which permitted an infinite series of gear ratios from 3.5 to 1 to 9 to 1 thanks to a pulley, the diameter of which could be increased or decreased, and the rear wheel, which could be moved forward or backward, sliding along special grooves).

Indian was one of the first companies in the world to produce high-powered narrow angle V-twin engines. These engines were a great success in the years leading up to the First World War and were used on racing vehicles as well as high-performance, high-reliability mass-produced bikes. In 1914, a few mass-produced Indians were given electric lights and starters. This was also one of the first companies to use twistgrip throttle controls. Indian remained faithful to the V-twin formula throughout its career, despite producing some interesting engines of different design.

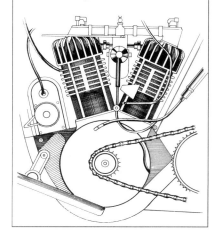

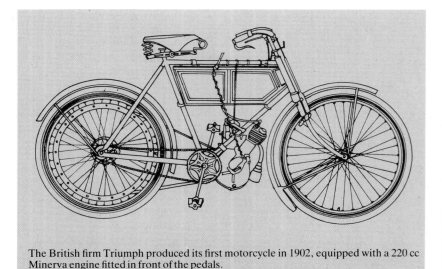

The British firm Triumph produced its first motorcycle in 1902, equipped with a 220 cc Minerva engine fitted in front of the pedals.

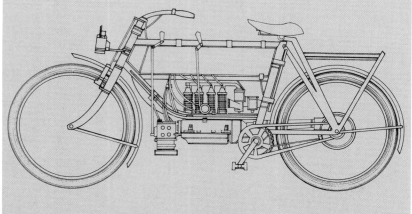

The first four-cylinder by the Belgian company FN was built in 1904. The cylinder-in-line engine had a displacement of 362 cc, spray carburetor fuel feed and magneto ignition. It had shaft final drive.

The first Indian of 1901 had a 1.75 HP single-cylinder engine fitted above the pedals (it was in fact a motor bicycle) and chain drive. Various changes were made to this model, such as the addition of a throttle control and a spring front fork. In 1906, the power was increased to 2.5 HP. In 1905, Indian brought out its first twin-cylinder.

Thanks to the Gradua transmission Zenith also proved unbeatable, with the result that a number of organizations refused to enter it in their races, thus providing it with free publicity which increased sales.

The engine of the 1904 Douglas was in an original position: the horizontally opposed twin cylinder was fitted longitudinally to the frame, very high up, below the fuel tank and above the pedals. In 1907, Douglas built a machine with a 696 cc four-cylinder engine composed of two 80 degree V-twins, with an external flywheel, no gears and no clutch. The one model built is still in perfect working order.

In 1901 FN of Belgium, a big weapons manufacturer, built a motorcycle with a single-cylinder engine but the company only became famous in 1904 when it brought out a model with a 362 cc engine with four cylinders in line,

which had a spray carburetor with a constant level float chamber, ignition magneto, pedal start and shaft final drive with a crown and pinion enclosed in an oil bath box. Over the next few years, the machine was constantly improved: the displacement was increased to 412 cc in 1908, rising to no less than 748 cc delivering 7 HP in 1914. In this last version, lubrication was by means of a pump operated by the engine: it had three-speed gears.

The term Motosacoche means, basically, engine in a bag, and at the beginning of the century the Swiss brothers Henri and Armand Dufaux brought out an auxiliary engine that was contained in a type of sleeve and could be fitted beneath the crossbar of any bicycle. The various controls and drive belt were connected, and success was achieved. In later years, the engine sleeve was supplied in steel plate or leather.

The Swiss company adopted the word Motosacoche as its trademark and produced other, conventional single- or twin-cylinder motorcycles under the same name. In 1907 it brought out a prototype seven-cylinder radial engine which could be attached to the side of the rear wheel of any bicycle, but it was never exploited commercially, probably because it was too expensive and complex to produce.

The Neckarsulmer bicycle factory, founded in 1886, was named after the German town of Neckarsulm. In 1900 it brought out a bicycle with a single-cylinder engine. In 1905 it produced a V-twin as well and, having adopted the NSU trademark, the company became enormously successful with its single- and twin-cylinder models. In 1914 it introduced a bicycle which was highly progressive for the time: delivering 6 HP, it had elastic front

and rear suspension, three-speed gears and chain primary and secondary drive.

Dozens of motorcycle factories were established in the United States too: according to Floyd Clymer, pioneer motorcycle journalist and publisher of articles of great historical value, there were estimated to be over a hundred factories, nearly all of which have now disappeared.

Indian, which was to become the most famous American brand, was established in 1901. Its first bike was a 1.75 HP single-cylinder with a backward-sloping engine incorporated in the frame in place of the saddle support tube. In 1904 a much improved version of this machine was even fitted with a twistgrip throttle control, which was quite extraordinary when you consider that the use of such devices instead of levers for controlling the fuel and air supplies did not become the norm

17

until after World War One. In 1905 Indian produced its first V-twin and established a worldwide reputation over the years, so much so that in 1914 its annual output was 35,000 units. The 1914 model had a 9 HP V-twin engine, two-speed gears, elastic rear suspension using five-leaf quarter elliptic springs and even electric start, thanks to a small motor fitted in front of the crankcase. This device was abolished the following year, because electrical installations still left much to be desired in 1914: however, one cannot help but admire the engineers of that great American company, given that electric starter motors really began to be used worldwide only in the seventies, and even today there are many motorcycles without them.

The other big American company – and the only one which is

still going strong – was Harley-Davidson. In 1903 it brought out its first single-cylinder machine, which was quite successful, followed by its first V-twin in 1909. The company did so well that its workforce increased from little more than a dozen in 1908 to over a thousand in 1912. The first Harley-Davidson V-twin with all-chain drive was introduced in 1913. The following year the company brought out a much-improved model with two-speed hub-type gears and controlled inlet and exhaust valves.

The first motorcycle by the American company Excelsior (not to be confused with the British company of the same name) came out in 1907. It had a single-cylinder engine with no gears and belt drive. In 1911 the single-cylinder model was joined by a V-twin. In subsequent years ma-

chines of this type specially prepared for racing earned a reputation for being unbeatable. At that period (in 1913, to be precise) the big X trademark appeared on the petrol tank of Excelsior machines, and immediately became famous.

A truly outstanding machine was the Cyclone, produced from 1912 to 1916, with a 42 degree V-twin engine which even had an overhead camshaft timing system at a time when the use of overhead valves was still a rarity.

Another interesting machine was the Underslung of 1912, with an open frame, small-diameter wheels and a steering wheel in place of handlebars. After World War One it was named Militaire. American motorcycles of the period included the Pierce and the Henderson.

The Pierce of 1909 had a 750 cc

engine with four cylinders in line and shaft final drive; the frame was made up of thick tubes which also served as petrol and oil tanks. Known as the Arrowmodel, it remained virtually unchanged until World War One.

The Henderson of 1911 had a 780 cc engine with four cylinders in line, an aluminum crankcase and chain drive. Apart from constant increases in displacement, this machine remained unaltered in subsequent years; the 1914 model had a displacement of 1076 cc, a cone clutch and two-speed gearbox.

The first motorcycle with eight cylinders, produced by motorcycle and aviation pioneer Glenn Hammond Curtiss, is preserved at the National Air Museum of the Smithsonian Institution in the United States. In 1906 Curtiss had built an eight-cylinder V-type

This bicycle, with a 1.5 HP Zedel single-cylinder engine fitted forward of the front tube of the frame, was issued under the Neckarsulmer trademark in 1903. It had a rigid front fork and was in fact the first NSU machine.

The single-cylinder engine built by the Dufaux brothers in the early 1900s was contained in a type of metal "sleeve" which could be fitted to the frame of any bicycle. The Motosacoche had been invented.

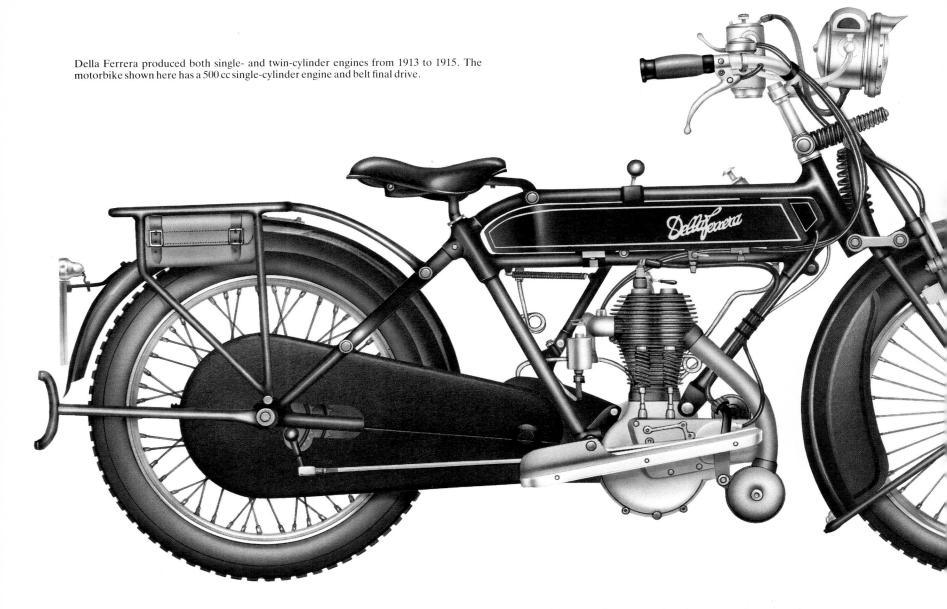

Della Ferrera produced both single- and twin-cylinder engines from 1913 to 1915. The motorbike shown here has a 500 cc single-cylinder engine and belt final drive.

engine which he wanted to test thoroughly before fitting it to an aircraft. He therefore prepared a special motorcycle frame and in 1907 clocked up nearly 219 km/h (136 mph) over a mile with a flying start – the highest speed ever achieved by a land vehicle at that time, and one which would not be exceeded for some years.

On the eve of World War I

From 1905 to World War I other motorcycle companies were established in Britain, which were to be world-famous for decades.

The first BSA motorcycle was made in 1905, but was not mass-produced. In 1909 the company designed a machine (available the following year) with a 500 cc German NSU engine and belt final drive. By 1914 BSA's output was quite considerable, including models with belt drive, mixed chain and belt and all-chain drive, to satisfy the diverse needs

of the public.

An extraordinary machine was the Wilkinson TAC of 1909, with an open frame, V-twin engine and steering wheel. In 1911, Wilkinson (at the time a famous manufacturer of swords and side arms, whereas nowadays they only make razor blades) brought out a new model called TMC, which was produced until 1913. It had the same characteristics as the previous one, apart from the fact that it had handlebars instead of a steering wheel, and the 848 cc engine was water-cooled.

In 1909 John Wooler brought out his first motorcycle, dubbed "flying banana" on account of its distinctive torpedo-shaped petrol tank incorporating the steering head: manufactured until 1914 without any substantial changes, it had a two-stroke twin-cylinder engine with complex valve gear.

In 1910 Veloce took up motorcycle production, adopting the Velocette trademark, for which it

was to become famous, shortly after the war. In 1912, John Marston's Sunbeam company began motorcycle production. In the same year his son Charles founded the Villiers engine works, which was to flood the world with two-stroke engines of all displacements and produced the first flywheel magneto at the outbreak of World War I.

The Rudge Whitworth, the first Rudge model of 1910, was followed the next year by the Multi, with belt drive and variable transmission, which permitted a number of gear ratios by varying the diameter of the engine pulley and drive-belt rim.

Motorcycle companies destined to become famous were established in Italy, too, from 1906 to 1914. The most important was Frera, founded in 1906, which stocked various single- and twin-cylinder models with displacements from 320 to 795 cc. It was the biggest wartime supplier of

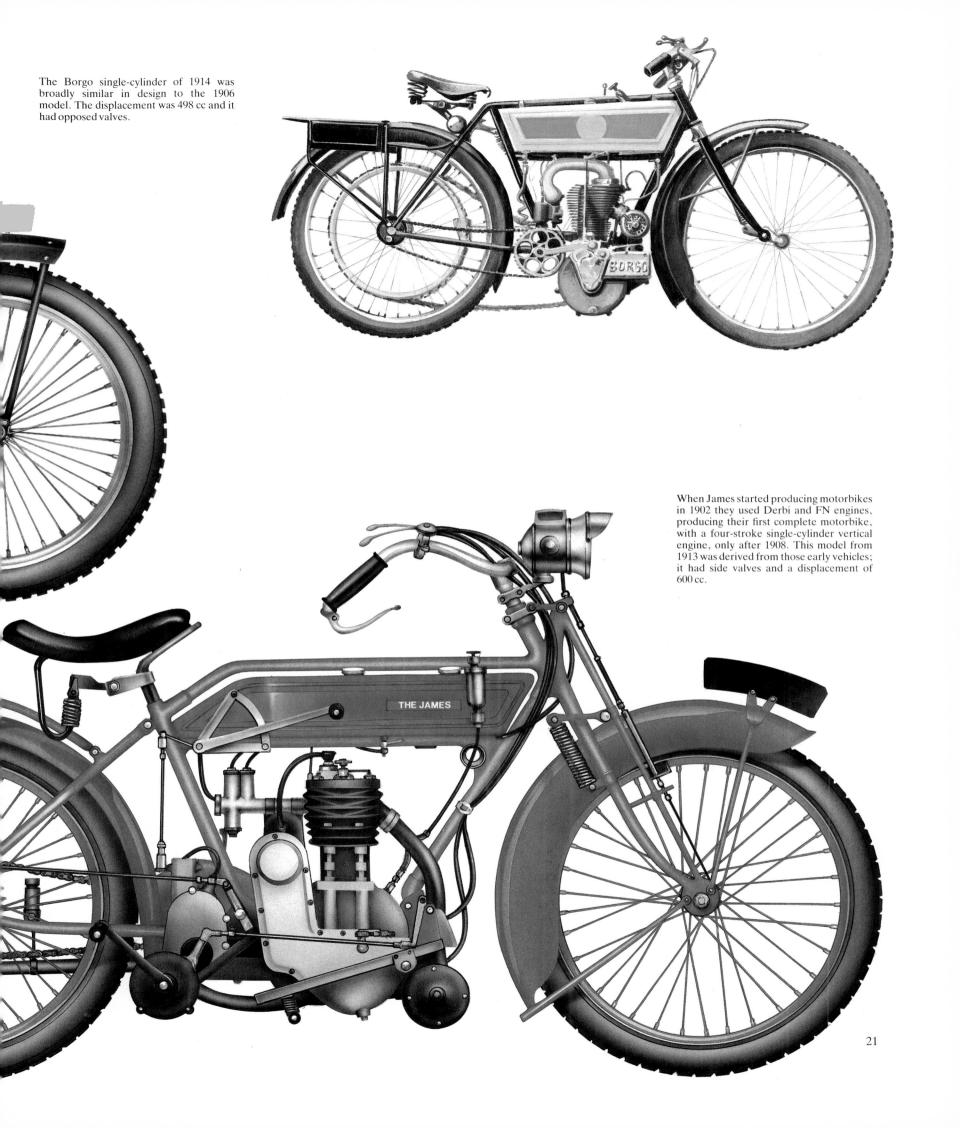

The Borgo single-cylinder of 1914 was broadly similar in design to the 1906 model. The displacement was 498 cc and it had opposed valves.

When James started producing motorbikes in 1902 they used Derbi and FN engines, producing their first complete motorbike, with a four-stroke single-cylinder vertical engine, only after 1908. This model from 1913 was derived from those early vehicles; it had side valves and a displacement of 600 cc.

THE JAMES

21

MOTORCYCLE TECHNOLOGY ON THE EVE OF WORLD WAR I

By 1914, on the eve of World War I the motorcycle had achieved a high level of technical development. Compared with a model from 1905, the differences were enormous. For example, the motorcycle of 1905 had a tall frame, which was rather short from front to back; the engine was fitted to the frame very high up; it was set in motion by push start or pedalling with the rear wheel off the ground; an ignition coil with a battery and contact breaker was used; the inlet valve was automatic; it had belt drive with fixed front and rear pulleys; lubrication was by hand pump and the front fork was often elastic (spring-type), but the rear fork was rigid and the bicycle-type saddle was unsprung.

The motorcycle of 1914 had a long, low frame; the engine was installed in the lowest possible position in the frame; it was started by a pedal, with the wheels on the ground, and from a stationary position thanks to the addition of a clutch; the pedals had very often been eliminated; the final drive used a rubber belt rather than a leather one, with an expanding pulley, although increasingly often chain and belt or all-chain drive was used, with gears in the hub or in the "cradle" of the frame; lubrication was by automatic pump; magneto ignition was used; both valves of the timing system were controlled and the brakes were generally foot-operated.

In 1914, motorcycles were classified according to their displacement, not their power, as had been the case previously (since the rated output no longer corresponded to the effective horsepower (brake horsepower) of the engines, classification by displacement seemed a better idea). If you examine the statistics of the time, you will note that up to 1914 the commonest type of engine was the four-stroke single-cylinder, and the type preferred by customers had a rated horsepower of 3.5 HP, corresponding to a displacement of 500 cc. Most twin-cylinder engines were V-type, but in Britain many companies still preferred engines with two horizontally opposed cylinders fitted longitudinally to the frame. A number of three- and four-cylinder radial engines – the Rivierre, for example – were also built up to 1914, but were not a success.

Two-stroke engines were quite common but were mainly used with displacements below 300 cc, four-stroke engines being preferred for machines of higher capacity. This pattern was to continue for several decades, except in German-speaking countries.

By 1914, the magneto had virtually replaced all other forms of ignition. Automatic inlet valves gradually disappeared too, mechanically controlled valves proving more efficient. Side valves were still common up to 1914, the exhaust valve being at the side and the inlet one at the top, operated by a push rod and rocker arm. Rotary valves were used very occasionally, and slide valve mechanisms were also tried.

Spray carburetors were now universally adopted, while lubrication by hand pump was still the norm, although gear pumps which recovered the oil and sent it back into circulation were coming into use.

Belt drive was still very common in 1914, although chain drive was starting to gain ground. A good compromise between the two systems was chain and belt drive, or a chain from the engine to the gearbox and a belt from the gearbox to the rear wheel. Variable-diameter pulleys delayed the adoption of chains, but drive belts were not to survive World War I.

Clutches were nearly always of the disc type, either dry or oil bath, cone clutches being an exception. They were foot-operated, a characteristic which American motorcycles have kept to this day, whereas in other countries after World War One the clutch was operated by a lever on the handlebars.

We have already said that motorcycle frames in 1914 were longer and lower than previously. Low-capacity machines also normally had an unbroken cradle, while those of higher displacement had a two-piece cradle. Front forks were now all of the spring type, usually having two arms with springs at the sides or a big central spring, although several examples of deformable parallelogram front forks with a big central spring were seen and friction shock absorbers were introduced after the war, thereafter becoming the commonest type of front suspension. Rear suspension, on the other hand, was most uncommon. Wheels normally had spurred tyres, with longitudinal grooves to improve roadholding. In many cases, however, the grooves were replaced by square or round tread blocks. Most tyres measured 26 inches (66 cm) in diameter and 2 to 2.5 inches (5–6.35 cm) in cross-section.

At the beginning of the century, lighting was by oil lamp; after 1905 acetylene lamps were used, these gradually being replaced in turn, in about 1914, by electric lights powered by accumulators or by a friction dynamo on the wheel, similar to those used on bicycles today.

Drum brakes began to prevail by about 1914. After the Great War, internally expanding drum brakes took over completely from the pad and belt types.

motorcycles to the Army, including sidecars with machine guns and sidecars with stretchers for carrying the wounded.

The first Della Ferrera, of 1909, had a 330cc engine (increased shortly afterward to 499cc). The company constantly improved its models in subsequent years. The works in Turin produced only a few vehicles a month, the emphasis being on quality: their motorcycles were carefully finished and virtually custom-built. The existing range of single-cylinder and V-twin models was joined in 1915 by a magnificent 500cc single-cylinder with a timing system employing four overhead valves, variable transmission, belt final drive, large cross-section tyres and brakes on both wheels.

Giuseppe Gilera, an accomplished racer and a brilliant engineer, built his first motorcycle in Milan in 1909, with a 317cc vertical single-cylinder, which was followed by other, single- and twin-cylinder models.

Moto Borgo was founded in Turin in 1906. Their best machine was a 498cc single-cylinder with magneto ignition and opposed-valves, which was also given highly efficient variable transmission in 1914. In 1911 Borgo also began producing pistons for cars and motorcycles, and this later became its sole activity.

In 1913, Adalberto Garelli built the prototype of a motorcycle that became famous on European racing circuits shortly after the war. He tested it by climbing Montecenisio on 10 January 1914, reaching the pass at an altitude of 1,925 meters (6,135 ft) without difficulty. Although not the first to think of using a split-cylinder engine, Adalberto Garelli was the one who perfected it: the 349cc Garelli engine was a two-stroke with two vertical cylinder barrels side by side, with a shared combustion chamber. The two pistons were fixed to a single pin and they also used the same connecting rod, with the result that their movement was parallel and synchronous. The left-hand barrel had transfer ports at the base through which fresh gases entered the cylinder, while after the expansion phase the combusted gases poured out of the exhaust ports, which were situated at the base of the right-hand barrel. Belt drive was used to begin with, but chain drive was fitted when the motorcycle went into production in 1919.

As regards unconventional

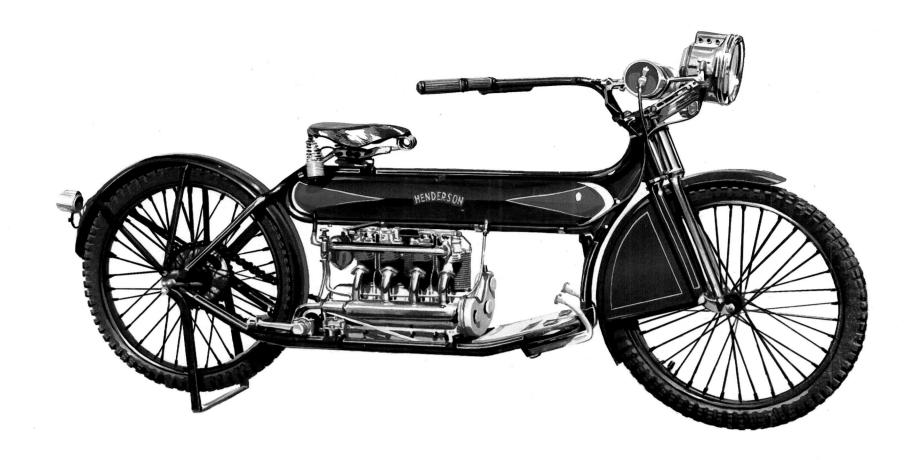

This is the 1913 Henderson, with four vertical cylinders in line and opposed valves. It
had chain drive and delivered 7 HP.

The highly original German Megola of 1921, with an upholstered seat. The engine was a
640 cc five-cylinder radial (bore and stroke = 32 x 60 mm). The brake was on the rear
wheel, the front one being completely taken up by the cylinders (which turned with it).
Speed 110 km/h (68 mph).

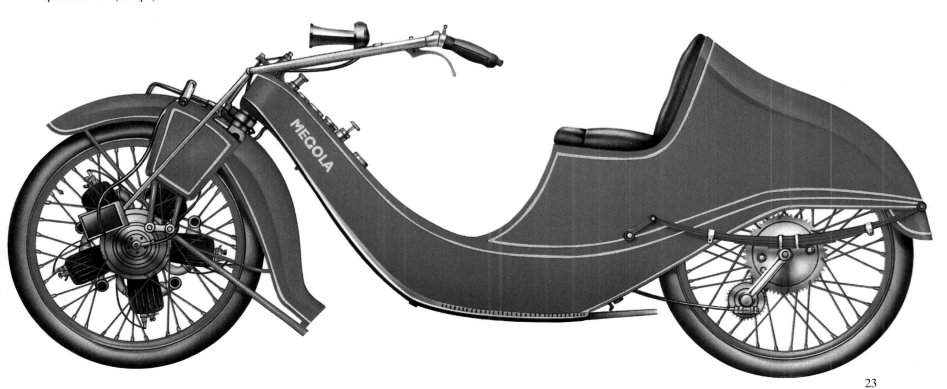

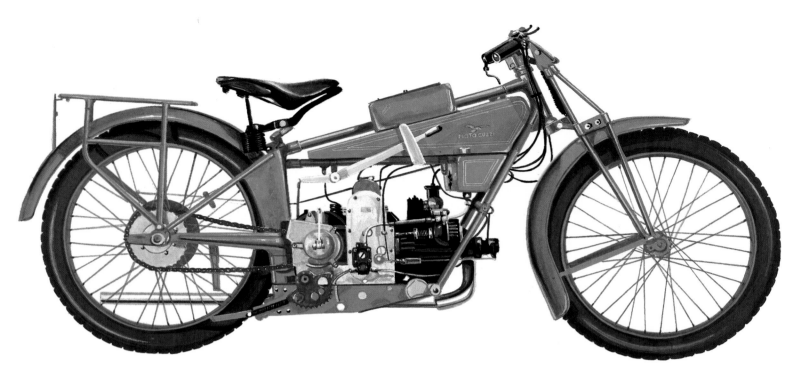

two-stroke engines, the one that was used for the 1914 Pony by the English company Premier is worth mentioning. It was a 322cc model with twin cylinders in line and a special connecting rod with a curved bar which caused the piston to rotate 30 degrees on itself, apart from accomplishing the normal stroke from top dead center to bottom dead center and vice versa. This was required by the complex timing system. However, the machine was never mass-produced and no more was heard of it after the war.

The first woman motorcyclist was Muriel Hind, who in 1902 purchased a Singer with a radial engine in the rear wheel and redesigned the frame, thus becoming the first woman motorcycle designer as well. She was also the first woman to obtain a racing license (in 1905) and in 1910 joined the staff of *Motor Cycling* magazine to become the first woman editor in this field.

Postwar trends

The 1914–18 war forced most motorcycle companies to close down, or switch production to providing transport for the Army.

In Italy, the companies that built military motorcycles included Frera, Bianchi and Borgo; in Britain, the main producers were Douglas, Triumph and P & M (the latter for the Air Force only); in France, Peugeot, Terrot and René

Gillet; in the United States, the most notable were Indian and Harley-Davidson, although the four-cylinder Henderson with sidecar and 279cc two-stroke Cleveland won a fair number of orders. The Germans mainly used NSUs, Brennabors and Wanderers, while the only military machine built in Austria was the Puch.

Motorcycles were widely used during World War I, chiefly for liaison and communications. In the years from 1918 to 1925 motorcycle technology drew on the experience gained in the war and bicycle pedals, hub gears and belt drive were finally abandoned. Front forks were greatly improved, using deformable parallelogram suspension with a big central spring and friction shock absorbers at the sides. Frames were usually rigid, although elastic suspension began to be adopted. Better materials were available to the industry, and manufacturing techniques were also greatly improved.

In Europe, the top limit for displacement tended to be 500cc, with a few models up to 750cc, while in the United States displacements of 750 to 1200cc were preferred for V-twin engines. Overhead valves were normally used, operated by push rods and rocker arms, although all companies continued to produce models with side valves, which were still in demand; opposed valves

Moto Guzzi produced their first motorbike in 1921. The engine was a 499 cc horizontal single-cylinder (88 x 82 mm) with opposed valves. It had a tubular cradle frame with a parallelogram front fork. The drum brake was on the rear wheel.

This Böhmerland was a three-seater model from 1928. There was room for two passengers on the very long frame and a third could fit onto a saddle over the rear wheel, which had a supplementary fuel tank on either side. The engine was a 598 cc vertical single-cylinder with push rod valve gear. The wheels were of cast aluminum alloy. ▼

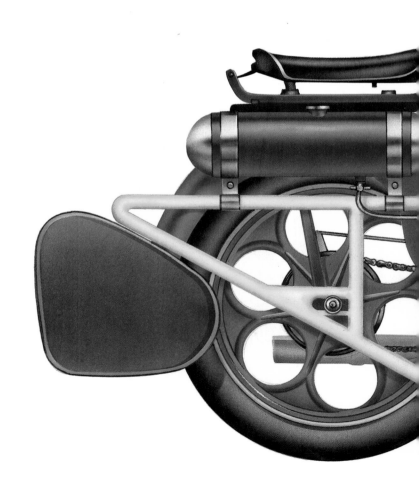

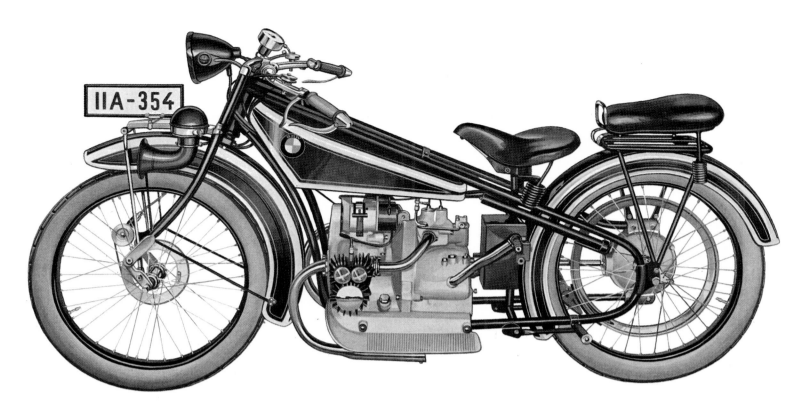

The BMW R 32 designed by Max Friz was first seen at the 1923 Paris Automobile Show. The boxer engine was fitted transversely. It had a displacement of 486 cc, delivering 8.5 HP at 3300 rpm. The frame was of the tubular type with shaft final drive.

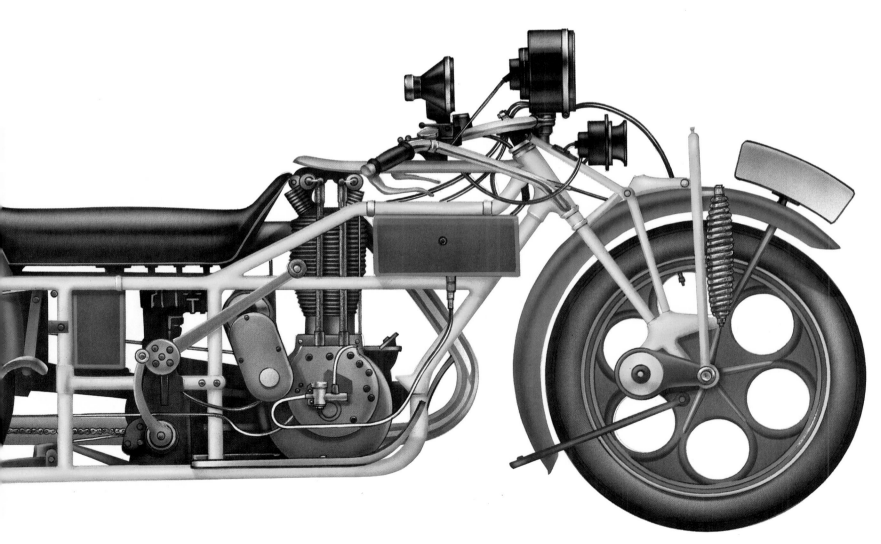

had disappeared by then.

Still on the subject of valve gear, Rudge caused a sensation with their 350cc model of 1924, which had a timing system with four overhead valves arranged radially. But the following year's model reverted to the use of four parallel valves. However, valve gear with one or even two overhead camshafts was increasingly used for racing models.

Most engines were four-stroke, but two-stroke engines were quite popular, particularly in Austria, Germany and Britain: apart from Garelli, the Austrian company Puch used split-cylinder two-stroke engines.

Cylinder blocks were normally made of cast iron, with a separate cylinder head (also in cast iron), although light alloy was used very occasionally. The bronze cylinder heads fitted to Garelli and Frera machines were an exception, partly because of their very high cost.

Aluminum pistons were used in Europe; cast iron ones in the United States. Engines with aluminum cylinders and cast iron or steel piston skirts began to be seen, but technical difficulties and high cost restricted their use.

The spoked wheels were 26 or 28 inches (66 or 71cm) in diameter, with tyres 2.25 or 3 inches (5.7 or 7.6cm) in cross-section. Wheels with an extractable pin began to be popular, enabling the wheel to be removed without disturbing the rear crown and chain. Practically all motorcycles had drum brakes; high-voltage ignition magnetos were used, or flywheel magnetos in the case of two-stroke engines.

Lighting systems were far from perfect in the early postwar years: most companies made motorcycles without lamps, the customer then purchasing his own oil or acetylene lamps. The first machines complete with electric headlamps and rear lights appeared in about 1925, after which all other lighting systems rapidly disappeared.

In 1924, the German company Bosch decided to publish tables of heat grades for its spark plugs to help motorcyclists choose the correct type. This was the famous "Bosch scale" which later served as a frame of reference for heat grades of plugs by other companies. Spark plugs had been greatly improved by that time and could produce enough sparks even for engines with very high rotational speeds.

Manual lubrication had completely disappeared by 1925, fully automatic oil pumps being fitted outside the crankcase, or very occasionally inside it.

Variable transmission using a drive belt with an expanding pulley had also disappeared and motorcycles now had transmission with sliding gears, giving two and increasingly three speeds. The 1921 Della Ferrera, with a four-speed constant mesh gearbox, was an exception. The gears were controlled by a hand lever at the side of the petrol tank, bikes with foot-operated controls being rare. The vast majority had chain final drive, just a few having shaft drive.

Frames were sturdy and much lower and were gradually built with a continuous duplex cradle passing beneath the crankcase or with a two-piece cradle, in which the front and rear portions were connected by the crankcase. Frames in pressed steel were regularly used only in Germany, being either of the U cross-section or metal shell type.

In the early postwar years, apart from true motorcycles, motorized bicycles with a bicycle frame, pedals and engine of not more than 175cc displacement were quite common. Dozens of factories producing motor bicycles appeared throughout Europe, but by 1925 the craze was over and these machines disappeared. The fashion was revived after the end of World War II, in the form of a bicycle with an auxiliary motor first, a motor bicycle second.

The first scooters appeared at the same time: around 1910 in America; from 1919 only in Europe. To begin with they were virtually motorized versions of the child's scooter, the rider standing on a platform supported by two very small-diameter wheels: then they began to look more like modern scooters, being ridden from a seated position. But the only scooter that truly resembled those in circulation today was the Unibus of 1921, which was no more successful than the others.

There is not room to mention all the different companies that were founded or developed at that period. Moto Guzzi and Benelli, who established themselves immediately in the racing sector and soon became world-famous, brought out their first motorbikes in 1921. In 1919 Garelli began mass-producing their split-cylinder model, with a unit construction two-speed gearbox and chain drive. The Garelli stayed in production, with minor changes, until 1930 and the exploits of the company's racing and speed

THE NEW LOOK

Around 1930 chromium plating began to be used – first on the petrol tank, then on the handlebars and other parts of the frame that had formerly just been painted. Frames were nearly always of the closed-cradle type with one or two tubes, the tube from the steering head to the saddle no longer being horizontal but inclined to enable the saddle to be set still further down; the saddle was very comfortable, broad, sprung and increasingly anatomical in shape.

Petrol tanks were curved, roughly triangular and fitted astride the crossbar with the broadest part at the steering head and the narrowest part at the saddle. Special rubber "kneepad" tanks became fashionable.

Efficient electric headlamps and rear lights were now available to customers as a matter of routine. The gearbox, which was separate from the engine because many companies preferred to buy this from specialist firms (like Burman and Sturmey Archer in Britain), normally had three transmission ratios, although there were four-speed gearboxes. The gears were still operated by a hand lever at the side of the petrol tank, although pedal controls with a single lever or rocker were found.

Immediately after World War I rear suspension seemed to be gaining ground quite rapidly, but in later years (around 1930 in particular), it tended to disappear and many companies who had been using it reverted to rigid frames.

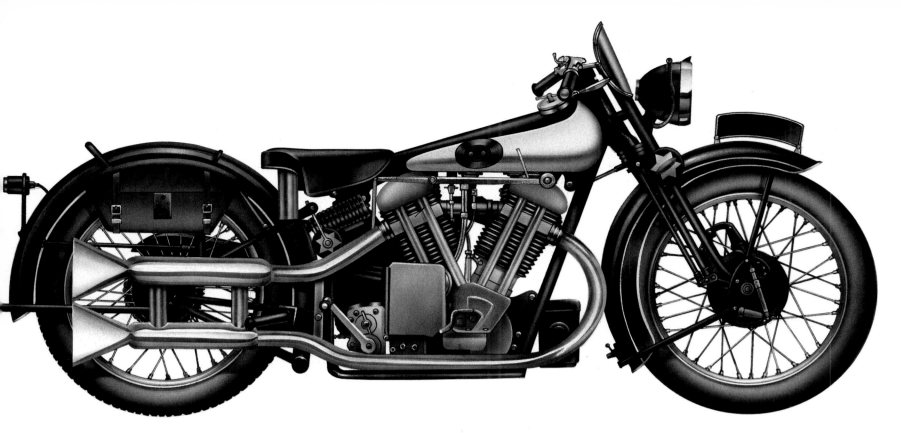

The 1930 Brough Superior model SS 100 had a JAP 980 cc twin-cylinder V-type engine, or later, a Matchless 998 cc. In both cases, push rod valve gear was used. The different versions of this motorbike were a great success and it stayed in production until 1940.

Motosacoche is the most famous Swiss firm. The 1930 Jubilee Grand Touring model had a twin-cylinder V-type engine. The 350 cc version had push rod valve gear, while the 500 cc model had side valves.

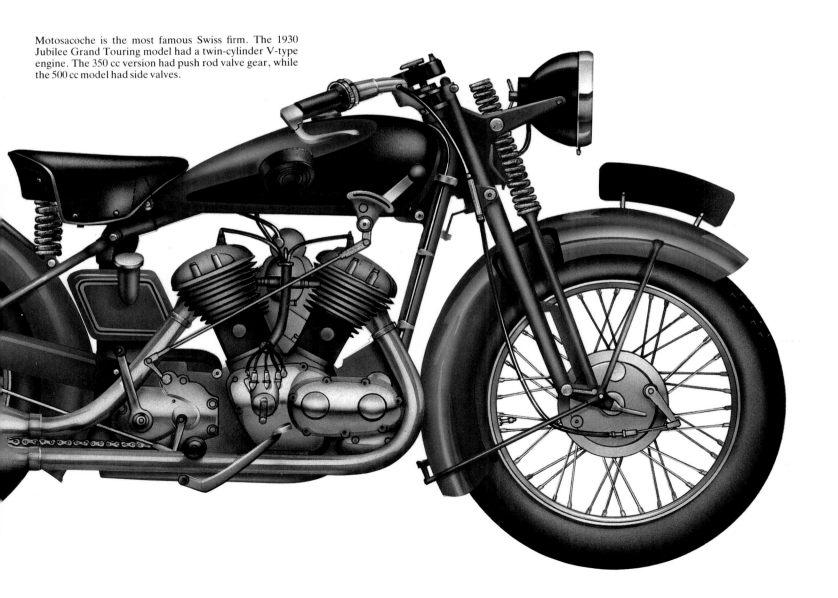

record models attracted world-wide admiration and acclaim in the twenties.

In 1919 Gilera resumed production, having moved from Milan to Arcore. In 1922 Garabello produced a fine machine with four cylinders in line, which was not, however, a success.

In Germany, DKW was established in 1919. Like Zündapp (founded in 1921) and BMW (founded in 1917), it was to become world-famous.

In Britain, the famous Brough Superior came out in 1925: with a 680 cc JAP V-twin engine, it was produced in much the same form until 1935.

In 1919, Royal Enfield designed a 675 cc two-stroke engine with three cylinders in line and an 846 cc with four cylinders in line, neither of which was mass-produced.

In the same year, Granville Bradshaw designed a new ABC which had an engine with two horizontally opposed cylinders fitted transversely to the frame, with cast iron cylinder heads,

hemispherical combustion chambers and overhead valves controlled by push rods and rocker arms. This machine, which had four-speed gears, a cone clutch and chain drive, was then manufactured under license by the French company Gnome & Rhône. It was the first machine to fit horizontally opposed cylinders transversely rather than longitudinally to the frame.

In Germany in 1921 Cockerell designed the Megola, an extraordinary machine with a five-cylinder radial engine in the front wheel, an open frame with complete bodywork finish, an upholstered seat and elastic front and rear suspension. The Megola, a racing version of which achieved an average speed of 145 km/h (90 mph) on the track at Avus in 1923, disappeared from the market in 1925.

Another interesting machine which had an open frame and bodywork finish was the American Ner-a-Car with a two-stroke engine, built in 1921 and sold immediately afterward to a British

company, who manufactured it under license with a four-stroke engine. But this new version was no more successful than the first.

The British Eta of 1921 had a three-cylinder engine (two of them were fitted transversely and horizontally opposed, while the third was vertical and installed in the center, between the other two), a displacement of 807 cc, shaft drive, half leaf spring front suspension and whole leaf spring rear suspension.

In 1921 Triumph brought out the model R, which had a timing system with four overhead valves operated by push rods and rocker arms. Designed by the famous Ricardo, it was the fastest British mass-produced model and was manufactured until 1927.

In 1920, C. R. Redrup used a

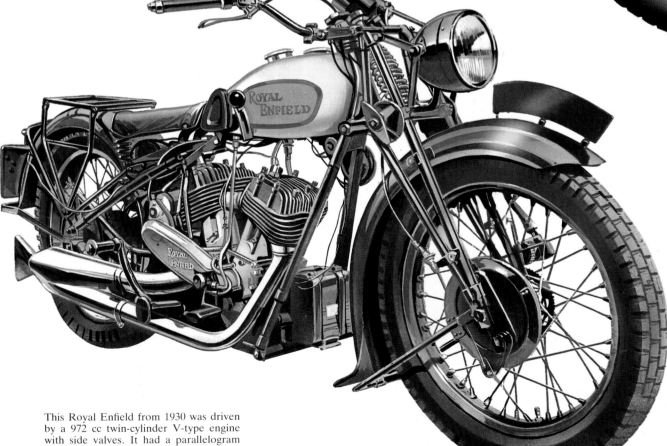

This Royal Enfield from 1930 was driven by a 972 cc twin-cylinder V-type engine with side valves. It had a parallelogram front fork and drum brakes.

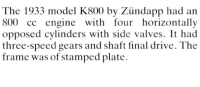

The 1933 model K800 by Zündapp had an 800 cc engine with four horizontally opposed cylinders with side valves. It had three-speed gears and shaft final drive. The frame was of stamped plate.

309 cc three-cylinder radial engine which he had designed in 1913, as the basis for a 618 cc six-cylinder radial engine.

In the years from 1926 to 1930, the motorcycle's appearance was transformed: it became more rounded, less angular than before and thus more aesthetic. The British call this the *new look* period and you need only compare a machine from 1930 with one from a few years earlier to see that the motorcycle as we know it stemmed from that period.

The birth of the four-cylinder

At the beginning of the thirties, the public showed particular interest in four-cylinder motorcycles: articles were published in the specialized press; many readers submitted their own designs; and the four-cylinder was regarded as the ideal motorcycle of the future. The success of today's big multi-cylinder machines shows that this view was not mistaken.

Yet not many four-cylinder bikes were successful.

Of the models before World War I, the Binks of 1903 (which became the Evart Hall in 1904) and the Durkopp are worth mentioning. The Low of 1922, with a two-stroke engine with horizontally opposed cylinders, was another, followed by – all with cylinders in line, as was the fashion – the Widhoff of 1927, the Mat of 1928, the Ragot of 1929 and finally the Bradshaw also of 1929.

In the United States, after the disappearance of the Pierce Arrow in 1914, the Militaire (derived from the Underslung), also with four cylinders in line, became available in 1915. The company failed in 1917, re-formed shortly afterwards under the name Militor, and finally closed down completely in 1922.

The four-cylinder-in-line Henderson was acquired in 1917 by Excelsior, who sold it with the Henderson trademark superimposed on the big X of their own logo and produced it, with continual improvements, until 1931 when Excelsior closed down because of the Depression. This machine was the first to use force-feed lubrication for the three main bearings and four big-end bearings.

Meanwhile William Henderson, who had left Excelsior in 1919, designed a new model with four cylinders in line named Ace, which was an enormous success. But high costs and the death of Henderson in an accident in 1924 halted production. After many vicissitudes, the Ace was acquired in 1927 by Indian, who marketed it as the Indian-Ace until 1929. In 1929 the Ace tradename was abandoned; the machine was updated and given the name Indian Four, which it kept until 1940. Up to 1937 it was virtually unchanged, but it was completely redesigned in 1938 and turned into a magnificent machine which was even fitted with telescopic rear suspension in 1939.

A motorcycle with four cylinders in line which had a long history, if no outstanding success, was the Danish Nimbus, introduced in 1926 and produced with

29

The range of Norton motorcycles in 1936 included this 500 cc (79 x 100 mm) model with push rod valve gear and dry-sump lubrication.

very few changes until after World War II. Another machine with a long and successful career was the famous Ariel Square Four, with four cylinders arranged in a square, which came out in 1930 and was produced until the mid fifties.

Other vehicles with four cylinders in line included the Brough Superior of 1928 with a Swiss MAG engine, designed by George Brough (who had brought out a model with a four-cylinder V-type engine the previous year) and the Brough Superior of 1931 with an Austin engine; the splendid Brough Superior Dream of 1937, in which the four cylinders were horizontally opposed, was not produced because of World War II.

Worth mentioning are the AJW, Chaise, Motobécane, Motoconfort, Train and Hess; the 1933 Zündapp with four horizontally opposed cylinders; the 1936 Puch with a four-stroke engine with four horizontally opposed cylinders fitted transversely; the magnificent but unsuccessful Matchless Silver Hawk of 1930 with a four-cylinder 26 degree narrow V-type engine and the AJS of 1935 with a four-cylinder 50 degree V-type engine.

In Italy, unsuccessful multi-cylinder machines included the 500 cc 1931 Moto Guzzi racing model, with four horizontal cylinders side by side; the 1932 Moto Guzzi with three horizontal cylinders side by side; the 1931 Zappoli with four horizontally opposed cylinders; the 1933 Super Itala with a four-cylinder V-type engine; the 1938 Galbusera 250 with a four-cylinder V-type engine and the 500 with an eight-cylinder V-type engine, and the 1939/1940 Moto Guzzi with three cylinders side by side, which was abandoned because of the war.

New prewar models

So many good brands of motorcycle were introduced in the decade from 1931 to 1940 that it is impossible to name them all. We shall mention only the most outstanding.

In 1933, the British company Scott designed a new 747 cc model, unveiled at the London Show. It had a final displacement of 986 cc and a three-cylinder in-line engine, but was never mass-produced. In 1935 Scott brought out another original engine, a 650 cc with two cylinders in line which was fitted to the frame upside down, but this was not mass-produced either.

Between 1929 and 1934, the French company Majestic built several models of motorcycle with displacements of 350 to 1000 cc, frames of pressed steel and fully faired bodies. These machines had vertical arm front suspension, with telescopic shock absorbers and strong helical springs, but do not appear to have had much success.

The 600 cc and 800 cc Zündapp models of 1935, with four horizontally opposed cylinders, were derived from the earlier 400 cc and 500 cc models with two horizontally opposed cylinders. All these machines had three-speed gears with duplex chain linkage between the primary and secondary drive shafts. Shaft final drive was used.

The Austrian company Puch, which had merged with Austro Daimler in 1928, was united with Steyr in 1934 to form the powerful Steyr-Daimler-Puch AG group. In 1936 it produced an 800 cc motorcycle complete with sidecar, with a horizontally opposed four-cylinder engine fitted transversely to the frame. This machine, which was intended for the Army, had a side-valve timing system, bevel gear primary drive from the engine to the gearbox and chain gear (final) drive from

the gearbox to the rear wheel. The frame was a mixture of tubular and stamped elements, with a deformable parallelogram type front fork in pressed steel. This model was, however, abandoned directly after the Nazi invasion of Austria.

Various conventional types of motorcycle were built in the Soviet Union in the years leading up to World War II; they were very sturdy, but not very fast, two- or four-stroke, and were generally inspired by German motorcycles.

Apart from a racing model with a compressor, built in 1935, the Czechoslovakian company Jawa brought out in 1937 the 98 cc Robot lightweight motorbike, which was a great success before World War II.

In 1933 Frera, which had been the biggest Italian motorcycle producer before World War I, disappeared from the market. After a few months, the company was revived by a group of shareholders and resumed production. Another very famous company that disappeared in 1936 was Garelli, but it started up again after the war, producing the famous Mosquito auxiliary engine.

Shortly before the war Gilera brought out a fine sporting machine, the 500 VTGS, which immediately became known as "Otto Bulloni" (Eight Bolts) and could hold its own against true racing models; and the Saturno, also with a displacement of 500 cc.

A splendid machine was built in 1939 by Miller Balsamo of Milan: it had a 200 cc two-stroke engine and very modern-looking fairing, but was virtually abandoned because of the war.

In 1931 Officine Meccaniche Fausto Alberti of Milan, who had been manufacturing various types of instruments and machine tools since 1922, brought out a fine 175 cc motorcycle under the Sertum trademark, which was followed by 250 cc single-cylinder and 500 cc twin-cylinder models. During the thirties, Sertum became one of the five top Italian producers of motorcycles and distinguished itself in reliability trials.

An interesting and very modern machine was the Altea, built by engineer Alberico Seiling in 1939; it had a 196 cc four-stroke single-cylinder engine and original elastic rear suspension with a

swinging fork controlled by a single vertical spring.

In 1932, the British company Coventry Eagle introduced the Silent Superb, with a 150 cc two-stroke engine and pressed steel frame with removable side panels. Coventry Eagle claimed to be the first motorcycle manufacturer to have moved the headlamp from the top of the front fork to a position lower down, between the two arms of the fork.

The BSA auxiliary motor for bicycles, with a fixed central axle, a rotating toric cylinder and a displacement of 34 cc, was not mass-produced – probably due to high manufacturing costs but also because, being designed in 1938, it was shelved on account of the war, like many other experimental engines.

In 1939 Rudge, which had been one of the top British makes, was forced to close down, and disappeared from the market.

The decade from 1931 to 1940 was certainly not an easy one for motorcycles. After the Wall Street crash, caused by frantic speculation on the New York Stock Exchange, all the United States motorcycle producers disappeared from the market, with the exception of Indian and Harley-Davidson.

Then the effects of the Depression began to be felt in Europe as well, causing the slump of the early thirties and the consequent closure of dozens of factories.

The BSA M 20, which appeared at the end of the thirties, was widely used as a military vehicle during World War II. It had a 500 cc single-cylinder side-valve engine and four-speed gearbox.

This is the Manxman model of 1937 by Excelsior, which was produced in 250, 350 and 500 cc displacements, all with a single-cylinder engine and overhead-camshaft valve gear.

TECHNICAL DEVELOPMENT IN THE TWENTIES AND THIRTIES

At the end of the thirties the majority of motorcycle engines were single-cylinder, the cylinder usually being fitted vertically or tilted forward slightly, as in a number of British models; the horizontal cylinder used by Moto Guzzi was quite exceptional.

Twin-cylinder engines, which were common at the beginning of the twenties, had become very rare. Horizontally opposed cylinders fitted longitudinally to the frame had disappeared and a few engines of this type, such as those of BMW, had transverse cylinders. V-twin engines were hardly used any more, except in the United States.

Twin-cylinder engines with two forward-facing parallel cylinders (like the one fitted to the 1937 Triumph) were also rare, although this arrangement was to be enormously successful after World War II.

In Europe, high-capacity machines with displacements from 750 to 1200 cc had disappeared, the commonest displacements being 250 and 350 cc. The use of light alloys were common, especially for the cylinder heads: cylinder blocks were still normally made of cast iron, although many companies sold models with both sections made of light alloy.

Overhead-valve timing systems had won the day by the end of the thirties, but most manufacturers still stocked models with side valves and continued to do so, above all in Britain, even in the years immediately following the Second World War. Overhead valves were usually operated by push rods and rocker arms, although a few models had high-cam valve gear in which the camshaft, instead of being at the base of the engine, was positioned higher up (roughly halfway between the base of the cylinder block and the cylinder head): high-cam valve gear used very short push rods, which were more rigid and lighter than the very long normal type. Only a few machines were fitted with overhead camshafts.

As far as two-stroke engines were concerned most of these were of small or medium displacement, except in Germany and Austria, where they were also used for high-capacity machines. Most two-stroke engines had normal valve gear with three ports, although there were models with rotary valves or, as in the 1934 DKW, reed valves. Speaking of DKW, this company had revolutionized techniques for building two-stroke engines in the years before World War II, thanks to the system of scavenging using two transfer ports invented by engineer Schnürle. After winning the War the Allies appropriated this system – which had been the prerogative of DKW, who had patented it – and began producing two-stroke engines in Britain and the United States which were a copy of those made by DKW. Engines with split cylinders were also built in those years and in 1934, Puch even brought out an engine with two split cylinders – in other words, with two combustion chambers and four cylinder barrels.

Towards the end of the thirties most motorcycles had four-speed gears and an increasing number were foot-operated, generally with a single lever because the rocker type was still a luxury.

Chain final drive was used: in Germany this was often enclosed in an oil bath box, while in Italy it was still exposed to the elements. A few brands, like Ollearo in Italy and BMW in Germany, had shaft final drive. In 1938 BMW equipped its motorcycles with a drive shaft with universal joints, making it possible to use elastic rear suspension.

The motorcycle at the end of the thirties was several kilograms lighter than one of the same capacity from the twenties, despite carrying a full complement of electrical equipment and all the accessories which were now routine, whereas the motorcycle of the twenties had been sold virtually naked. This weight reduction was partly due to the use of light alloys and partly to improvements in materials, with the result, for example, that thinner tubes could be used. The pressed steel frames favoured in Germany were barely seen in Britain, France and Italy.

Wheels were spoked, with a removable pin and a smaller diameter than those of the twenties, the standard measurement in this period being about 19 inches (48 cm). Tyres had a grooved or sculpted tread and punctures were now a rarity, thanks to better-quality rubber and, above all, vast improvements in the roads.

Front forks were of the deformable parallelogram type with friction shock absorbers at the sides and a big central spring, although the first telescopic front forks were coming into use and were to replace the parallelogram type completely after World War II. The German company BMW were pioneers in this field, abandoning the leaf-spring front fork in 1935 in favour of an elegant and functional telescopic fork.

Elastic rear suspension began to be quite common toward the end of the thirties, manufacturers offering versions with elastic frames alongside the rigid-framed models.

The old system of elastic rear suspension using leaf springs was abandoned in favour of more efficient methods, such as trailing-arm rear forks connected to the frame by friction shock absorbers or telescopic vertical shock absorbers connecting the top section of the rear fork to the top tube of the frame.

Various brands even had the frame's rear triangle of the trailing type, instead of just the fork, with springs in a wide variety of positions: beneath the crankcase in a horizontal metal box (Moto Guzzi); with a single, large oblique spring (Gilera); with a single, large-diameter vertical spring (Altea); with helical springs in a container fitted obliquely (Vincent-HRD), helical springs fitted vertically (ONC), or beneath the saddle (Draper).

When the effects of the economic crisis were starting to ease off a little (1933–1935), a period of political instability followed, leading up to the wars in Spain and Ethiopia, a prelude to World War II.

And yet it was in those very years of economic crisis and political instability that the motorcycle entered a phase of exceptional development. Towards the end of the twenties, it had become a thoroughly reliable vehicle on which one could travel with peace of mind, sure of reaching one's destination safely. No longer plagued by the need to solve problems concerning the reliability of the various components of the motorcycle (for example, at the beginning of the twenties it was still advisable to carry at least one spare valve), engineers could now concentrate on improving its performance, enhancing its appearance and making it more comfortable. Accordingly, by the end of the thirties the motorcycle had reached a very high level of aesthetics and performance and could satisfy the demands of motorcyclists in these respects, until factories could start producing new models again.

The 1933 Puch 500 had the technical features typical of motorbikes by this company, with a split-single-cylinder two-stroke engine.

The 500 cc Gilera Saturno with a unit construction four-ratio gearbox was introduced in 1939, but went into production only in 1946. The 84 x 90 mm single-cylinder engine, with push rod valve gear, delivered 18 HP at 4500 rpm in the touring version and 22 HP at 5000 rpm in the sports version.

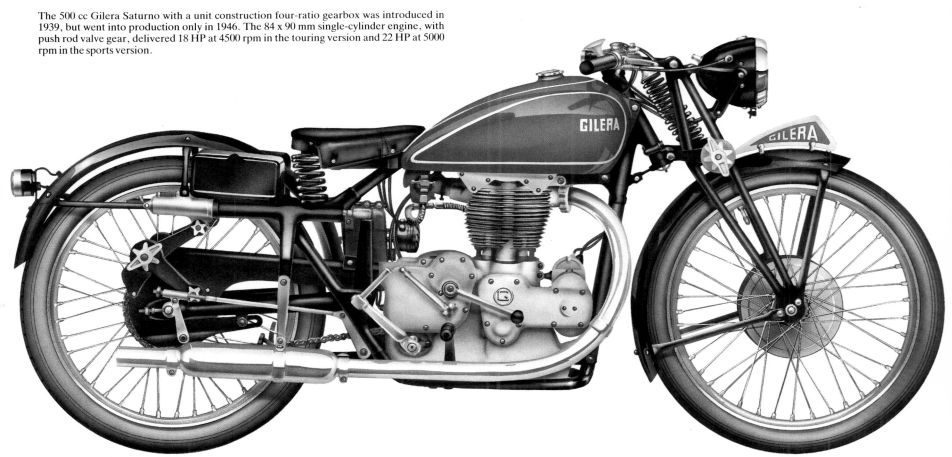

The idea of the first motorcycle race as a contest between two lucky owners of two-wheeled motor vehicles, battling it out on dusty, bumpy roads at the end of the last century, is picturesque but not very realistic. The earliest competitions were in fact exhausting long-distance journeys along roads that were open to traffic. The first such events were held in France, from 1894. The starting point was always Paris, the target destination being Rouen, or Marseilles, Bordeaux, Toulouse, then further and further afield, to Vienna and Madrid.

The first competitions were open to steam- and petrol-engined cars, motor tricycles and two-wheeled motor vehicles, without any regulations or semblance of separate classification. One cannot therefore speak of racing technique in that pioneering period: anybody with a motor vehicle of any description could take part, the sole aim being to reach the finish point.

Matters were a little better organized by the beginning of the century, two-wheeled vehicles becoming increasingly independent of three- and four-wheeled vehicles. The types of technical solution used in the early years of the century differed enormously. The 1901 Werner was powered by a vertical single-cylinder of 2.75 HP. It won the Paris–Vienna and Paris–Madrid races the following year and also did well in Italy, being appreciated for its staying power as well as its slim profile and small displacement. Other famous bikes were the colossal Buchet driven by a huge twin-cylinder with a total capacity of 2.5 to 3 liters and a speed of over 120 km/h (75 mph) and the first narrow-angle V-twins, which were to figure prominently in motorcycle racing for a number of years. The first bikes of this type to be used for racing were powered by Peugeot engines, but the Griffon-Zedel, Czech Laurin & Klement of 1905 and German NSU are also worth mentioning.

An historic occasion was the birth of the Tourist Trophy, which was contested for the first time on 28 May 1907 and was to become the most prestigious, demanding and lethal motorcycle race in the world, judging by the more than one hundred riders who have lost their lives in the various types of competition held on that circuit.

The active British motorcycle industry was longing to follow in the footsteps of France, but was hampered by the categorical refusal of the authorities to close down stretches of road to allow motorcycle races to take place on them, and the equally strict prohibition on motor vehicles exceeding a speed of 36 km/h (22.5 mph). The Auto-Cycle Union therefore took advantage of the fact that the Isle of Man in the Irish Sea had independent legislation and found a circuit about 25.5 km (16 miles) long, which could be closed to traffic for the duration of the race. The Tourist Trophy was

The highly successful Griffon V-twin with opposed valves, which came out in 1902.

FROM THE FIRST COMPETITIONS TO 1940

In 1903 the artisan Buchet built this extraordinary machine for the rider Fournier. It had a twin-cylinder engine of over two liters displacement.

thus held on a closed circuit, the bikes participating being divided into two separate classes, one for single- and one for twin-cylinders. There were no limits to weight or displacement, only fuel consumption.

The first edition of the Tourist Trophy, or TT for short, was won by a Norton in the twin-cylinder category and a Matchless in the single-cylinder category. The former, piloted by Rem Fowler, achieved a lower average speed than the "single," as it was stopped several times by punctured tyres; it nonetheless managed to establish the fastest ever lap speed at 69 km/h (42.87 mph). It was powered by a 726 cc Peugeot narrow-angle V-twin with automatic inlet valves and side exhaust valves, no gearbox or clutch and direct belt drive. Charles Collier came first in the other category, riding a Matchless vertical-cylinder machine of about half a liter's displacement.

Thus began the epic deeds of the Tourist Trophy, an extremely demanding contest in terms of both the route and the fact that the contestants were started off in separate pairs, the result being a sort of race against the clock during which the rider could not check the position of his opponents by eye. The Collier brothers won the next two editions as well. Harry won the single-class race for the 1909 season on a Matchless with a 738 cc JAP narrow-angle V-twin and managed to raise the average lap speed to nearly 85 km/h (53 mph). Charles repeated his success with the same bike in 1910.

The following year the British competition was structured differently, being subdivided into two classes: Senior (500 cc) and Junior (350 cc). In the higher displacement the first three places went to American Indian V-twins. The big American machines of this type with a 1000 cc displacement – by Indian, Excelsior and above all Harley-Davidson, who in 1916 designed a racing engine with four push rod-operated valves per cylinder – often beat the lighter European bikes before the war, when they were able to race on fast stretches or autodromes. On that topic, in the all-important year of 1907 the track with cambered turns at Brooklands near London was also inaugurated; here it was possible to attain high speeds and attempt records. The Scott was very successful at the TT for a few years. This was an original 489 cc two-stroke water-cooled "oversquare" twin (70 × 63.5 mm), which won in 1912 and 1913. Excellent results were also obtained by the Douglas, with two horizontally opposed cylinders mounted longitudinally.

But the strongest interest was in the tough, straightforward single-cylinder, closely related to the production models which had by then achieved an acceptable general standard of reliability. After 1910 came the 490 cc (79 × 100 mm) Norton with side valves, two gear ratios and adjustable belt drive and the 499 cc

Norton entered this slimline V-twin with a Peugeot engine of about 5 HP in the first edition of the Tourist Trophy, which took place in 1907.

(85 × 88 mm) Rudge Multi, with an overhead valve engine and transmission by an adjustable pulley operated by a hand lever, on which Pullin won the last prewar TT.

In Italy motorcycle racing started off on the wrong foot at the beginning of the century, as had happened a few years earlier in France: using very long courses on roads, velodromes and – given the topography of the country – even hills. The riders normally used foreign bikes, as there were very few Italian models at that time which could be adapted for racing. Those that could included the sloping-cylinder 2.5 HP Rosselli and the Marchand, made in Piacenza. Italian bikes did not take on a more sporting character until a few years later. In 1909 Giuseppe Gilera built his first bike. Driven by a 317 cc push rod-operated overhead valve vertical single-cylinder, it could do 100 km/h (62 mph) and its builder, who was also a competent rider, won some notable victories on it.

The Grand Prix model designed for Peugeot by the Swiss engineer Henry in 1913 was quite outstanding. It had two parallel vertical cylinders of 498 cc (62 × 82 mm), a gear-driven double overhead camshaft valve mechanism, unit construction three-speed gearbox and chain final drive; it developed 15 HP.

New international regulations

In the period immediately following the First World War racing received a considerable boost, uniform regulations being introduced which were valid internationally, including subdivision into classes according to displacement: up to 250, 350 and 500 cc; up to 175 cc and sidecar category. In the space of a few years the European countries most closely involved – apart from Britain, which had resumed the contest for the Tourist Trophy from 1920, and France – introduced their own

annual Grand Prix, with an established venue. Belgium fixed hers at Spa-Francorchamps in the Ardennes (in 1921); Italy at the new autodrome at Monza (in 1922); Ulster at the Clady triangle near Belfast (also in 1922); Germany at the Avis autodrome in Berlin (in 1924) and Holland at the Assen circuit (in 1925). These were decidedly fast courses, on which the famous average of 100 km/h (62 mph) was exceeded almost immediately despite stops for refuelling, which were unavoidable because of the length of the courses.

Somewhat surprisingly the new courses, rather than favouring the big, powerful American-style twin-cylinders, virtually spelled their doom because the more agile, latest-generation European singles soon proved more efficient on all types of ground. The 1000 cc class was banned from official races, the last notable victory of an American twin-cylinder being achieved at Monza in 1922 by Amedeo Ruggeri on a Harley-Davidson.

The 1909 Indian 1000 made the American company famous in Europe too. The engine was a narrow-angle V-twin with an opposed valve timing system.

In 1916 the great American company Harley-Davidson built a twin-cylinder racing bike with four valves per cylinder and a displacement of 1000 cc.

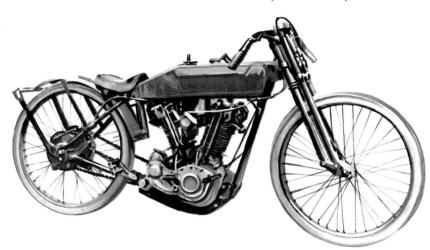

In 1913 Peugeot brought out a 500 with a sensational new twin-cylinder engine: the first to use a (gear-driven) double overhead camshaft timing system; there were four valves per cylinder.

For the 500 class, which was the largest capacity permitted by the regulations and the most exciting, the British and Italian makers chose single-cylinder engines with overhead valves. In Great Britain Norton, Triumph, Sunbeam, Rudge and AJS bikes were push rod-operated. The Norton TT of 1923–1924 had just two valves angled at 100°, a displacement of 490 cc (79 × 100 mm), developed about 25 HP and could do 150 km/h (93 mph). The contemporary 498 cc Sunbeam, with a very long stroke (77 × 105 mm) and just two valves angled at 90°, offered similar performance; likewise the Rudge 497 cc (85 × 88 mm) with four overhead valves, two inlet and two exhaust. The 500 cc Triumph Ricardo with four valves in the cylinder head was short-lived, while the AJS did well in the lower displacement with the 348 cc (74 × 81 mm) Big Port, also winning the Senior Class Tourist Trophy in 1921. Overhead camshaft valve gear seemed the best solution for racing engines. The first of this type was the Peugeot 495 cc

(62 × 82 mm) twin-cylinder, with 27 HP at 5000 rpm, which won the French G.P. in 1923 and the G.P. des Nations (International G.P.) at Monza with Gillard, but was soon outclassed by the British and Italian single-cylinder machines. On the French bike, the top part of the timing system was operated by a shaft with bevel gears. This system was also used on most of the new single-cylinder racing machines.

The year 1924 saw the successful launch of the 499 cc (88 × 82 mm) four-valve Moto Guzzi, which was built on similar lines to the first production models designed by Carlo Guzzi, namely "oversquare" cylinder dimensions, a horizontal cylinder axis and external flywheel, to which were added a cylinder head with four valves and an overhead camshaft operated by shaft and bevel gears. The Guzzi "four-valve" distinguished itself that year at the Lario Circuit (Ghersi), at the G.P. des Nations at Monza (Mentasti) against the official Norton and Peugeot machines, and at the German

G.P. at Avus (Ghersi). In the same year the 348 cc (74 × 81 mm) Bianchi Freccia Celeste came out; this developed over 20 HP and could do over 140 km/h (87 mph) right from the outset. Designed by Mario Baldi, it was the first racing single-cylinder with a double overhead camshaft and proved virtually unbeatable for about six years (at least in national competitions), performing equally well on very fast tracks like the one at Monza and on tortuous routes like the Lario circuit. Credit for the victories achieved by this machine was of course also due to its top-class riders, notably Tazio Nuvolari and Achille Varzi.

In 1926 the Moto Guzzi half-liter, which had in the meantime suffered from the "resurgence" of the British bikes, was joined by the 247 cc "square" (68 × 68 mm). Size apart, this was very similar to the 500, with a triangular oil tank fitted above the fuel tank. It had the same overhead camshaft valve gear operated by shaft and bevel gears, but with just two

All motorbikes by Scott had water-cooled two-stroke twin-cylinder engines. This is the 1922 "Squirrel," with which the company won the Tourist Trophy brand event.

One of the most famous racing bikes of the twenties was the AJS 350 "Big Port," which delivered about 20 HP and won the Tourist Trophy in 1921, 1922 and 1923. It had push rod valve gear.

The Moto Guzzi 500 single-cylinder seen on racecourses in 1924 had some very interesting technical features, such as the use of four valves (two inlet and two exhaust) and a higher bore than stroke (88 mm and 82 mm). The valve mechanism was of the single-camshaft type, operated by a shaft and bevel gearing. It had dry-sump lubrication (the oil tank was fitted above the fuel tank), a 3-speed unit construction gearbox and a power of about 22 HP at 5500 rpm.

inclined valves. The engine developed about 15 HP, which was enough to give the vehicle a speed of over 130 km/h (81 mph). The little Guzzi gained a reputation for being unbeatable on all types of circuit from the straight stretches of Monza to the bends of Lario, and this was to continue for years.

In Great Britain too, conversion to overhead camshaft valve gear was fairly rapid. Velocette used this type on their 348 cc model of 1926 with two overhead valves angled at 80° and similar performance to that of the Bianchi. It was immediately successful in the TT, piloted by Alec Bennett. A year later it was the turn of the Norton 490 cc (79 × 100 mm) designed by Walter Moore. The Velocette, which won the TT with Willis in 1927, and the Norton, which triumphed in the 500 class in the same year with the indefatigable Bennett, both had bevel shaft-operated overhead valve gear. An identical system was used for a 498 cc (80 × 99 mm) machine which Moore, having moved to

Germany, designed in 1930 for the German company NSU, stirring up a hornet's nest of nationalist indignation.

In those years more attention was paid to the bicycle side of motorbikes, refinements being made to the frame and brakes and the first foot-operated gearboxes being introduced. Nonetheless, the part that most distinguished racing models from normal machines was still the valve gear. Apart from the very popular shaft and bevel gears, overhead camshafts were operated by two other systems: chain drive (used on AJS 250, 350 and 500 cc vertical single-cylinders in 1927) and cascaded gears (used by Benelli for their 172 cc "oversquare" engined lightweight motorbike). The AJS single-camshaft in the various displacements was not an unqualified success, despite the 500 cc model piloted by Hicks winning the Grand Prix des Nations at Monza in 1931, while Benelli established a virtual monopoly of 175 class events which lasted for several years.

The only types of opposition to the classic single-cylinder overhead valve engine were two-stroke engines. The updated edition of the 500 cc Scott "Squirrel" performed very creditably until 1928, but without the prowess of the prewar period. The biggest innovations came from Italy, Germany and to a lesser extent Austria, with their famous Puch single-cylinder.

During the war engineer Adalberto Garelli had been working on an original engine with two cylinders side by side and a shared connecting rod and ignition chamber. The engine was lubricated by a high percentage of oil, had a total displacement of 349 cc (50 × 89 mm) and delivered approximately 15 HP. This agile bike could exceed 110 km/h (68 mph) in the first version, rising to over 130 km/h (80 mph) in subsequent ones. The most outstanding achievements of the Garelli 350 split-single-cylinder model included winning the Milan–Naples race in 1919; the Lario Circuit and Milan–Naples in 1921; the

One of the most famous racing bikes produced in Italy between the two World Wars was undoubtedly the Bianchi 350 double-camshaft, which became known as the "Freccia Celeste" (Blue Arrow). The single-cylinder engine had two valves but the exhaust was divided in two, two pipes emerging from the cylinder head. With a bore of 74 mm and stroke of 81 mm, the final version of this engine could deliver about 30 HP. The two camshafts were operated by a vertical shaft and bevel gearing. This machine dominated the racing scene from 1924 to 1930.

The Motosacoche 500 of the early twenties (this is the 1923 version) had a V-twin engine with push rod valve gear.

The Peugeot 500 twin-cylinder of 1923 had single-camshaft valve gear with two valves per cylinder. It delivered about 27 HP at 5000 rpm.

In the years following World War One Indian V-twins derived from series models (this is a 1924 1000 cc) were very successful in Europe too.

British JAP engines were extremely popular for years, being fitted to both production and racing bikes. This is the Brough Superior, with which Bert Le Vack established a world speed record (191.59 km/h = 119 mph) in 1924. The engine was a 1000 cc JAP twin-cylinder, delivering 50 HP.

In 1923 Norton brought out a new single-cylinder 500 with push rod valve gear, which was very successful. The engine, with a 79 mm bore and 100 mm stroke (measurements used by the company for many years) delivered about 25 HP.

The Belgian company Saroléa was very successful in competitions in the mid twenties, using 350 and 500 cc models derived from their production machines. They had single-cylinder engines with push rod valve gear. This is the 1926 500 cc version.

North–South Rally, Lario Circuit, French G.P. at Strasbourg and G.P. des Nations at Monza in 1922. With a modified bore:stroke ratio and lubrication fitted with oil in a separate tank, the Garelli engine was still a strong protagonist in 1923 when a very youthful Achille Varzi won the Lario Circuit and Italian Championship, while a series of important victories was achieved by Isacco Mariani. After that the Lombard machine was overtaken by the progressive establishment of British four-stroke engines.

DKW, founded in Saxony immediately after the Great War by the Dane Rasmussen, has always and only built two-stroke engines. The company's first racing bike was a 175 cc in 1926; its vertical single-cylinder engine was water-cooled and had a supercharger consisting of a horizontal cylinder-pump, the connecting rod of which was operated by the drive shaft. In the course of three or four seasons the DKW proved quite competitive but inferior overall, despite beating the single-camshaft Benelli on the Monza track in 1928.

Ten years of technical progress

The technical situation at the end of the twenties can be summarized as follows: over 30 HP and 170 km/h (105 mph) for the best half-liter machines; about 25 HP and 160 km/h (100 mph) for the 350s; about 20 HP and nearly 150 km/h (93 mph) for the 250s, of

which the single-camshaft Moto Guzzi was still by far the most successful example; about 12 HP and 120 km/h (75 mph) for the 175s.

In the higher displacement, the Norton which won the TT in 1927 was opposed for several seasons by the best "push rod" bikes around. During that period the strongest opposition in the half-liter category was considered to be the Sunbeam, which in fact won the TT in 1928 and 1929 (the rider was Dodson); the Grand Prix des Nations at Monza in 1926 (Varzi), 1927 (Arcangeli), 1928 (Franconi) and 1929 (Varzi); the Ulster G.P. in 1926 (Walker); the Belgian G.P. in 1928 and 1929 (Dodson); the Lario Circuit in 1927 (Arcangeli); 1928 (Arcangeli) and 1929 (Colombo).

Of shorter duration, but equally magnificent, was the golden age of Rudge. The 500 with four valves in parallel pairs had won the Ulster G.P. in 1928, at an average speed of over 135 km/h (84 mph), and the Dutch G.P. with Graham Walker. Then, in 1930, the British company prepared a 346 cc (70 × 90 mm) with four push rod-operated radial valves, which developed over 25 HP and had a speed of over 150 km/h (93 mph). This machine took the first three places at the TT with Tyrrell Smith, Nott and Walker at record average speeds, while Walter Handley won the 500 class with the type with four parallel valves, at an average of nearly 120 km/h (75 mph). The same half-liter bike also won most

of the top continental competitions. Rudge's fortunes were subsequently entrusted to the 250 cc (62.5 × 81 mm) which won the Tourist Trophy in 1931 and 1934, the numerous "Replica" models sold in Britain and on the Continent, and separate engines available under the Phyton trademark and used by such Italian bikes as the Miller Balsamo, Ancora and Linx.

After 1930 the major competitions went through a "static" period which lasted for quite some time. Italian marques dominated the lower-displacement classes. In 1930 the Benelli lightweight motorbike was given a new "square" (60.5 × 60.5) power unit of 174 cc, with double overhead camshaft valve gear driven by cascaded gears, with which it continued to excel until 1934. One of its chief rivals was another Italian machine, the chain-operated single-camshaft MM made in Bologna, which proved equally fast on more than one occasion. The Moto Guzzi 250 single-camshaft had foot-operated gears which were soon split up into four gear ratios; it continued to be a formidable contestant in the class for that displacement, although many of the competitions were won by British bikes (like the single-camshaft Excelsior or push rod-operated New Imperial) and, occasionally, by German DKWs.

In the higher displacements there was an almost monotonous prevalence of the Norton (redesigned in 1930 by Joe Craig) in the 500

The Husqvarna 500 single-cylinder was fitted both with an engine specially made by the Swedish company and with a JAP engine; this is the 1930 version.

In 1925 Harley-Davidson made a 350 cc single-cylinder model from which was derived a sports version which took part in many European competitions.

Calthorpe never took part officially in races but produced excellent single-cylinder 350s for privateers, with single-camshaft valve gear (1926).

Rudge was famous for its 350 and 500 cc single-cylinder engines with push rod valve gear using four valves (fitted radially in some models). This is the 500 ("Ulster" model) of 1928. A 250 cc engine was later produced as well.

Toward the end of the twenties the Sunbeam was one of the best bikes in the 500 cc class and did well in a number of very important races. The single-cylinder engine had push rod valve gear. This is the 1928 version.

In 1926 Scott, ever faithful to the water-cooled two-stroke twin-cylinder with rotary valve induction, built this "Flying Squirrel," a 500 cc machine suitably modified versions of which were used for racing by various riders.

The Velocette 350 racing model originated in 1926 and was mass-produced for privateers from 1929, distinguished by the letters KTT. The engine was a single-cylinder with a single-camshaft valve mechanism (operated by a shaft and bevel gears), an arrangement ◄ used by the company until the second half of the forties. This is the 1929 version, which delivered about 28 HP.

One of the most famous bikes of the first half of the twenties was the Garelli 350 two-stroke with a split cylinder. This bike, which had a 3-speed unit construction gearbox, also established many world speed records on the Monza track. This is the 1924 version, which delivered 20 HP at 4500 rpm compared with the 15 of the original model.

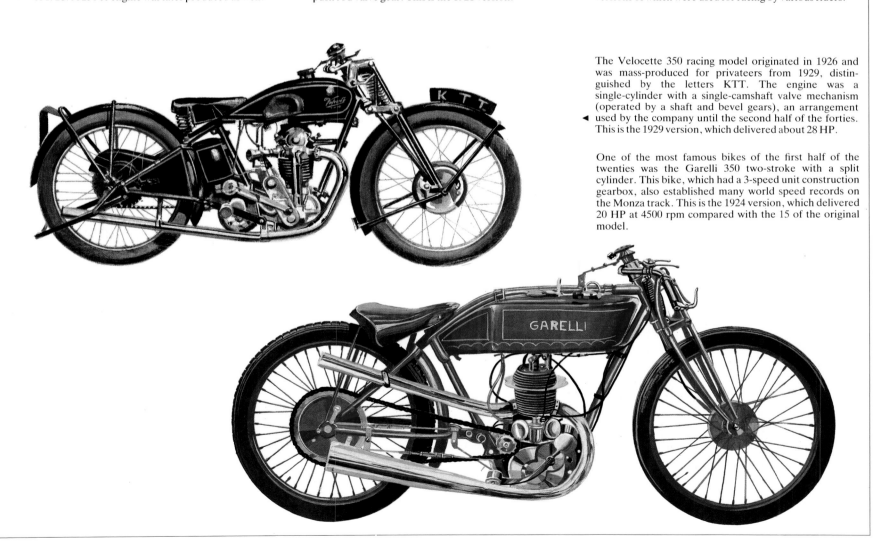

and 350 classes, a 348 cc single-camshaft single-cylinder (71 × 88 mm) having been prepared for the latter. Modifications included the vertical shaft of the valve gear, the frames and the separate Sturmey-Archer gearbox with three gear ratios, for which a pedal control was fitted. Nortons won most of the international motorcycling Grands Prix up to 1935, as their performance was excellent (30 HP and 160 km/h = 100 mph for the 350 cc and 40 HP and 180 km/h = 112 mph for the half-liters). These models were acknowledged masterpieces of mechanical rationality and general reliability, but one must not forget that the British company could also count on the top riders of the day, from Stanley Woods to Tim Hunt and Jimmy Guthrie.

Those who worked hardest to oppose British supremacy in the 500 class were the Swedish company Husqvarna in 1932–1933 and Moto Guzzi, both of whom preferred twin-cylinder engines. The Swedish bike had a power unit consisting of a 498 cc (65 × 75 mm) narrow-angle V-twin, mounted longitudinally as on the old American machines, and push rod-operated overhead valves; this engine developed about 45 HP. On the Italian bike, the V between the longitudinal cylinders was much broader – 120° – this being basically an engine which Carlo Guzzi had produced by adding a second cylinder, angled toward the back of the bike, to the proven 250 cc single-camshaft horizontal-cylinder model. The displacement was 494 cc (68 × 68 mm) and the power similar to that of the Husqvarna, 44–45 HP. Both these twins had a top speed of nearly 200 km/h (125 mph).

The racing successes of the Husqvarna were confined to national competitions, notably the Swedish Grand Prix. Stanley Woods also clocked up the fastest lap speed at the 1934 TT, and a smaller 350 cc version ridden by Sundqvist performed well at Monza in 1936.

The Moto Guzzi 250 single-camshaft single-cylinder began its career in 1926 with a power of about 15 HP, and was constantly updated and improved until the end of the thirties (by which time, partly thanks to supercharging, it could deliver 38 HP). This is the 1930 version, which developed 20 HP at 6800 rpm.

The Moto Guzzi twin-cylinder, on the other hand, had an extremely long and successful career, continuing to compete until 1951.

Partly due to outstanding riders like Omobono Tenni – who was considered on a par with the top British aces – and Stanley Woods himself, the bike from Mandello did brilliantly, winning the top Italian competition in 1934, 1935 and 1936, and an exciting edition of the TT with Stanley Woods in 1935. Performance was very good on all types of circuit and permitted record average lap speeds: in 1935 Woods touched 140 km/h (87 mph) at the TT and Omoboni Tenni achieved an average of nearly 178 km/h (110.6 mph) on the long, straight stretches of the Mellaha circuit in Tripoli.

The year 1935 was an historic one for the development of racing bikes. The smaller displacements were abandoned, and as a result some of the companies which had been producing them turned their attention to the displacements immediately above: the 250 cc and, to some extent, the 350 cc. There were also the first rational attempts at fitting racing bikes with elastic rear suspension; these were subsequently developed in various different

ways but were an immediate success in Italy, thanks to Moto Guzzi. Finally – and this was the most important factor – supercharged engines began to establish a foothold: they were to influence racing bike engineering in the second half of the thirties, up to the outbreak of World War Two.

As far as the first of these factors is concerned, the acknowledged supremacy of the tireless Moto Guzzi 250 – against which the conventional single-cylinders of the British school had very little chance of defending themselves in a direct confrontation – began to be undermined by the supercharged DKW split-cylinder models as well as the new Benelli, which was a sort of enlarged version of the multivictorious 175 cc. New bikes in the 350 cc class were developed by DKW and the Italian company MM, which had been a strong protagonist in the lightweight category.

The elastic rear suspension used in the spring of 1935 was quite complex, but functional. It consisted of hydraulic, horizontal shock absorbers fitted at the sides of the rear wheel, outside the triangle of the frame and accompanied by friction shock absorbers. Later, the two shock absorbers and their springs were placed side by side beneath the horizontal cylinder. Beween 1935 and 1937 the German BMW and DKW, British Norton and AJS and Italian Bianchi, Benelli and MM used a system of rear springing known as "vertical sliding hub" consisting of vertical, hydraulic shock absorbers fitted parallel to the rear mounts of the frame, the sliding elements of which were pivoted on the tip of the wheel axle; sometimes this system was also given a big rear fork, as in the DKW and Benelli bikes. The most functional system of springs was, however, that used by Velocette in 1938, with hydraulic shock absorbers incorporating the springs which acted as a simple joint between the swinging fork and the top part of the

The single-cylinder Norton "Inter national," derived from the official models, was sold to "privateers" from 1932. This machine, which had an engine with a single-camshaft valve mechanism (operated by a vertical shaft and bevel gears) was built in two versions, one of 350 and the other of 500 cc. This is the higher displacement version of 1936, which could deliver 40 HP at 6000 rpm. It had a separate, foot-operated 4-speed gearbox.

The second half of the thirties was the era of supercharging for racing bikes. BMW achieved great success with its 500 cc twin-cylinder models with a "split single camshaft" valve mechanism (operated by shafting and bevel gears), which competed from 1935. This type of machine, with a Zöller vane supercharger (the 1939 version is shown here) delivered 80 HP at 8000 rpm. It had telescopic fork front suspension and plunger rear suspension.

frame; this system, despite being highly progressive at the time, is still in favour today. Also worth mentioning is the fact that in those same years first BMW then Norton introduced telescopic hydraulic fork front suspension, although most racing bikes kept to the old, deformable parallelogram fork with a compressed central spring, pivoting levers and adjustable friction shock absorbers. These forks were usually made of round cross-section steel tubes but a few companies, like Gilera, used pressed steel forks.

The era of supercharging

A supercharger is a mechanical device which enables more fuel/air mixture to enter the cylinder than is normally drawn in by the induction stroke of the piston. The supercharger thus fills the cylinder up more, thereby enabling a greater specific power to be obtained from it: hence the distinction between "aspirated" and "pressure feed" or "supercharged" engines.

The application of such devices to fast motorcycle engines was limited to quite a short period, being virtually confined to the second half of the thirties, although there were earlier examples mainly intended for speed record bikes. To begin with the use of superchargers on motorcycles was partly conditioned by their weight, by the sometimes rudimentary systems used to transmit motion to them from the engine, and by the amount of power it took to operate them. But after 1935 Grand Prix motorbike engines were expressly designed to have superchargers, a gear mechanism usually being fitted to operate them through the drive shaft, gears in the gearbox or primary drive.

Supercharged bikes had a short and splendid season, nearly all the top European makers producing highly original, progressive models.

At that period the most widely used method of supercharging for Grand Prix automobiles was the Roots (lobe) type. The only important motorcycle to use this variety was the four-cylinder Rondine (Swallow), which later became the Gilera. The cylinder-pump system was confined to two-stroke engines and the first to use it was DKW, who produced various different sorts. The majority of motorcycle companies – from BMW to Moto Guzzi, Benelli, Bianchi, NSU, AJS and Velocette – used the vane type (Cozette, Centric or Zöller).

The Rondine, designed in Rome at the beginning of 1935, was the product of research carried out ten years earlier by two young engineers, Pietro Remor and Carlo Giannini. These two engineers were in fact the first to try to produce a four-stroke racing engine with four forward-facing cylinders, overhead camshaft valve gear and first air then mixed cooling, specifically for sporting use. After a number of attempts at artisan-type production and a few promising if not triumphant racing experiences, Giannini and Remor were given the opportunity of working with better finances for the Compagnia Nazionale Aeronautica (National Aeronautical Company) in 1935. The result was a new 493 cc (52×58 mm) engine angled 45° forward, which had water cooling, using a radiator fitted between the two front bars of the frame and a Roots-type supercharger operated by the primary drive mechanism. The engine's power was very high, about 80 HP at 9000 rpm, with the result that the bike, which had a pressed steel frame and partial fairing on some models, could touch 220 km/h (137 mph),

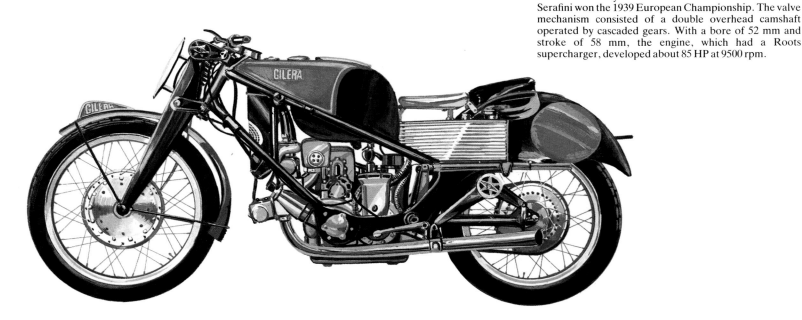

This is the four-cylinder water-cooled Gilera 500 on which Serafini won the 1939 European Championship. The valve mechanism consisted of a double overhead camshaft operated by cascaded gears. With a bore of 52 mm and stroke of 58 mm, the engine, which had a Roots supercharger, developed about 85 HP at 9500 rpm.

making it quite outstanding in circuit races and world speed championships.

The Rondine's top rider in 1935 was another young engineer from Latium, Piero Taruffi, who won two important races in Tripoli and Pescara, also setting a 500 class world speed record for the flying kilometer on a more extensively faired version, at an average of over 244 km/h (152 mph). Partly as a result of internal politics, the company that had built the Rondine was forced to surrender the equipment (six bikes and their respective spare parts), which was taken up by Gilera in 1936. The company appointed first Taruffi as engineer and test rider, then Remor also, and made a few changes to the drive shaft, supercharger and rear suspension. In 1937 the bike did brilliantly at Monza, beating Tenni's Guzzi and Gall's BMW, having established a dizzy record average lap speed of over 177 km/h (110 mph). Taruffi raised the world hour record to an average of 195 km/h (121 mph) and the record for the flying kilometer to an average of 274 km/h (170 mph).

In 1938 the European Championship was introduced with multiple trials, and in the higher displacement the supercharged Gilera four-cylinder was overshadowed by BMW's superior reliability and organization. But the improvements carried out by Gilera paid off and the bike won two completely different competitions, the long haul from Milan to Taranto (with Aldrighetti) and the tortuous Lario Circuit (with Serafini). In 1939 Serafini also won the most coveted award for Gilera, the European 500 Class title, after three consecutive victories on the circuits of Ulster, Sweden and Germany. Even the severest British critics recognized the overall superiority of the Italian machine which, in the faired record version piloted by Taruffi, raised the

hour world speed record to an average of 205 km/h (127 mph).

German engineers were the strongest champions of the other two methods of supercharging (cylinder-pump and vane) for some years. Oddly enough, however, in spite of this fact, Germany had transferred her main national motorcycling event in 1927 from the fast Avus circuit to the tortuous Nürburgring, and from 1934 to the Hoenstein road circuit in Saxony, which only permitted medium-fast speeds and had a somewhat dubious surface. In 1926 one of the very first BMW racing machines with a "boxer" engine established an average speed of 126.60 km/h (78.66 mph) at Avus; while in 1933, in a brief reappearance on the Berlin circuit which had in the meantime been given cambered turns, the supercharged BMW bike clocked up an average of 161.30 km/h (100.23 mph). Compare that with the best averages achieved at Nürburgring in 1933 by Guthrie's Norton (111.50 km/h = 69.28 mph) and Hoenstein in 1939 by Serafini's Gilera (141 km/h = 87.61 mph).

While all this chopping and changing was taking place, the Italians remained faithful to the Monza autodrome and the British to the almost impregnable fortress of the terrible Tourist Trophy.

German engineering prowess

To return to technical matters: the cylinder-pump fitted to DKW 175 and 250 cc two-stroke single-cylinders built up to 1930 did not live up to expectations at all, with the result that in 1931 the head of the racing department, engineer Zöller, designed a split-cylinder engine with a single combustion chamber which was fairly similar to the Garelli type, except for the connecting rod system and

arrangement of the pistons, which were fitted longitudinally in line, one behind the other. The two cylinders had slightly different capacities (the back one was a bit smaller than the front one). The cylinder-pump operated by an extra connecting rod was fitted horizontally at the front.

This machine, called URe, developed a power of over 25 HP and speed of about 170 km/h (105 mph), but took a few years to achieve the necessary reliability to counter the Moto Guzzi on all terrain. Its rider Winkler won the Grands Prix in Holland and Switzerland in 1934, in Holland again and Germany in 1935 and for the third time in Holland in 1937. The URe preferred fast tracks: it in fact won the Ulster G.P. in 1935 with Geiss and in 1937 with the British rider Thomas. Woods achieved the fastest lap speed at an average of 122.60 km/h (76.18 mph) at the 1936 TT (his last race before retirement), while a year later in Monza the DKWs were behind the Moto Guzzis of Pagani and Tenni.

For the 1938 season DKW prepared a new 250, the ULd, the completely redesigned engine of which had a third cylinder fitted at the front, in addition to the two longitudinal cylinders which acted as a compressor-pump; induction was controlled by a rotary valve. The ULd, which had a power of over 30 HP at 7000 rpm and speed of 180 km/h (112 mph), immediately became the machine to beat, despite its considerable weight, very high fuel consumption (it needed a 32 liter = 7 imperial gallon petrol tank) and somewhat precarious roadholding. The specialist Ewald Klüge, who was very clever at exploiting the bike's speed and, above all, acceleration, won the European Championship in 1938 and 1939, based on the sum of the points achieved in the various Grands Prix. In 1938 Klüge gained the

DKW has always raced motorcycles fitted with two-stroke engines, achieving excellent results. In the thirties in particular this famous German company was respected by engineers the world over for its highly progressive production and racing models. The URe 250 first appeared around 1934. The engine was of the split-cylinder type (two pistons in two adjacent cylinder barrels, with a single combustion chamber) with water cooling and a piston-type scavenge pump of nearly twice the displacement of the engine (this permitted a considerable degree of supercharging). This is the 1937 version, delivering over 26 HP at about 5000 rpm.

The URe 250 was replaced in 1938 by the ULd 250, with a completely redesigned engine. The piston-operated scavenge pump was fitted vertically, immediately in front of the split cylinder of the engine, and had its own crankshaft. Induction of the air-fuel mixture drawn in by the pump was controlled by a rotary valve, and this model also had a (thermosiphon type) water cooling system. As with the previous engine, the two pistons were connected to the drive shaft by a main connecting rod plus a link rod. This engine could deliver about 31 HP at 7000 rpm.

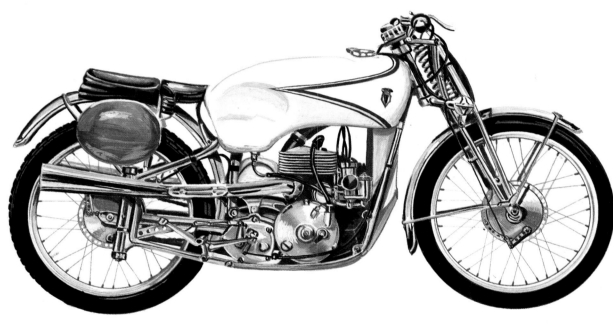

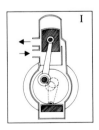 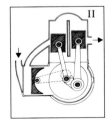 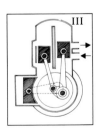 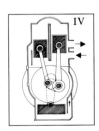

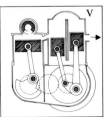 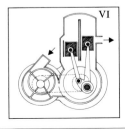 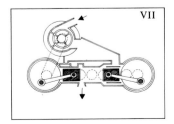

These diagrams show the evolution of DKW racing engines. The first engine, fitted with a piston scavenge pump (located at the bottom of the crankcase) was the 1927 ARe 175 (I), from which was developed a 250 cc version which delivered 17 HP at 5000 rpm. After that the company switched to the use of split cylinders, still with a piston scavenge pump (but fitted horizontally at the front of the engine, and with a reed-type inlet valve). This arrangement was used for the URe 250 and 175 (II). Engines for privateers were developed at the same time (UL 250), in which the inner part of the piston pump did the work (the air-fuel mixture thus being drawn into and precompressed in the cylinder block). The power in 1935 was about 20 HP at 4500 rpm (III). 350 and 500 cc engines with four pistons (or two split cylinders) were produced on the lines shown in Diagram IV. Diagram V shows the design used for the formidable ULd, with a vertical scavenge pump with its own crankshaft fitted in front of the split cylinder. A vane supercharger was subsequently fitted to the front of the engine (VI). The final stage in the evolution of supercharged two-stroke DKW engines is represented by Diagram VII, referring to the prototype GS 250 with opposed pistons and two crankshafts connected by a gear train, which should have developed about 46 HP.

title by winning the TT and the Belgian, Dutch, Swiss and French G.P.s. In 1939 he did so again by winning the Belgian, Dutch, French and Swedish G.P.s (but not the TT, which was won by Mellors' "aspirated" Benelli) and the top national event at Hoenstein, where the DKWs were thoroughly beaten by the Moto Guzzi supercharged single-cylinder.

The best results for a bike with a vane supercharger were undoubtedly achieved by BMW, who in 1923 built their first engine with two horizontally opposed cylinders, a unit construction gearbox and cardan shaft final drive. The company passed from side-valve engines to ones with push rod-operated overhead valves and displacements of 500 and 750 cc, which were also used for speed competitions. In 1929 a Zöller vane supercharger was adapted for these engines and fitted above the gearbox. The 750 cc model, which developed over 70 HP, powered motorcycles with increasingly extensive fairing, whose main purpose was to break the world speed records for the flying kilometer, given that on circuits the BMW 500, despite having the considerable power of 55 HP, did well only in national competitions.

The 735 cc record BMW, still piloted by Ernst Henne, first set a world speed record for the flying kilometer in 1929 (average 216.750 km/h = 135 mph), then repeated this achievement in 1930 (221.540 and then 244.400 km/h = 138/152 mph), in 1934 (246.061 km/h = 153 mph), in 1935 (252.831 km/h = 157 mph) and in 1936 (256.056 km/h = 159 mph). The competitions on circuits began to be a more worthwhile undertaking for BMW from 1935, when a new 493 cc "boxer" twin was designed which developed about 80 HP and had a double overhead camshaft and Zöller supercharger with vanes keyed to the front end of the drive shaft. The rise of the BMW bike to the top took some time. The final versions of the Norton – subsequently provided with light alloy cylinders and cylinder heads, double overhead camshaft valve gear and with displacement increased to 499 cc by a slight increase in bore – were still able to oppose the supercharged multi-cylinders for a couple of seasons, due to their great strength and endurance, greater maneuverability and, in particular, the sheer class of riders like Jimmy Guthrie, Freddie Frith and Harold Daniell. The single-cylinders from Birmingham were able to defend themselves with dignity up to 1936–1937, at least on certain circuits, despite developing only 50 HP and a speed of barely 200 km/h (124 mph) using special fuel mixtures.

Velocette made a strong comeback in the 350 class, which was not given much thought by continental companies except DKW, who derived a 350 from an enlargement of the more famous 250, and NSU, who brought out a reduced version of the 500 twin-cylinder. Around 1930 Veloce Ltd. had been involved in the construction of KTT models, which were replicas of the official bikes and were sold to private riders. This bike, which was very light and easy to handle, could do 140 km/h (87 mph) at that period if fuelled by petrol and 160 (100 mph) if fuelled by alcohol with a different compression ratio.

Velocette KTTs were used as back-ups for a few years by isolated competitors, achieving excellent placings, and returned to the front line after 1937 with the Mark 8 model, with more extensive light alloy finning and a swinging rear fork, a few half-liter versions of which were also built. The vitality of the machine and quality of its riders (from Woods to Ted Mellors and Bob Foster) meant that the single-camshaft version, which at that point developed 35 HP and 170 km/h (105 mph), was able to beat the better-organized and better-qualified Norton on several occasions. The two European Championships in 1938 and 1939 were won by Mellors, and Woods won the Tourist Trophy in the same year, still with the 350 cc machine.

Apart from the two famous British marques, there were no great novelties in the "aspirated" sector in the second half of the thirties. French Terrots with push rod-operated overhead valves and the new editions of the AJS single-cylinder with chain-operated single-camshaft valve gear played a marginal role. The best was offered by the "old" and continually rejuvenated Moto Guzzi 250 and the more recent Benelli double-camshaft of the same displacement. The latter was in fact redesigned in 1938 and given new bore and stroke measurements (65 × 75 mm instead of 67 × 70) with a total displacement of 249 cc, power of 27 HP at 9500 rpm and maximum speed of over 170 km/h (105 mph). Benelli won the Italian title in 1938 and put three machines in the first three places at the Monza International Grand Prix, and in 1939 Mellors won the TT, beating Klüge's supercharged DKW.

The other conventional single-cylinders fulfilled a subordinate role of mainly national significance. This was true of the British Rudge, New Imperial and Excelsior and the German single-camshaft NSU, which survived up to the war in a 600 cc version as well, for sidecar competitions. In Italy after 1930 Bianchi replaced its magnificent 350 cc double-camshaft by a similar but more up-to-date half-liter model. The engine of the "170," as this bike was designated, was a 496 cc (84 × 94 mm) double-camshaft which developed nearly 35 HP and permitted a speed of about 180 km/h (112 mph). At the same time Alfonso Morini, the designer for MM, devised a single-cylinder "3½" with single-camshaft valve gear, using a chain-driven camshaft like the old 175.

The 345 cc MM "square" engine with a 76 mm bore and stroke was not up to the standard of the contemporary Velocettes and best Nortons. A special record version established flying kilometer and flying mile world speed records in 1936, at an average of about 186 km/h (116 mph). The circuit model won the Italian Championship in 1938 thanks to the Roman Mangione, who also won the Lario event in 1938 and 1939.

The Moto Guzzi and Benelli 250s were the only two single-cylinders adapted to use a supercharger. The single-camshaft model from Mandello had a Cozette volumetric device fitted above the gearbox, which enabled the bike to touch 40 HP and 200 km/h (124 mph) and counter the supercharged DKWs. The Guzzi's biggest successes were in the world speed record sector, where it achieved an average of 180.5 km/h (112 mph) for the hour event and 213 km/h (132 mph) for the flying kilometer. However, the supercharged bike took part in the European Championship in 1939 and also won the German Grand Prix. The double-camshaft model from Pesaro, which had a centrifugal blower operated by the drive shaft, was entered experimentally in a few races only, and from the limited information available its performance appears to have been slightly below that of the Moto Guzzi machines.

Toward the end of the thirties the quest for absolute supremacy in the 500 class was basically confined to the BMW twin- and Gilera four-cylinder, both of which were supercharged. The German bike – which had won the Dutch and German G.P.s with Karl Gall in 1937 and established a world record for the flying kilometer at an average of 279.5 km/h (173.7 mph) – piloted by Henne, dominated the 1938 season. Its new number one rider, Georg Meier, became European Champion after winning the Belgian, Dutch, German and International Grands Prix. In 1939 he was stopped by an accident after winning the TT with ease and the Belgian and Dutch G.P.s with greater difficulty, leaving the way clear for Serafini, who won the title of European Champion with the Gilera four-cylinder, by triumphing at Ulster and in Sweden and Germany.

There was no longer any doubt that supercharged engines could not be opposed, and in the two years before World War Two there was a ferment of activity by the Italians, Germans and – somewhat surprisingly – the British, who were usually strictly conservative. In Germany the BMW was joined in 1939 by the 345 cc (56 × 70 mm) NSU with two cylinders (angled slightly forward) and two overhead camshafts driven by an unusual system: two shafts with bevel gears in the block, which operated the valve gear at the top. The engine developed about 60 HP but the bike did not have a chance to prove its

The Benelli 250 double-camshaft was derived from the 175, which started out with single-camshaft valve gear but was later given a dohc. This bike, of very modern design, came out in 1934 but did not really distinguish itself until four years later with some prestigious racing successes. A machine of this type piloted by Mellors won the TT in 1939. This is the 1938 version, which developed 27 HP at 9500 rpm. Bore and stroke = 65 x 75 mm; separate 4-speed gearbox.

worth until the immediate postwar period, when a 500 cc version achieved some important world records.

In Italy, supercharged multicylinders were developed by Benelli, Bianchi and Moto Guzzi. The most original bike – and the only one to take part in a competition, albeit only once – was the Guzzi 492 cc three-cylinder (bore and stroke 59 × 60 mm), with the cylinders sloping forward at an angle of 45°, double-camshaft valve gear operated by a gear train and a Cozette supercharger fitted above the gearbox. It developed 80 HP, as did the Bianchi 493 cc (52 × 58 mm) four-cylinder of more conventional design, with vertical cylinders, bevel gear shaft-operated double-

camshaft valve gear and a gear-driven vane supercharger, also fitted above the gearbox. The highest performance levels, in theory at least, were achieved by the Benelli 249 cc (42 × 45 mm) four-cylinder introduced in 1940. The cylinders were angled forward and water-cooled; the double-camshaft valve gear used a gear train on the right of the block and the Cozette supercharger was driven by the transmission. It developed nearly 60 HP and was faster than the best half-liters of the time, but apart from a few brief initial trials nothing became of it.

In Britain, AJS was the first company to build a four-cylinder in 1938, of 495 cc (50 × 63 mm), the cylinders being mounted longi-

tudinally as two narrow-angle V-twins; it had chain-driven valve gear, first air then water cooling and a Centric supercharger, which was also chain-driven and fitted in front of the crankcase. The Roarer twin-cylinder by Velocette was also unusual, being a half-liter bike produced by fitting two (forward-facing) 250 cc engines with double-camshaft valve gear operated by a shaft and bevel driving gears, air cooling, cardan shaft final drive and a positive displacement vane supercharger. This machine was tested only, at the 1939 Tourist Trophy.

Having used single-cylinder racing bikes for years (first single-, then double-camshaft), NSU decided to fit a new model with a more up-to-date, twin-cylinder engine. This hefty racing machine, designed by Albert Roder, came out in 1939 with a displacement of 350 cc and was soon followed by a 500 cc version. It had a vane supercharger and double overhead camshaft valve gear. The outbreak of World War Two stopped development of this very interesting motorcycle.

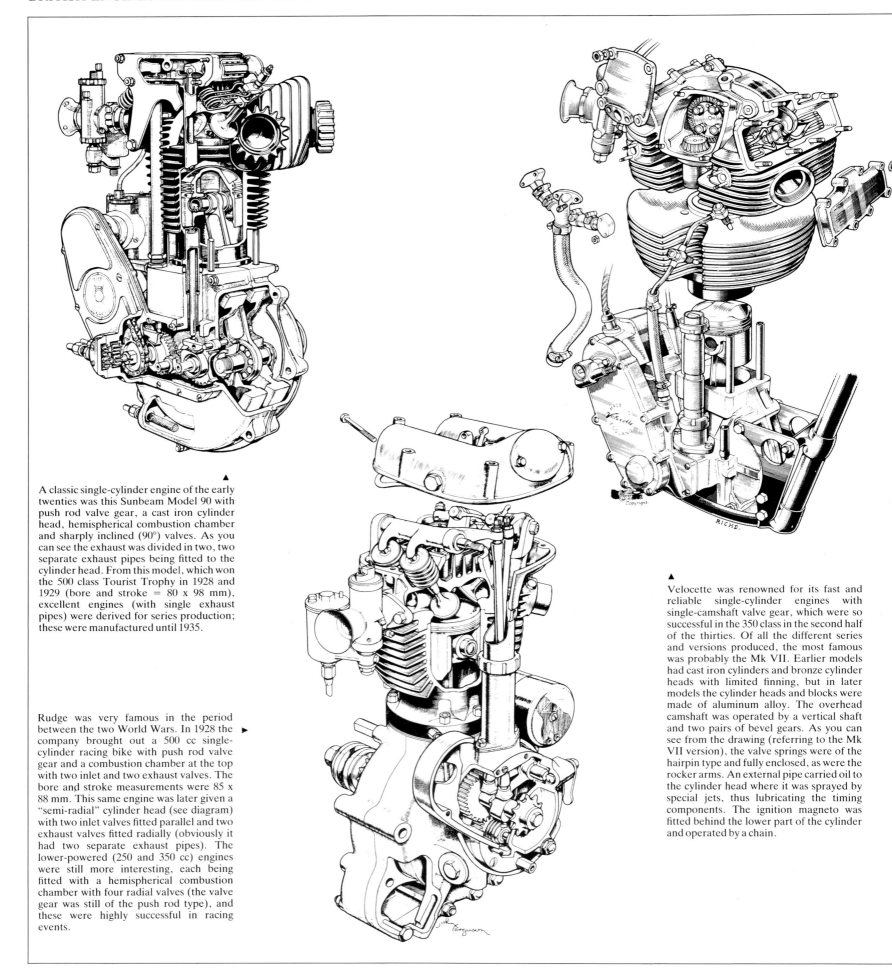

A classic single-cylinder engine of the early twenties was this Sunbeam Model 90 with push rod valve gear, a cast iron cylinder head, hemispherical combustion chamber and sharply inclined (90°) valves. As you can see the exhaust was divided in two, two separate exhaust pipes being fitted to the cylinder head. From this model, which won the 500 class Tourist Trophy in 1928 and 1929 (bore and stroke = 80 x 98 mm), excellent engines (with single exhaust pipes) were derived for series production; these were manufactured until 1935.

Rudge was very famous in the period between the two World Wars. In 1928 the company brought out a 500 cc single-cylinder racing bike with push rod valve gear and a combustion chamber at the top with two inlet and two exhaust valves. The bore and stroke measurements were 85 x 88 mm. This same engine was later given a "semi-radial" cylinder head (see diagram) with two inlet valves fitted parallel and two exhaust valves fitted radially (obviously it had two separate exhaust pipes). The lower-powered (250 and 350 cc) engines were still more interesting, each being fitted with a hemispherical combustion chamber with four radial valves (the valve gear was still of the push rod type), and these were highly successful in racing events.

Velocette was renowned for its fast and reliable single-cylinder engines with single-camshaft valve gear, which were so successful in the 350 class in the second half of the thirties. Of all the different series and versions produced, the most famous was probably the Mk VII. Earlier models had cast iron cylinders and bronze cylinder heads with limited finning, but in later models the cylinder heads and blocks were made of aluminum alloy. The overhead camshaft was operated by a vertical shaft and two pairs of bevel gears. As you can see from the drawing (referring to the Mk VII version), the valve springs were of the hairpin type and fully enclosed, as were the rocker arms. An external pipe carried oil to the cylinder head where it was sprayed by special jets, thus lubricating the timing components. The ignition magneto was fitted behind the lower part of the cylinder and operated by a chain.

One of the most sophisticated engines of ▶ the thirties was undoubtedly the Brough Superior, with four horizontally opposed cylinders and two crankshafts one above the other, meshed together by a pair of gears at the back. This engine, which was extremely quiet and totally free from vibrations, had push rod valve gear (the two camshafts in the cylinder block being operated by a roller chain fitted at the front). The cylinders were "integral" with the aluminum alloy block, which separated on a vertical plane. The cylinder barrels were of cast iron. Each crankshaft, of the composite type, had a single crank pin on which both connecting rods worked, one being of the forked type (i.e. an inner plus an outer connecting rod, as favoured by aeronautical engineers).

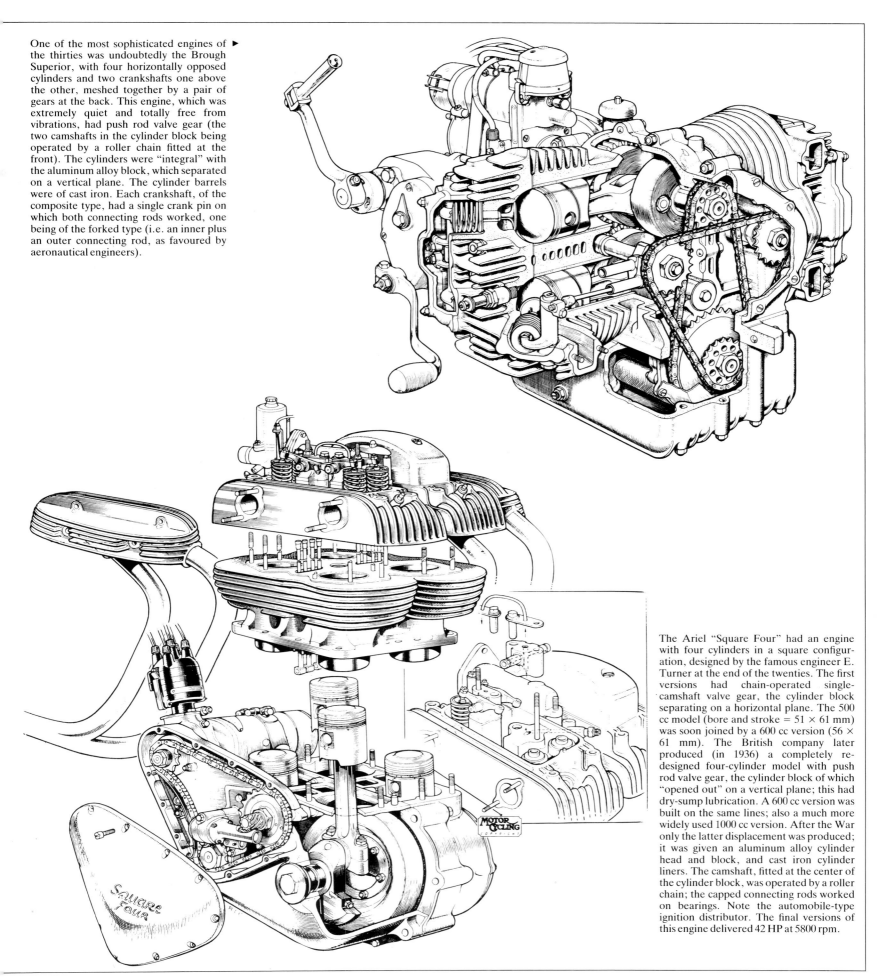

The Ariel "Square Four" had an engine with four cylinders in a square configuration, designed by the famous engineer E. Turner at the end of the twenties. The first versions had chain-operated single-camshaft valve gear, the cylinder block separating on a horizontal plane. The 500 cc model (bore and stroke = 51 × 61 mm) was soon joined by a 600 cc version (56 × 61 mm). The British company later produced (in 1936) a completely re-designed four-cylinder model with push rod valve gear, the cylinder block of which "opened out" on a vertical plane; this had dry-sump lubrication. A 600 cc version was built on the same lines; also a much more widely used 1000 cc version. After the War only the latter displacement was produced; it was given an aluminum alloy cylinder head and block, and cast iron cylinder liners. The camshaft, fitted at the center of the cylinder block, was operated by a roller chain; the capped connecting rods worked on bearings. Note the automobile-type ignition distributor. The final versions of this engine delivered 42 HP at 5800 rpm.

THE GREAT RECOVERY

The postwar years witnessed a real boom in motorcycling, which in Europe in the space of a few years reached levels that have never since been equalled. The almost total lack of individual and collective means of transport as a result of the destruction of war, combined with the need to travel to work (the movement of factories away from the big cities meant that many people were commuting – something virtually unheard of before) led large numbers of people to acquire motor vehicles. Before long, the undeniable advantages of individual motorization profoundly altered the lives and habits of everyone. It became important to be able to move around without the restrictions of public transport or the effort of riding a bicycle.

The existing stock of vehicles – already very limited in many countries – had been virtually wiped out; therefore none could be assigned for public use. Thus in the early days people bought up ex-Army vehicles.

Once the initial difficulties over the supply of raw materials and rebuilding of factories had been overcome, however, the national companies started reappearing on the market. They were also joined by many factories that had been used for wartime production and were obliged to look for new outlets to safeguard their own existence and keep their employees in work.

The Italian and French companies started out producing proprietary engines, or engines of small displacement which were sold separately and could be fitted

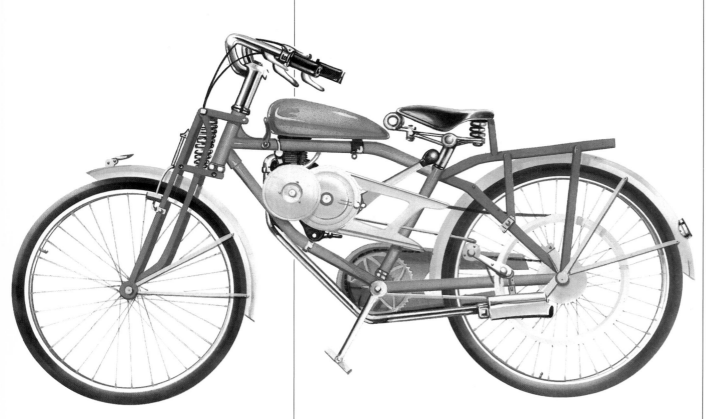

In Japan as elsewhere, the problem of transport in the immediate postwar period was largely solved by mopeds and auxiliary motors for bicycles. Here we see the first Honda machine of this type (from 1948); the 50 cc two-stroke engine delivered 1 HP at 5000 rpm.

to bicycles, which nearly everybody had. These clip-on engines were soon to be followed by mopeds, or vehicles still based on pedal cycles but expressly designed for motorization and thus without the typical defects of motorized bicycles – above all, their fragility.

The first clip-ons were designed in the final years of the war, and came on to the market at the end of 1945. They were mainly two-strokes of 35 to 50 cc displacement with no gearbox or clutch, and were fitted in all positions: at the center of the frame (Caproni, Galloni), near the pedals (CAB, G.M., Leone, Lince, Mosquito, M.T. 34, Vega), above the rear wheel (Gazzella, Giamas, Minimotor, Pony) or beside it, to the left or right (Alpino, ASPI, Carda, Folletto, GRIM, IMEX, Sirio). Transmission was normally by friction roller on the tyre, but chains and gears were also used. A few more sophisticated models, like the Alpino and Sirio, had two- or three-speed gears.

Italian producers included aeronautical companies like Caproni, automobile companies like SIATA (famous for the sports versions of the Topolino and Balilla), earlier designers who had returned to the limelight like Galloni and Garelli, and a long list of new names, bringing the total number of factories to more than fifty – but not one motorcycle company among them!

In France the most representative names were Peugeot, Poulain, Motobécane and VAP. The Vélosolex, which came under the category of a moped despite being very simple (friction roller drive on the front wheel; rigid, lady's

In the postwar period auxiliary motors for bicycles, followed by utilitarian mopeds, became widely used. The famous Garelli Mosquito started out with a displacement of 38.5 cc, increased to 49 cc by 1953. The final version had a 40 mm bore and 39 mm stroke and delivered 1 HP at 3800 rpm. This auxiliary motor was very easy to install and had roller drive.

In France, in 1950, Motobécane introduced the Mobylette moped, with two speeds and chain final drive, which soon became very popular and stayed in production for a very long time; the different versions were constantly updated but always faithful to the original design.

One of the very few examples of a moped with a four-stroke engine is the Motom 48, which came out in 1948 and was very popular in Italy. The single-cylinder engine with push rod valve gear developed 1.4 HP at 4500 rpm. It had ◄ 3-speed gears and a pressed steel frame.

The most famous German scooter of the ► fifties was in all probability the NSU Quickly, powered by a two-stroke single-cylinder engine with a baffle piston. It developed 1.4 HP at 5000 rpm. Bore and stroke = 40 × 39 mm; 2-speed gears.

◄ The Puch 48, introduced in the second half of the fifties, was a great success. This is the 1957 "Sport" version. The two-stroke engine had a fan-operated forced cooling system.

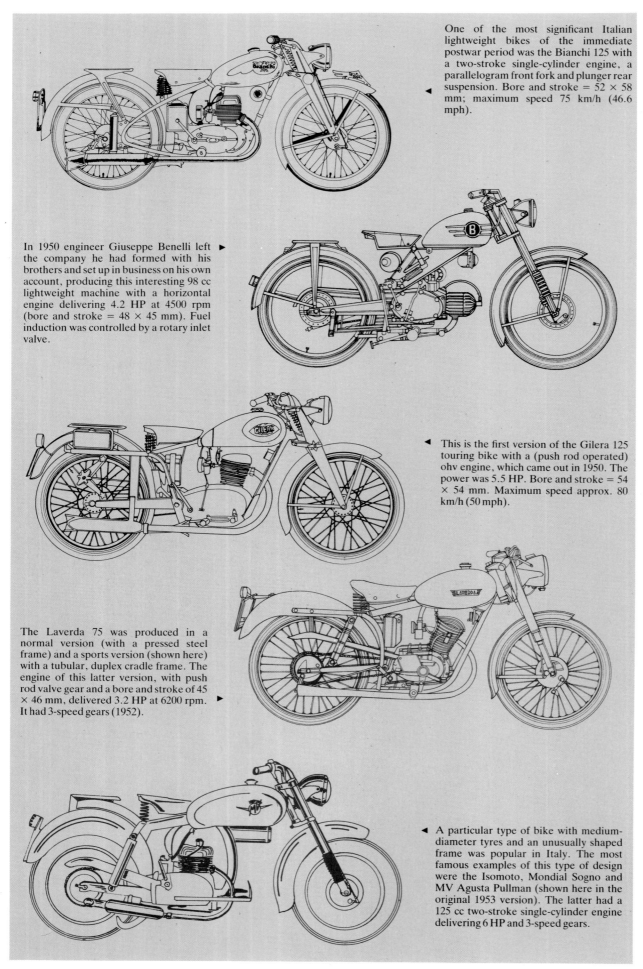

One of the most significant Italian lightweight bikes of the immediate postwar period was the Bianchi 125 with a two-stroke single-cylinder engine, a parallelogram front fork and plunger rear suspension. Bore and stroke = 52 × 58 mm; maximum speed 75 km/h (46.6 mph).

In 1950 engineer Giuseppe Benelli left the company he had formed with his brothers and set up in business on his own account, producing this interesting 98 cc lightweight machine with a horizontal engine delivering 4.2 HP at 4500 rpm (bore and stroke = 48 × 45 mm). Fuel induction was controlled by a rotary inlet valve.

This is the first version of the Gilera 125 touring bike with a (push rod operated) ohv engine, which came out in 1950. The power was 5.5 HP. Bore and stroke = 54 × 54 mm. Maximum speed approx. 80 km/h (50 mph).

The Laverda 75 was produced in a normal version (with a pressed steel frame) and a sports version (shown here) with a tubular, duplex cradle frame. The engine of this latter version, with push rod valve gear and a bore and stroke of 45 × 46 mm, delivered 3.2 HP at 6200 rpm. It had 3-speed gears (1952).

A particular type of bike with medium-diameter tyres and an unusually shaped frame was popular in Italy. The most famous examples of this type of design were the Isomoto, Mondial Sogno and MV Agusta Pullman (shown here in the original 1953 version). The latter had a 125 cc two-stroke single-cylinder engine delivering 6 HP and 3-speed gears.

bicycle type frame) was to be enormously popular.

Most of the French mopeds had automatic progressive transmission by belt and expanding pulley, which was simple and efficient and subsequently used on all types of utilitarian moped worldwide, right up to the present day.

The use of separate engines declined in about 1950, since people preferred complete mopeds.

At the same time as the clip-on engines were introduced, in the immediate postwar period, a number of lightweight motorbikes of no more than 125 cc displacement appeared. These vehicles were certainly more comfortable than ordinary motorized bicycles, but like them they were built for maximum simplicity. The most famous in Italy was undoubtedly the Moto Guzzi "65," which was used by so many people from all walks of life – manual workers, students, office workers, shopkeepers, craftsmen and professional people – that it became a legend in its own lifetime. Guzzi was also one of the few motorcycle companies – together with Bianchi – to have understood the new requirements and adapted to them immediately. All the other machines on the market were by companies which had modified their previous production, or completely new makes: Motobi, Ducati, Idroflex, Iso, Mondial, Morini, MV, Parilla, Rumi, Sterzi. In 1949 they were joined by Gilera, with a handsome four-stroke, three-speed 125.

There were very few new developments in the higher-displacement categories. Virtually all models were the same as the prewar ones, with minor modifications.

At the beginning of the fifties the German industry returned to the international scene. Germany took some time to recover from the destruction of war, but when conditions allowed, the Germans returned in a big way. Classic names like BMW, DKW, Horex, Adler, NSU, Sachs, TWN and Zündapp were joined by new companies like Hoffman, Lohmann, Kreidler, IMME and Maico. Because of the division of the country in 1945 into East and West Germany, the production plants of a few famous companies ended up in the East and were used to form new motorcycle marques. This was the case, for example, with IFA-MZ, who used the plant of DKW, who had migrated to the West. MZ, established in 1945, started out producing household goods, then switched to motorcycles – becoming, like DKW, a strong champion of two-stroke engines.

During this period the Spanish industry, which had been practically nonexistent before the war, also gathered strength and grew. A number of factories built bikes under license. These factories included Guzzi-Hispania, ISA (who produced the Mosquito), Isomotor, Lambretta-Locomociones, MV-Avello (called Emevue to begin with), Moto-Vespa and Derbi, who fitted Jawa engines. But several wholly Spanish workshops and factories were also established more or less everywhere, with the enthusiasm of beginners aroused by the prospect of conquering a virgin market which was virtually closed to direct importation. It was a tumultuous phenomenon, like the one that had occurred a few years earlier in Italy; it soon

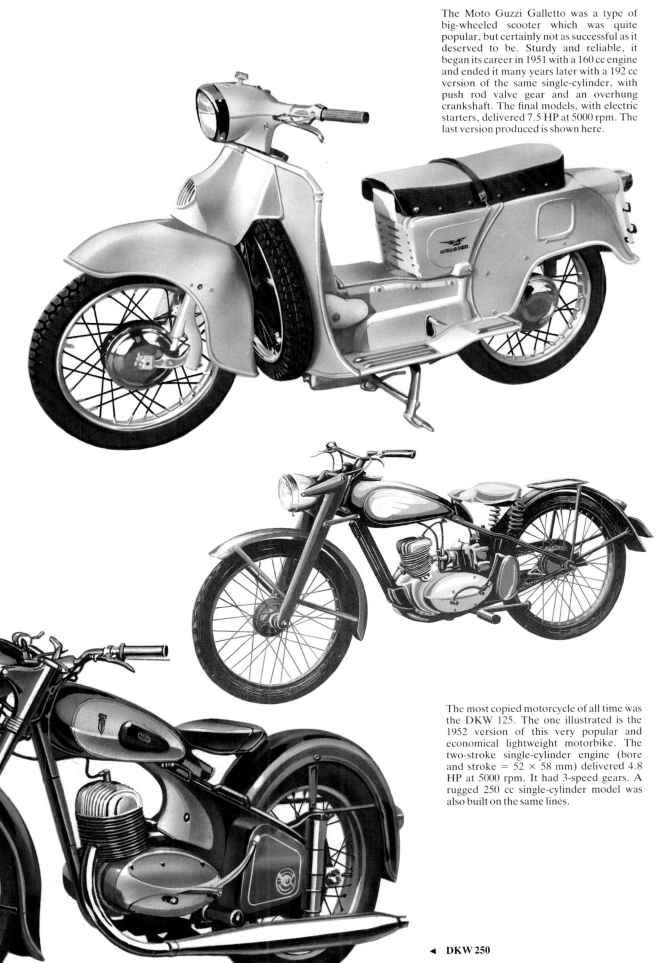

The Moto Guzzi Galletto was a type of big-wheeled scooter which was quite popular, but certainly not as successful as it deserved to be. Sturdy and reliable, it began its career in 1951 with a 160 cc engine and ended it many years later with a 192 cc version of the same single-cylinder, with push rod valve gear and an overhung crankshaft. The final models, with electric starters, delivered 7.5 HP at 5000 rpm. The last version produced is shown here.

The most copied motorcycle of all time was the DKW 125. The one illustrated is the 1952 version of this very popular and economical lightweight motorbike. The two-stroke single-cylinder engine (bore and stroke = 52 × 58 mm) delivered 4.8 HP at 5000 rpm. It had 3-speed gears. A rugged 250 cc single-cylinder model was also built on the same lines.

◄ DKW 250

51

died down, leaving many illusions in its wake. However, more serious and solid companies included Clua, Lube, Montesa (founded in 1945), Ossa (a manufacturer of cinematographic equipment), Rieju, and Soriano. Bultaco, one of the most illustrious Spanish companies, was founded a few years later when the technical manager of Montesa, Bultò, left to set up his own company. All of these companies built mopeds and lightweights with displacements not exceeding 200 cc; the one exception was Sanglas, which devoted itself to medium- and high-powered vehicles (350 to 500 cc), with push rod-operated four-stroke engines, rigid frames and telescopic forks, based on the most successful British models.

The period of maximum expansion for the motorcycle industry occurred in the mid fifties in Europe. The economy was settling down, living standards were improving almost everywhere, a number of motorcyclists were graduating to motorcars; but their place was filled by the new "emergent classes," so that the market was unaffected. But time had taken care of a lot of unsound businesses and overambitious projects, leaving only the best-prepared and most responsible firms.

Technical development

By about the mid fifties, "loose" engines had virtually disappeared. The bulk of French and German production was based on mopeds. These were of a very simple type in France, having two-stroke engines with an automatic clutch and no gearbox, or with automatic belt drive and almost always with rigid frames. German mopeds were more sophisticated with two- or three-speed gears, often with pressed steel frames and rather heavy lines. The most typical makes were Motobécane, Peugeot and Vélosolex in France, Kreidler and NSU in Germany and Puch in Austria.

In Italy the utilitarian moped was somewhat in decline, users preferring more powerful machines, which apart from anything else could carry a passenger. The most important names were Bianchi, Ducati, Garelli, Motom, Gilera, Innocenti and MV. On the other hand, high-performance sports mopeds became more popular (the 40 km/h = 25 mph speed limit had not yet been imposed), some with four-stroke engines, like the BM (with single-camshaft valve gear), Pegaso, and Somaschini. Two-strokes included the IMN, Itom, Mondial, Pirotta and Testi.

Production of lightweight motorbikes of up to 125 cc was considerable throughout Europe, including countries like Belgium, Holland, Sweden and Switzerland, which had a long history of motorcycle production, albeit in small numbers. In Italy, however, displacements were gradually increased, first to about 150–160 cc and then to 175–200 cc.

The typical Italian lightweight machine of the mid fifties was a fast four-stroke 175 with four-speed gears and a distinctly sporty riding position, low handlebars and rear-set footrests, capable of at least 130 km/h (80.77 mph) with ease. Some examples were the Beta Folgore, Bianchi Tonale, Guazzoni, Mondial, Morini Rebello and Parilla and perhaps the most "classic" of all, the MV Disco Volante (Flying Saucer). Later on they were joined by the Ducati and the Guzzi Lodola, also with single camshafts.

As already mentioned the higher displacements were in decline, although there would still have been a market for them if really new, up-to-date models had been available.

The situation in other countries was much the same: the Belgian and French medium- and high-powered bikes, though good, were disappearing one by one. The only companies to resist were the German BMW – with its classic boxer engines, impervious to the whims of fashion; NSU (who had designed a really modern and interesting 250 with a backbone frame of pressed steel and engine with a single camshaft operated by an original system of link rods, delivering 18 HP and with a top speed of 140 km/h = 87 mph); and the British, who only ever seemed interested in engines of 350 cc and over.

From 100 cc upward the vast majority of engines were four-stroke, normally with push rod valve gear but quite often with one or two overhead camshafts. Exceptions were the 125–250 cc models by the German companies DKW and MZ, the split-cylinder models of another German producer, TWN, the Italian Iso, and Czechoslovakian engines.

The Czech industry is interesting. With a long tradition (one of the very first motorcycle factories, Laurin & Klement, was established in Bohemia) it had basically been reduced by the end of the 1939-1945 war to two brands: Jawa and CZ, which had been nationalized and brought together under the same management. Production in the fifties was on strictly utilitarian lines, 125, 250 and 350 cc two-stroke models being designed, including twin-cylinders. Of modest performance but extremely durable and reliable, much the same type of models are available today, although obviously with improvements where necessary, and they have been widely distributed throughout East Europe and Asia.

Nearly all low-powered models had single-cylinder engines, for reasons of economy. There were few exceptions, nearly all Italian: the Benelli 250, Berneg 160, Capriolo 150 (a beautiful motorbike with a twin-cylinder boxer engine and pressed steel frame), the Motobi, Rumi two-stroke 125 and Iso two-stroke but with a split-single cylinder and – the last to appear – the Parilla 350 and Gilera 300, a very elegant and sophisticated bike which did not have the success it deserved.

Typical of the German industry were medium-powered two-stroke twins such as the Adler 250, Ardie 350, DKW 350 and Maico 350. The larger displacements – still with the exception of BMW and, for a little while longer, Zündapp – were the preserve of the British industry, which still built 350 and 500 cc singles, but concentrated on forward-facing twins. This type of design was not new (the Frenchman Werner used it in 1904) and was mechanically far from perfect, but it had the advantages of being compact and relatively simple. The engineers at Triumph (Val Page, followed by Edward Turner) were responsible for its revival in the mid thirties, and after that it was used by all makes: AJS, Ariel, BSA, Norton and Royal Enfield.

Great Britain could also boast three outstanding machines: the Sunbeam 500, Ariel 1000 and Vincent-HRD. Of the three the Sunbeam was the most modern, having been designed in 1946, with a longitudinal twin-cylinder in-line ohc engine, cardan shaft transmission, and thick tyres for maximum comfort. The Ariel, with a square four engine, was a worthy representative of the now extinct category of high-class motorcycles, designed for an elite set of customers who preferred elegance, "silent" operation and versatility to high performance. The Vincent was in a class of its own and embodied the British ideal of mechanical perfection. It had a 1000 cc longitudinal V-twin engine and was built with minute attention to detail and no expense spared. It had no chromium-plated parts which could go rusty, just stainless steel; every lever or pedal was adjustable and could be adapted to the build and habits of the rider. This machine is still a legend even today, despite its numerous faults (it had rather poor stability, its performance, though good, was a lot less than the promised 200 km/h (125 mph) and it had some needlessly complex features, such as the use of two separate brakes for each wheel when it would have been much better to have just one large one).

The highest-powered vehicles in those years were the American Harley-Davidsons, ever faithful to the longitudinal V-twin of somewhat antiquated design (some models still had side valves), albeit with refinements like hydraulic tappets; 750, 1000 and 1200 cc versions were available.

Practically all four-stroke motorcycles had wet-sump lubrication with a single supply pump, except for nearly all British and Guzzi engines, which had a separate tank with a double pump for supply and recovery (dry-sump lubrication). All engines were fed by carburetors. The vast majority had ignition magnetos of the traditional type or in the flywheel version, battery-coil ignition still being regarded with mistrust, both because it was considered too "sporty" and because of the vulnerability of electrical installations on motorcycles, which were exposed to knocks and bad weather, and were also

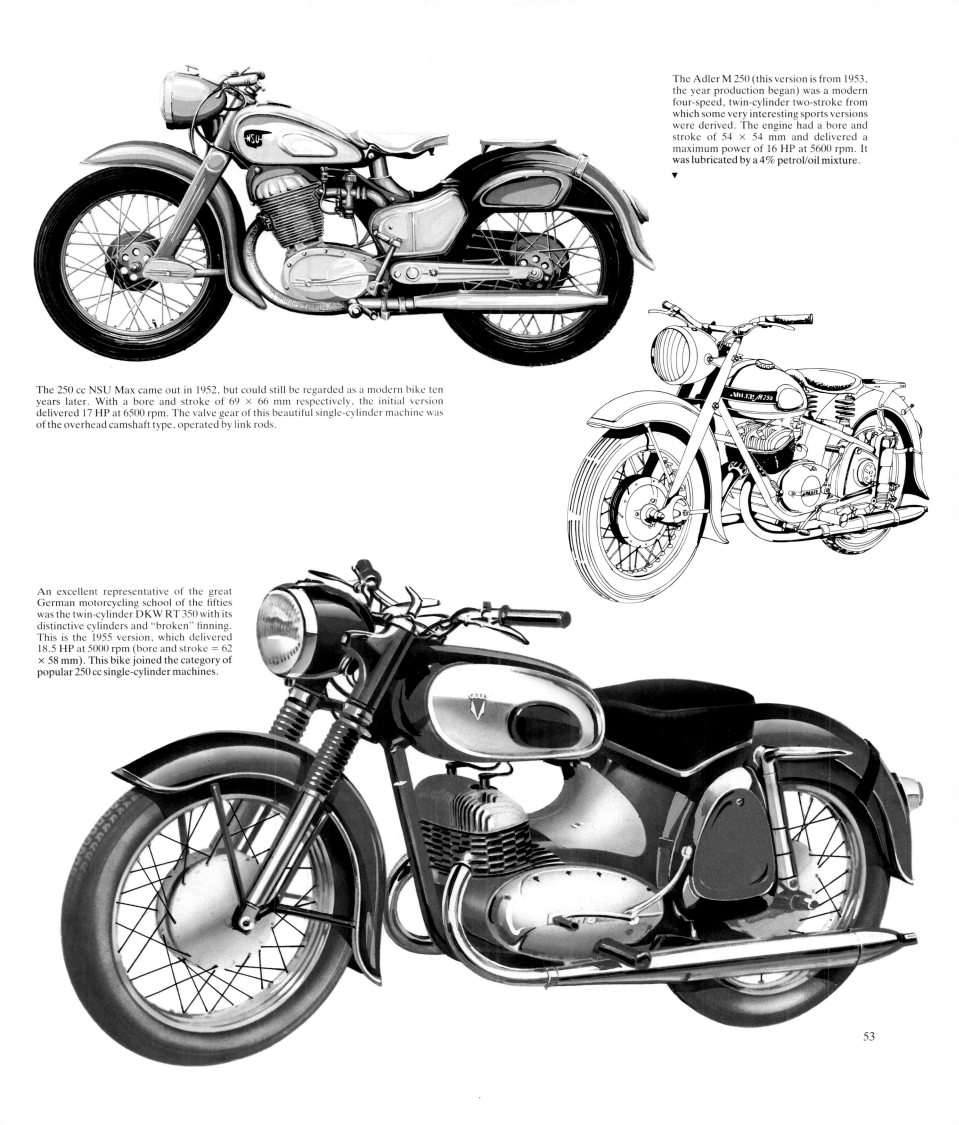

The Adler M 250 (this version is from 1953, the year production began) was a modern four-speed, twin-cylinder two-stroke from which some very interesting sports versions were derived. The engine had a bore and stroke of 54 × 54 mm and delivered a maximum power of 16 HP at 5600 rpm. It was lubricated by a 4% petrol/oil mixture.

▼

The 250 cc NSU Max came out in 1952, but could still be regarded as a modern bike ten years later. With a bore and stroke of 69 × 66 mm respectively, the initial version delivered 17 HP at 6500 rpm. The valve gear of this beautiful single-cylinder machine was of the overhead camshaft type, operated by link rods.

An excellent representative of the great German motorcycling school of the fifties was the twin-cylinder DKW RT 350 with its distinctive cylinders and "broken" finning. This is the 1955 version, which delivered 18.5 HP at 5000 rpm (bore and stroke = 62 × 58 mm). This bike joined the category of popular 250 cc single-cylinder machines.

53

A classic representative of the British school was the Velocette single-cylinder engine. This was produced in 350 and 500 cc versions with only slight differences. It had high-camshaft push rod valve gear. The main bearings were conical roller type, the big end bearings being caged-needle roller type. The crankshaft was in three pieces forged together. Other details included hairpin valve springs and a light alloy cylinder with a cast iron barrel. It had dry-sump lubrication. The sports models of this engine could deliver over 40 HP in the 500 cc version. Bore and stroke = 86 × 86 mm; inlet valve diameter 51 mm.

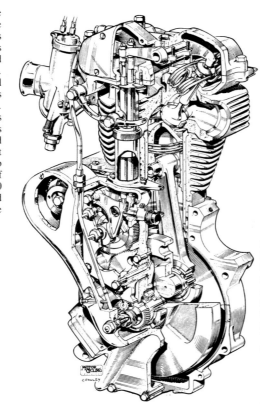

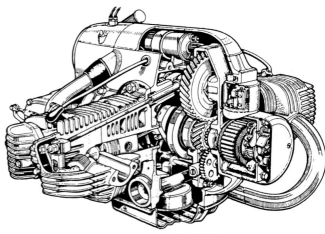

For many years the German industry remained faithful to boxer engines (i.e. with horizontally opposed cylinders) for high-powered bikes. The Zündapp KS 601 is a typical example of this type of engine in the postwar period. Its origins can in fact be traced back to the twin-cylinder side valve models of the thirties. This boxer, with push rod valve gear, was a much revised version of these, with a crankshaft in one piece and connecting rods with removable caps. The main bearings were ball type; the big end bearings were caged-needle roller type. The crankshaft operated the oil pump and camshaft through gears at the front. The light alloy cylinder block was of the tunnel type. The sports version of this engine (bore and stroke = 75 × 67.6 mm) delivered 34 HP at 6000 rpm.

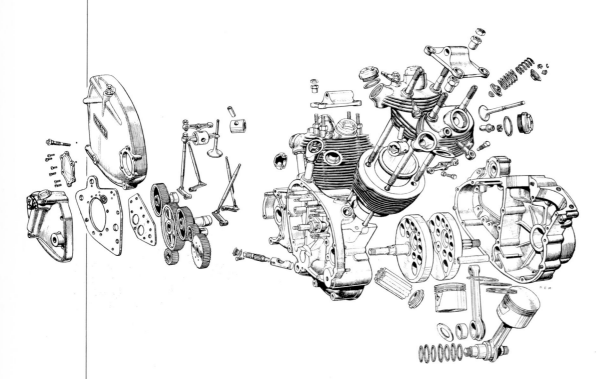

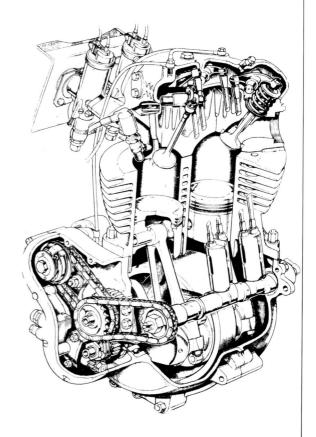

The last powerful V-twin to be mass-produced by the British motorcycle industry was the excellent Vincent 1000 cc. Here too the original design, by Australian engineer Irving, dated from the thirties, but after the war the project was completely revised. The angle between the cylinders was 50°. Among the most interesting characteristics of this engine were the double guides (one upper, one lower) for the valves and high camshaft valve gear. The cams acted on finger-type rockers which transmitted motion through short push rods to two-armed rockers which in turn operated the valves. The big ends of the two connecting rods worked side by side on the coupling axle. The sports version of this engine (bore and stroke 84 × 90 mm) had a power of about 55 HP at 5500 rpm.

The classic Norton twin-cylinder began life at the end of the forties with a displacement of 500 cc (it was designed by Bert Hopwood). Like most British postwar twin-cylinders, it was fairly narrow because just two main bearings were used. The single camshaft, which operated the valves through tappets, push rods and rocker arms, was fitted at the front at the base of the cylinders and controlled by a short roller chain. The two cylinders were cast from a single piece of iron. The forged aluminum connecting rods had removable caps. The displacement of this engine was increased over the years from the original 500 cc to 600, 650 and, in the Atlas and subsequent Commando models, 750 cc. The final versions were even in excess of 800 cc.

subject to vibrations.

Gears in a separate box were now used only by the British and Americans; all the other makers of low- and high-powered bikes housed the gears – together with the clutch and primary drive – in the crankcase, which was much more logical and was first thought of in Italy back in about 1910. There were a few examples of progressive hydraulic transmission: the Ducati Cruiser scooter, a luxury machine with electric start, used this type, while MV fitted a type patented by Badalini to a few models on an experimental basis. Chain final drive was always used except on the BMW, the big Zündapp, the Italian Iso 200 and a few British models (Douglas, Velocette twin-cylinder, Sunbeam).

The motorcycle of the fifties had as a rule a clearly defined structure with a tubular cradle frame, single or duplex, open or closed depending on the tastes of the designer and probable conditions of use. Telescopic front forks with sliding tubes had now replaced the deformable parallelogram type but, not being universally accepted, coexisted with lower link rod types as well as the English-invented Earles with long swinging arms, which was extremely popular at the time. At the back

Despite continuing to use two horizontally opposed cylinders for its high-powered bikes, BMW introduced several new models after the war. For many years the one with the highest performance was the 600 cc R 69. This is the R 69 "S" version of the sixties which, with a bore and stroke of 73 × 72 mm, delivered 42 HP at 7000 rpm. It had push rod valve gear.

The last model introduced by Horex before the market crisis which led to the closure of this famous German company was the single-cylinder Resident in the 350 (brought out in 1955) and subsequent 250 cc versions. The more powerful model (bore and stroke = 77 × 75 mm) delivered 24 HP at 6250 rpm.

The Black Shadow version (shown here) of the 1000 cc Vincent twin-cylinder was the fastest mass-produced bike of the fifties. The powerful engine (55 HP at 5500 rpm in the basic version) had push rod valve gear. The angle between the two cylinders was 50°. Bore and stroke = 84 × 90 mm.

swinging fork suspension was used, with telescopic elements at the sides of the wheel enclosing both the springs and hydraulic shock absorbers. This system, introduced by Velocette in 1938, combined structural simplicity and clean lines with the possibility of fitting spring units mass-produced by specialized firms. A few examples were, however, still seen of plunger (vertical sliding) suspension based on two short telescopes at the sides of the wheel. This type was readily adaptable to existing, rigid frames without big structural changes, but did not allow much travel.

There were quite a few motorcycles of unusual design – i.e. with frames partly or wholly of pressed steel, cast in light alloy, backbone type, or with partly or wholly unitized (bearing) bodies. These new types were developed for aesthetic reasons, in an effort to find cheaper methods of construction and to solve one of the basic drawbacks of motorcycles: the exposure of the occupants to the elements, road dust and engine oil. In many ways the scooter was the ideal solution, although it did not appeal to everyone both because of its small

wheels, which many mistrusted, and its low performance, which was unavoidable in a vehicle of such small displacement.

There was thus a whole crop of vehicles which tried to combine the advantages of the scooter with those of the classic motorbike, the results sometimes being extremely interesting. They can be subdivided into groups: large-wheeled scooters, the most famous of which was the Moto Guzzi Galletto with 17 in (432 mm) wheels, displacement gradually increased from 160 to 192 cc, and a four-stroke engine; bikes of conventional structure but wholly or partially faired, like the British Velocette LE with a four-stroke water-cooled boxer twin; the Aermacchi Corsaro 150 or Moto Guzzi Zigolo 98; and finally "pullman" type bikes with thick medium-diameter wheels (approx. 15 in = 380 mm), an anatomical saddle, broad handlebars and very soft suspension, suitable for gentle touring or everyday transport. They had two-stroke engines of about 125–160 cc, like the MV Pullman, Mondial Sogno or Parilla Bracco; or four-strokes like the earlier Motom Delfino, one of the most handsome and original of all.

Also worth mentioning is the Motom 98T with a 98 cc four-stroke engine, pressed steel frame, swinging arm suspension and 17 in (432 mm) wheels – a real gem of industrial design.

Those who could not or would not introduce many new technical and aesthetic features fitted bigger mudguards, tried to enclose at least the central part of the bike, or designed compact, rounded crankcases. In short, the bikes in those years tended to lose their sharp corners, softening the angles and adopting curved lines, with results that may have been appreciable in terms of comfort but were not always technically and aesthetically appropriate.

At the height of its expansion, however, the motorcycle industry was heading for a crisis. As large sections of the population became wealthier, many users abandoned the romantic world of two-wheeled transport for that of the more comfortable, utilitarian automobile. Cars were a dream now accessible to many, and even young people preferred sports cars – possibly open ones – to motorcycles. A sign of this crisis – which hit Italy in about 1960 but in richer countries like France and

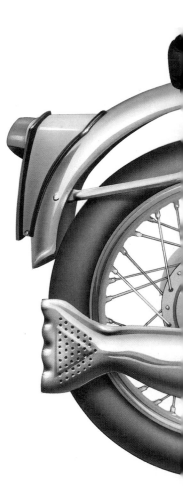

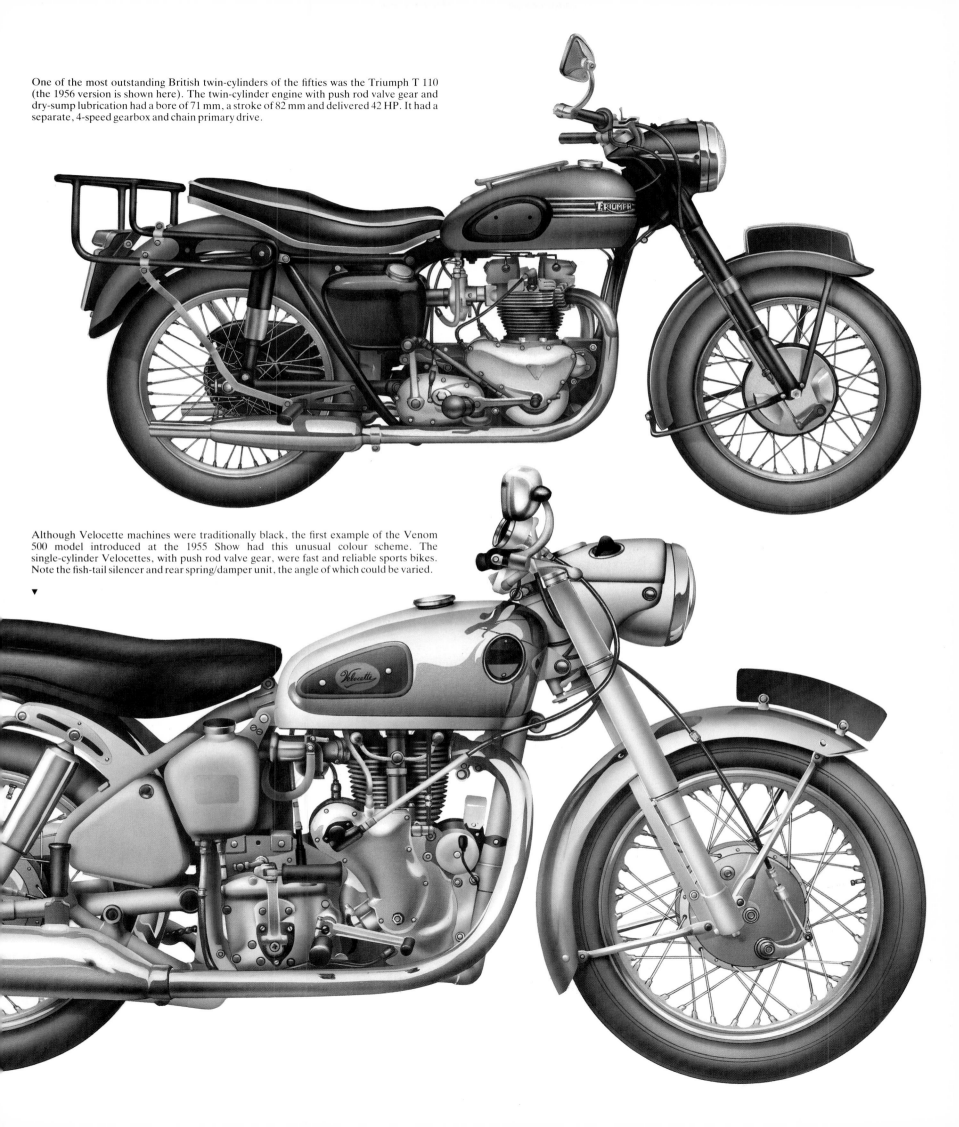

One of the most outstanding British twin-cylinders of the fifties was the Triumph T 110 (the 1956 version is shown here). The twin-cylinder engine with push rod valve gear and dry-sump lubrication had a bore of 71 mm, a stroke of 82 mm and delivered 42 HP. It had a separate, 4-speed gearbox and chain primary drive.

Although Velocette machines were traditionally black, the first example of the Venom 500 model introduced at the 1955 Show had this unusual colour scheme. The single-cylinder Velocettes, with push rod valve gear, were fast and reliable sports bikes. Note the fish-tail silencer and rear spring/damper unit, the angle of which could be varied.

▼

For many years Morini 125 and 150 cc single-cylinders (the first versions from the second half of the fifties were only 98 cc) were the mainstay of Italian motorcyclists. They were strong and reliable and their performance was so good that by the end of their career, which lasted nearly twenty years, they were fitted to a number of very successful trail bikes. They had push rod valve gear, a composite crankshaft which turned on three ball bearings (there were two side by side for the primary drive), a big end bearing consisting of a bush made of anti-friction material, gear primary drive and a light alloy cylinder with a cast iron barrel.

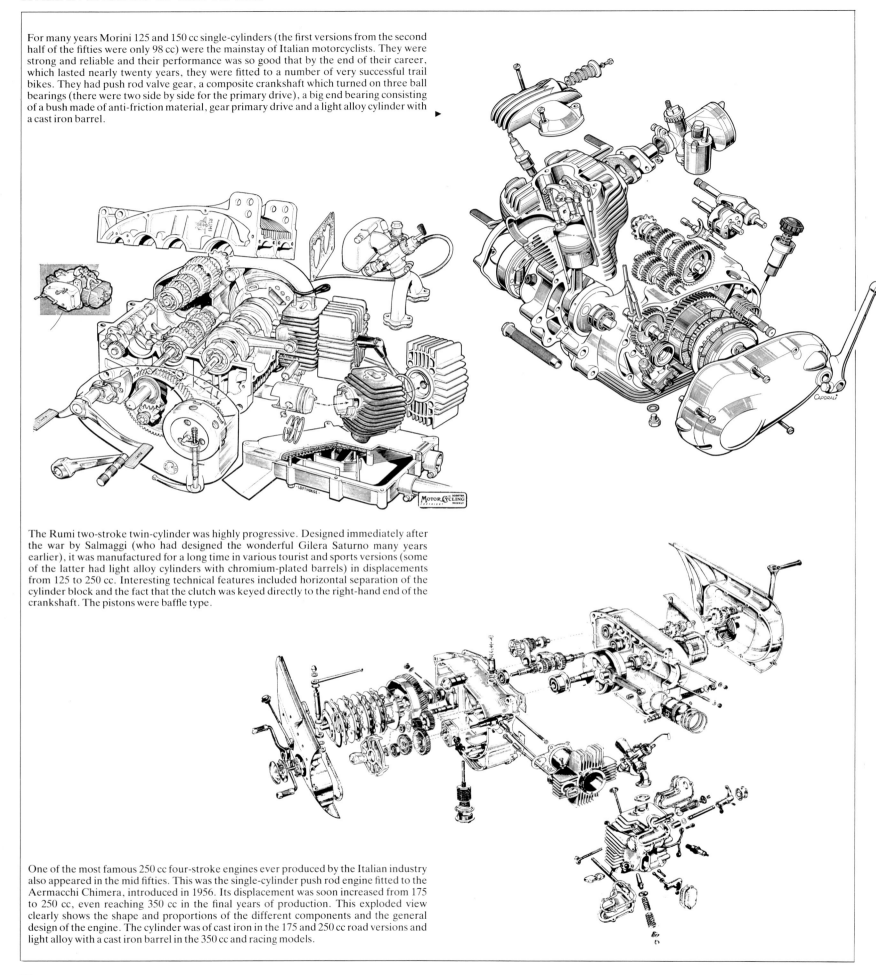

The Rumi two-stroke twin-cylinder was highly progressive. Designed immediately after the war by Salmaggi (who had designed the wonderful Gilera Saturno many years earlier), it was manufactured for a long time in various tourist and sports versions (some of the latter had light alloy cylinders with chromium-plated barrels) in displacements from 125 to 250 cc. Interesting technical features included horizontal separation of the cylinder block and the fact that the clutch was keyed directly to the right-hand end of the crankshaft. The pistons were baffle type.

One of the most famous 250 cc four-stroke engines ever produced by the Italian industry also appeared in the mid fifties. This was the single-cylinder push rod engine fitted to the Aermacchi Chimera, introduced in 1956. Its displacement was soon increased from 175 to 250 cc, even reaching 350 cc in the final years of production. This exploded view clearly shows the shape and proportions of the different components and the general design of the engine. The cylinder was of cast iron in the 175 and 250 cc road versions and light alloy with a cast iron barrel in the 350 cc and racing models.

At one time motocross, trail and even trials bikes were derived from road models, This is a magnificent Ariel four-stroke single-cylinder (Model HT 5) of 1957, with push rod valve gear, which was very successful in trials.

Germany had already begun to happen five years earlier – was the appearance of three- and four-wheeled mini vehicles, which a number of motorcycle companies brought out in the mid fifties in an effort to hold on to their motorcycling clientele.

Examples were the German Messerschmitt, designed by the famous aircraft builder and also manufactured under license by the Italian company Mival (the Mivalino); the Goggo; the Glas; the Zündapp Janus with seats back to back and the central boxer engine of the Elephant 600; the Piaggio Vespa, built in France, and the Italian Isetta, which was to be more successful in the BMW version than the Italian one.

Until 1960, however, the motorcycle industry as a whole resisted well, despite some initial casualties, especially in smaller and richer countries like Belgium, Holland and Switzerland, which could not count on a big internal market. Many companies, like Guzzi, Gilera, Mondial, AJS, Norton and DKW, drastically reduced their budgets, for instance by giving up direct participation in racing, and designed increasingly economical models such as mopeds. A few concentrated on rich customers, particularly the American market, which had discovered shortly before that European-style

This Mondial 175 of 1955, with single overhead camshaft valve gear, was not a great commercial success. The engine delivered over 10 HP at 6500 rpm.

The most successful 175 produced in Italy in the fifties was the Morini. This is the 1958 Tresette Sprint model. Bore and stroke = 60 × 61 mm; push rod valve gear; power 13 HP at 6500 rpm; maximum speed approx. 130 km/h (80 mph).

motorcycles had many advantages over the cumbersome American-designed twins. Thus in Germany BMW continued to produce their 500 and 600 cc twins, with new frames and suspension; NSU further improved their 250 with link rod valve gear; DKW and the Austrian Puch continued to build their sophisticated medium-powered models with two-stroke engines. The British also continued to produce high-powered bikes, for which they were still world leaders for the time being. In fact, they tended if anything to increase the displacement of their parallel twins, to as much as 600-700 cc (AJS, BSA, Matchless, Norton, Royal Enfield). A few models, like the Triumph Twenty-one or Norton Domina-tor, had partial fairing at the back, and bikes appeared with aero-dynamic fairing on the lines already used for some time for

Grand Prix models. Furthermore, the British industry was still sufficiently dynamic to come up with a few distinctly unorthodox designs, like the Ariel 250 with a two-stroke twin and pressed steel frame, available in both "naked" (Arrow) and fully enclosed (Lead-er) versions.

The big British engines designed in the forties or even before the war were beginning to show their age, normally through co-pious oil leakages. But for the time being the market had nothing better to offer for sheer per-formance; the British frames were still superior and could get the best out of a bike.

On the whole, however, four-stroke engines with overhead valve gear were on the decline, for economic reasons. At the same time there was renewed interest in two-strokes, which were increas-ingly closely scrutinized with a

view to improving their perform-ance. A number of manufacturers – Guzzi and Piaggio (Vespa), for example – used rotary valve induction, either disc type or as part of the connecting rod system. Following the example set by MZ, who had been incredibly success-ful with their Grand Prix engines with expansion chamber exhaust systems, people tried fitting this system to mass-produced bikes as well. The use of cylinders with chromium-plated barrels also in-creased: light alloy cylinders were used, the cast iron liners of which were replaced by a layer of chrome, whose properties were such that the percentage of oil in the mixture could be reduced to just 2%, greatly improving performance and smoothness of operation and reducing running costs.

There were no great changes to the cycle parts of the machine

In the sixties, four-stroke machines de-rived from series models were highly successful in reliability trials. This is the Gilera 125 with push rod valve gear and a 5-speed gearbox. Bore and stroke = 56 × 50 mm; power 10 HP at 8500 rpm.

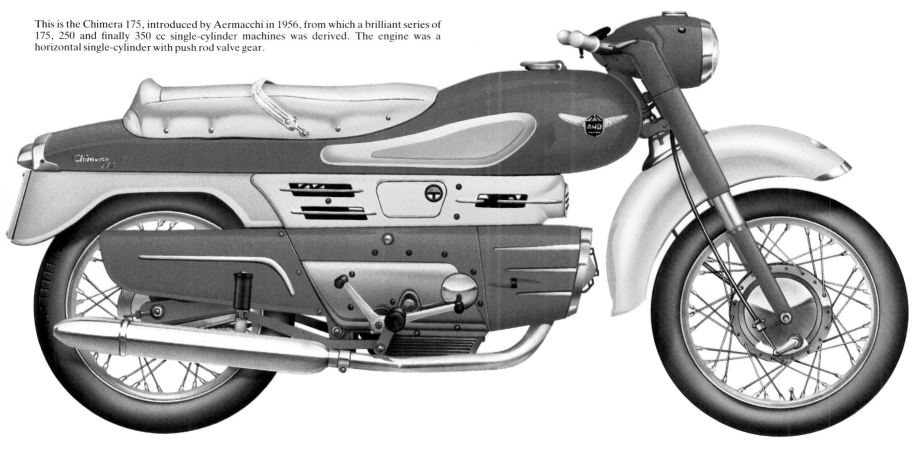

This is the Chimera 175, introduced by Aermacchi in 1956, from which a brilliant series of 175, 250 and finally 350 cc single-cylinder machines was derived. The engine was a horizontal single-cylinder with push rod valve gear.

except for some new models with pressed steel unitized bodies or with bodies fitted to the tubular frame, as on the Ariel already mentioned, and in Italy the 98 cc Parilla Slughi and the beautiful Aermacchi Chimera with a 175 cc horizontal-cylinder four-stroke engine. Later sports versions of this engine were to become world-famous: the Ala d'Oro (Gold Wing) of 175, 250 and 350 cc and over was to be the most widely used and popular bike for private racers in Europe throughout the sixties.

Nevertheless, sales continued to fall. At this point it would have been logical to look for new outlets and new markets like the almost wholly virgin territories of Asia, or to try and improve penetration in wealthy nations like the United States, where motorcycles obviously needed to be promoted not in terms of economy but as sporting and leisure vehicles for the young and young at heart, the non-conformist.

Very few tried the first approach; none had the courage to tackle the second in depth; apart from anything else, this would have required a very strong advertising campaign.

Japan set to conquer the motorcycle market

Shut off for centuries in splendid isolation, convinced of being at the height of perfection, Japan began opening up to the West and its inventions only toward the end of the nineteenth century, showing an immediate interest in vehicles with mechanical propulsion, above all for their possible military applications. Little information is available on the origins of the automobile and motorcycle industry in the Land of the Rising Sun. It is known that at the beginning of this century a number of motor vehicles were imported for comparative tests, obviously in order to select the best, while the first known automobile manufacturer was Kwai-shinsha, founded in 1911. Some time after that a number of two- and particularly three-wheeled vehicles appeared for carrying people and things, and these were popular in the twenties. In the decade before the last war there were already numerous factories building motor vehicles, although their total output was incredibly low: roughly 3000 a year. The engines were clearly based on British models, particularly those

by JAP, and the American Harley-Davidson and Indian.

At the end of the war the same conditions were created in Japan as had favoured the huge expansion of the motorcycle industry in Europe, and Italy in particular: the need for cheap, practical transport, the dismantling of big aeronautical and naval concerns and their conversion to peacetime production.

These enormous complexes – including dockyards, metallurgical companies and engineering plants – were obliged by the terms of the peace treaty to reduce their size and switch production, forming companies which were at least officially independent of the parent company, many of which devoted themselves to motorcycle production. To these were added other, new companies of varying size, including Honda. Soichiro Honda started out immediately after the war "recycling" pumps and electric generators left over from the Army. Then in 1948 he founded the Honda Motor Company with a capital of a million yen, equivalent of about 3,000 dollars at the time. He also began building clip-on engines and mopeds called Cub (like the Italian Cucciolo), which were even exported to the United States. He then graduated to a lightweight motorbike with a 150 cc engine, overhead valves and two-speed gearbox called the Dream, continually updated and improved versions of which were available for a number of years, and on which the company's fortunes were founded.

The principal Japanese marques in those years, apart from Honda, were Bridgestone, Fuji and Gasuden (with two-stroke engines), Hirano (single-speed scooter with automatic clutch), Meguro and Lilac. Suzuki, a huge manufacturer of textile machinery, entered the motorcycle sector in 1952 with a 36 cc clip-on which was followed by lightweight and normal bikes. In 1955 it was the turn of Yamaha, who made musical instruments. Kawasaki, the other big Japanese producer today, is an enormous industrial complex covering all different areas of activity which brought out its first bike in 1962. There were also quite a few manufacturers of tricars and three-wheeled sidecar models, which were also popular.

The Japanese bikes were nothing special, the best of them being faithful copies of British and German models; but after a few

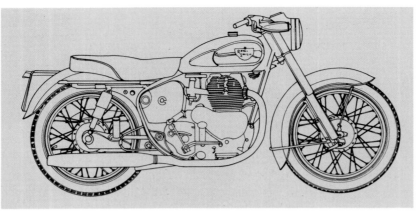

Unlike other heavy British bikes, the big Royal Enfield twin-cylinders had wet-sump lubrication and open cradle frames. They had push rod valve gear. This is the 692 cc Super Meteor of 1959 (bore and stroke = 70×90 mm).

years' apprenticeship and imitation the industry finally "took off," as had been the case in other areas. Thus toward the end of the fifties the Japanese, who had already secured the "poor" utilitarian oriental markets, decided that the time had come for a direct confrontation with the more advanced Western technology, obviously with a view to conquering its markets. They did this by taking part in what was the most famous race in the world at the time, the British Tourist Trophy (TT), a very rigorous test bench and the best possible publicity.

Honda entered five 125 cc machines which were not outstanding and were inspired by the best contemporary Italian and German machines: twin-cylinder engine with two overhead camshafts operated by a vertical shaft and bevel gears; ignition magneto; dry-plate clutch; six gear ratios. They also used a few systems, such as valve gear with four valves per cylinder, which had been around for decades (they were found on bikes by Guzzi, Rudge and Triumph between 1920 and 1930).

Despite the riders' lack of experience the Honda machines

did quite well, displaying excellent speed and endurance. In short, the Japanese had demonstrated their most typical qualities: no outstanding innovations – which in any case were impossible now in the field of internal combustion engines – but a great ability to make the most complex systems functional, combined with large-scale investment, organizational spirit and a meticulous approach. The concept of white-glove engineering originated at this time. Within a few years the Japanese were to dominate the racing sector, especially in the small and medium displacements. Meanwhile, many small factories which had sprung up in the initial enthusiasm had already disappeared, and those that were left had reached a potential capable of crushing all competitors.

From crisis to recovery

In the sixties, however, the crisis in Europe reached its peak. Even many famous factories found themselves in serious financial difficulties; others closed down for good. Production was now focused on mopeds and very lightweight models only. In Italy, Moto Guzzi was saved at the eleventh hour by a pool of banks; Aermacchi, Benelli, Bianchi, Garelli, Gilera and Motobi merged with other, stronger industrial groups; Ducati continued thanks to EFIM; Alpino, Capriolo, Iso, Itom, Mival, Mondial, Motom, Parilla and even Innocenti were forced to close down or would do so shortly afterward. This left the huge Piaggio company and MV, which kept going more through the will of its owner, Count Domenico Agusta, than for the profits that could be made from it; and a few small firms, saved by their modest size and particularly successful products: Guazzoni, Italjet, Laverda, Morini and Testi.

Of course, things were no better in the rest of Europe. France was reduced to making mopeds only, albeit in very large numbers, with just a few factories operating: Motobécane, Peugeot, Vélosolex. In Germany only BMW, Kreidler, Maico, DKW, Sachs (and its affiliate Hercules) and Zündapp survived. In Sweden Husqvarna resisted, also subsidized more as a hobby than for profit by a big metallurgical and mechanical con-

TWO-STROKE HORIZONTAL CYLINDER ENGINES OF THE SIXTIES

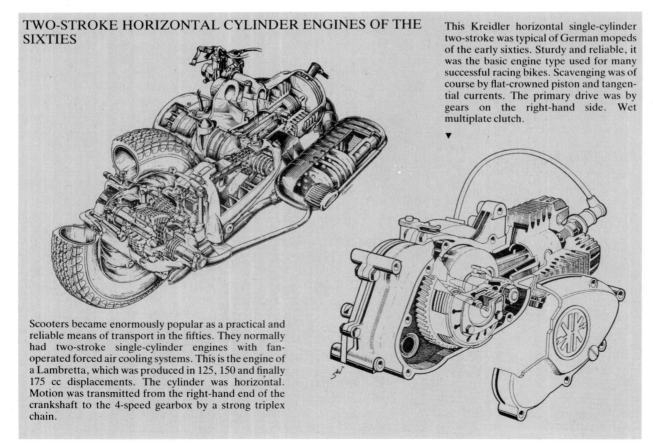

This Kreidler horizontal single-cylinder two-stroke was typical of German mopeds of the early sixties. Sturdy and reliable, it was the basic engine type used for many successful racing bikes. Scavenging was of course by flat-crowned piston and tangential currents. The primary drive was by gears on the right-hand side. Wet multiplate clutch.

▼

Scooters became enormously popular as a practical and reliable means of transport in the fifties. They normally had two-stroke single-cylinder engines with fan-operated forced air cooling systems. This is the engine of a Lambretta, which was produced in 125, 150 and finally 175 cc displacements. The cylinder was horizontal. Motion was transmitted from the right-hand end of the crankshaft to the 4-speed gearbox by a strong triplex chain.

The single-cylinder BSA B 34 Gold Star was one of the most brilliant 500 cc sports bikes for years. It had push rod valve gear and chain primary drive with a separate gearbox. This is the 1960 version, delivering about 38 HP at 6500 rpm (bore and stroke = 85 × 88 mm).

One of the bikes which helped to establish Honda on European markets was the 250 twin-cylinder. It had a chain-operated single overhead camshaft, a pressed steel frame and swinging link front suspension. This is the 1960 version.

cern. The British were still going strong with their immutable twin-cylinders, although the continuous concentration of brands heralded the impending crisis there too. The Swiss, Dutch and Belgian industries had virtually disappeared, except for a few producers of mopeds. The Spanish and East European industries, on the other hand, were still doing well – particularly those of East Germany and Czechoslovakia, which could count on a huge utilitarian market. Shortly afterward, however, almost unexpectedly, things began to change for the better even in old Europe. Following the example of America, where Japanese penetration was beginning to bear fruit, new categories of user were becoming interested in motorbikes.

This was the last big break for the British industry, the only one producing large motorbikes at the time and therefore the only one capable of satisfying the wishes of the new customers immediately. The various twin-cylinders were "blown up" still further to 800–850 cc and the last big British creation appeared: the 750 cc push rod engine with three cylinders side by side, sold with slight modifications under the BSA & Triumph trademark, these companies also having merged. Very high-performance vehicles were derived from it, perhaps the first of those available to the general public which were genuinely capable of 200 km/h (124 mph): easy to handle like all British bikes, stable and with good brakes. But they were not an overwhelming success and were soon over-

shadowed by Japanese products, which were being imported in increasing numbers into Europe too and had many good selling points. These included many accessories, like electric starters, to which motorcyclists were not accustomed; very full instrumentation, and numerous technical features directly derived from the competition: four-cylinder engines, single or double overhead camshaft valve gear and five- or six-speed gears – all designed to satisfy the motorcyclist's every whim.

The new medium-powered Honda twins and above all the fabulous 750 cc four-cylinder, the extraordinary Kawasaki 500 triple-cylinder two-stroke – with outstanding acceleration (and fuel consumption) – and the more leisurely and dignified Suzuki and

Yamaha two-stroke twins stole the show because they really had something new to offer.

The British industry, at one time the most powerful in the world, was soon on its knees.

Only BMW could withstand the Japanese onslaught. This company had always depended on a particular type of discerning clientele and had improved its engines (although they were still twin-cylinder boxers) and cycle parts at that time. The Italians did not have the capacity of the Germans and Japanese, but were still capable of being quick off the mark. Thus in about the mid sixties in Italy brand new "superbikes" appeared which at long last were thoroughly up to date: the Moto Guzzi V7 with a transverse-mounted 700 cc V-twin engine and shaft final drive; the

TWO CLASSIC BRITISH ENGINES

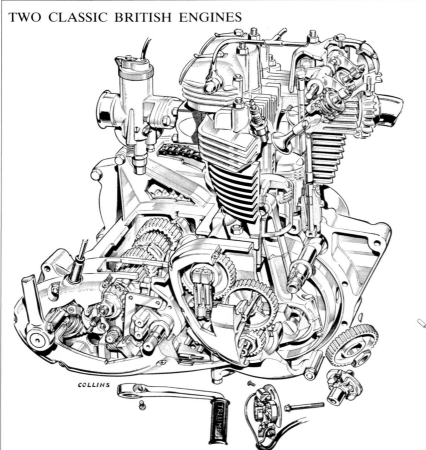

The classic Triumph twin-cylinder (this is the 650 cc single-carburetor version of the mid sixties) was derived from a 1938 design by Edward Turner. The cylinder head and block were originally made of cast iron, but a light alloy cylinder head was used after the war. The 650 cc version came out in 1950 (bore and stroke = 71 × 82 mm) and in the Bonneville model of the second half of the sixties delivered 46 HP at 6500 rpm. The valve gear was of the push rod type, with one camshaft fitted at the front of the base of the cylinders and the other behind it. The crankshaft had a big central flywheel fixed by screws. The connecting rods were of forged aluminum alloy. The main bearings were roller type; the big end bearings, friction type. It had dry-sump lubrication with a piston oil pump.

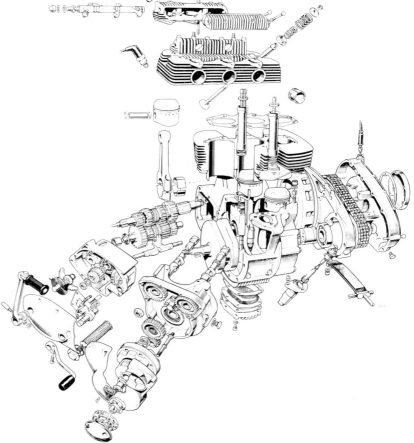

The three-cylinder engine of the Triumph Trident and BSA "Rocket 3" was the last major product by the British motorcycle industry. It was closely related to the 500 cc twin-cylinder. Here too, the valve mechanism was of the push rod type with two gear-driven camshafts in the cylinder block, but unlike the twin-cylinder models it had a steel crankshaft forged in one piece, with four journals. The connecting rods were of aluminum alloy and also worked on thin-walled bearings; the crank pins were set at 120°. The cylinder block was of aluminum with cast iron cylinder liners.

Toward the end of the sixties Norton produced the Commando model, using the 750 cc version of their by then old twin-cylinder engine (designed in 1947) with push rod valve gear, cast iron cylinders and just two main bearings. It sold well, thanks to its good looks and high performance, but could not compare with the latest Japanese, German and Italian models in reliability and durability. This engine, different variants of which were produced for a number of years, was very much the swan song of this illustrious British company. This version is from 1969–70 and developed 58 HP at 6800 rpm. Bore and stroke = 73 × 89 mm.

In 1968 the BSA-Triumph group brought out a handsome, very high-performance triple-cylinder with push rod valve gear. The engine was basically a 500 cc Triumph twin to which an extra cylinder had been added in the center. The oil radiator was fitted in series. The final versions of this bike (those produced by Triumph were called "Trident," those by BSA, "Rocket 3") were given disc brakes and later electric starters too. The one shown is from 1971–72 (power 60 HP at 7250 rpm). Bore and stroke = 67 × 70 mm. Maximum speed 195 km/h (121 mph).

Laverda 650 and 750 twins with single-camshaft valve gear and the MV 600, with a superb double-camshaft four-cylinder closely related to the company's G.P. racing models. The Guzzi was a big, unshakable grand touring bike; the Laverdas were fast and powerful sports bikes; the MV was an exclusive vehicle despite its sporty characteristics, designed to be sold to a few customers only, carefully selected by the manufacturers.

By the beginning of the seventies the motorcycling scene had thus changed rapidly: there were still many mopeds on the market, a number of 125 cc lightweight models which were becoming the typical form of transport for those too young to drive more powerful vehicles; scooters were still doing well, even if virtually the only producer in the world now was the Italian company Piaggio; and there were a few medium-displacement bikes and quite a lot

of "supers" from 500 cc to 1000 cc and over. Four-stroke engines were the most widely used, but two-strokes were rapidly gaining ground. In fact, recent studies on valve gear, the perfection of the Schnürle system taken to the extremes of five, six and seven transfer ports, separate lubrication with an automatic pump and the use of rotary and reed inlet valves had finally enabled the two-stroke engine to beat its old rival in terms of performance.

High-capacity multicylinder engines thus appeared, with outstanding performance, if at the cost of very high fuel consumption.

The motorbike was no longer a practical means of transport for the poor; therefore designers no longer had any hesitation in using costly and complex technical solutions. Four-cylinders were increasingly common, even for medium-small displacements like 350 cc (Honda followed by Moto

For a number of years the Titan 500 was the most powerful bike produced by Suzuki. The two-stroke twin-cylinder engine with air cooling and separate lubrication delivered 47 HP at 7000 rpm (bore and stroke = 70 × 64 mm). It had gear primary drive, a 5-speed gearbox and a continuous, tubular steel duplex cradle frame. The final versions of this bike (which went into production in the second half of the sixties) were fitted with disc brakes and then aluminum alloy spoked wheels.

Ducati Desmo single-cylinders were the first series bikes to be fitted with desmodromic valve gear. These high-performance machines were introduced in 1970 in 250, 350 and 450 cc versions and produced until 1974.

Kawasaki two-stroke triple-cylinders were pacesetters in terms of performance. This is the 350 cc S2 model (1971) which could deliver 45 HP and had a maximum speed of 170 km/h (105 mph). Weight 150 kg (330 lb).

The new BMW twin-cylinder boxer came out in 1969. Initially produced in 500, 600 and 750 cc versions, the displacement was later taken to 800, 900 and 1000 cc thanks to constant increases in bore (the stroke in all versions stayed at 70.6 mm). The cylinders were of aluminum alloy with cast-in iron barrels (but the final versions had Nikasil liners). The crankshaft was of forged steel, in one piece. It had thin-walled main and big end bearings. The valve gear was of the push rod type with a camshaft low down in the block, driven by a duplex chain.

The Morini twin-cylinder which came out in 1973 with a displacement of 350 cc (bore and stroke = 62 × 57 mm) was later produced in 250 and 500 cc versions as well. It had push rod valve gear with a camshaft at the center of the (72° angle) V formed by the cylinders, driven by a short toothed belt. The forged steel crankshaft turned on two ball bearings; the connecting rods worked side by side on the single crank pin and were fitted with bearings. The clutch was of the dry multiplate type and there was a 6-speed gearbox.

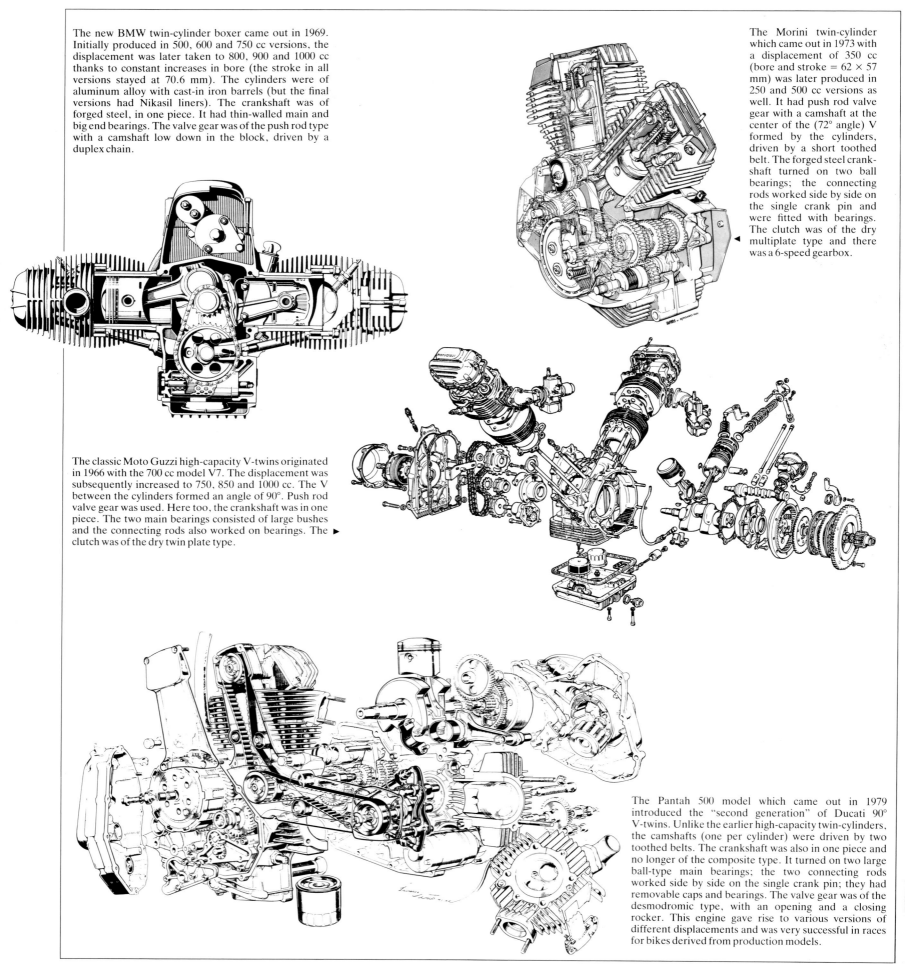

The classic Moto Guzzi high-capacity V-twins originated in 1966 with the 700 cc model V7. The displacement was subsequently increased to 750, 850 and 1000 cc. The V between the cylinders formed an angle of 90°. Push rod valve gear was used. Here too, the crankshaft was in one piece. The two main bearings consisted of large bushes and the connecting rods also worked on bearings. The ▶ clutch was of the dry twin plate type.

The Pantah 500 model which came out in 1979 introduced the "second generation" of Ducati 90° V-twins. Unlike the earlier high-capacity twin-cylinders, the camshafts (one per cylinder) were driven by two toothed belts. The crankshaft was also in one piece and no longer of the composite type. It turned on two large ball-type main bearings; the two connecting rods worked side by side on the single crank pin; they had removable caps and bearings. The valve gear was of the desmodromic type, with an opening and a closing rocker. This engine gave rise to various versions of different displacements and was very successful in races for bikes derived from production models.

Motobi horizontal-cylinder four-strokes were produced for many years (the design originated in the mid-fifties) in 125, 175, 200 and 250 cc displacements. At a later stage these bikes, with pressed steel backbone frames, were also sold under the Benelli trademark (the two companies having merged). This is the 250 cc version of 1971, delivering 18 HP and capable of over 135 km/h (84 mph). Bore and stroke = 74 × 74 mm; push rod valve gear. Weight 108 kg (238 lb).

Very few bikes have influenced technical development and market trends as much as the first Honda four-cylinders with single-camshaft valve gear. The first, and most famous, was the 750 introduced in 1969, which was soon followed by the 500 and then the CB 500 Four, launched in 1971. The engine delivered 48 HP at 9000 rpm, which gave a top speed of over 170 km/h (105 mph). Bore and stroke = 56 × 50.6 mm. Primary drive by Morse chain and a pair of gears; continuous, duplex cradle frame; hydraulically actuated front disc brake; electric start. Weight 183 kg (403 lb).

The big Moto Guzzi 90° V-twins began their career in the second half of the sixties, with a 700 cc displacement and 4-speed gearbox. When the displacement was upped to 750 cc, the normal models were joined by sports versions. This is the V7 750 "S" of 1974 with a twin-disc front brake. The engine, with a bore and stroke of 82.5 × 70 mm, delivered 70 HP at 7000 rpm. It had push rod valve gear, a 5-speed gearbox and shaft final drive. Maximum speed 206 km/h (128 mph).

Guzzi), or even 250 cc (Guzzi again). Luxurious six-cylinder machines also appeared, first by Benelli (750 then 900 cc), then Honda (1000 CBX). Many bikes had valve gear with one or two overhead camshafts and the gearboxes always had at least five speeds. The frames, which were nearly all tubular, duplex cradle type, had telehydraulic suspension with spring preload and damping adjustment, to adapt to different conditions of loading and use.

One area which was doing increasingly well from the early sixties was the off-road bike sector. To begin with the Japanese were not too interested in this field, as it did not yet provide a big enough market for their tastes; but before long they became involved in a big way – Honda, Kawasaki and Suzuki finally overtaking all their European rivals.

Nowadays the image of the motorcycle is essentially a sporting one, "normal" bikes almost being a thing of the past. Modern machines are all based on competition bikes, whether for speed or cross-country use. The road bikes look increasingly like Grand Prix models, as well as incorporating their latest technical features.

Virtually all have more or less extensive fairing, which in many cases is in fact part of the vehicle's structure. In the off-road sector bikes of up to 125 cc, which were very fashionable with young people a few years ago, are now somewhat in decline. Conversely, the larger displacements are becoming more popular – from 600 cc upward, single- and twin-cylinder four-strokes – designed for American-style "enduro" competitions and racing in the desert, which is the one remaining area where man can still live out his spirit of adventure.

"Dream bikes" deserve a special mention. These are machines created to satisfy the American taste for size, which have also had some success in Europe. They combine a powerful engine with all the most ostentatious features imaginable: fairing, trunks, flashing lights and stereo, the whole lot weighing anything up to 400 kg (882 lb). The type was of course pioneered by Harley-Davidson, with their 1340 cc Tour Glide twin-cylinder. This was followed by the Honda Aspencade 1200 with a four-cylinder boxer engine, the Kawasaki Voyager 1300 six-cylinder, Suzuki Cavalcade 1400 V-four built to order, and the

Yamaha Venture Royale, a 1200 cc V-four.

Nowadays the market is shared between two- and four-stroke engines. Four-strokes dominate the medium and large displacements from 350 cc upward, mainly for reasons of fuel economy and pollution control. Two-strokes, with numerous refinements – the latest being automatic partializing valves on the exhaust (sometimes combined with compensating chambers) to improve air flow and pull at low rpm – dominate the smaller displacements, with a few in the medium displacements.

All possible subdivisions of displacement are used nowadays, from the classic singles to twins, four and up to six cylinders, in a wide range of designs. The cylinders can be vertical, horizontal, in line, boxer, longitudinal and transverse Vee. Liquid cooling is increasingly used, as apart from anything else it ensures a more even temperature in the various parts of the engine; this is very important in multicylinders in general and in two-strokes, which now have so many ports in the cylinders that they are subject to considerable distortion.

Ignition is generally of the capacitive discharge type, which can produce very high voltage sparks at the plugs. Simple ignition magnetos are used only on the smallest and most economical models.

The majority of engines are still fed by carburetors but injection systems are found, at least on the most prestigious models. Turbochargers, on the other hand, never really caught on. Lubrication is almost always of the wet-sump type; simple gear pumps have been joined by efficient trochoidal pumps, which can ensure high pressure. Very often, the wheels of the gear mechanism are also pressure-lubricated.

The transmission is always of the mechanical type, with foot-operated constant-mesh gears with five or six ratios. The only modern example of automatic transmission with a hydraulic

Laverda twin-cylinders went into production in 1968 with a displacement of 650 cc, which was soon increased to 750 cc (bore and stroke = 80×74 mm). This is the 1972 version of the 750 SF. The single-camshaft engine delivered 57 HP at 6500 rpm. It had chain primary drive and a 5-speed gearbox.

This 1975 150 cc Gilera four-stroke single-cylinder (Arcore model) with push rod valve gear and a 5-speed gearbox was quite popular. Bore and stroke 60 × 54 mm; power 14.5 HP at 8250 rpm.

A typical Italian moped of the mid seventies, this 50 HP Gilera had a two-stroke single-cylinder engine (38.4 × 43 mm) delivering 1.4 HP at 4500 rpm and a 5-speed gearbox.

Trail bikes became increasingly popular from the early seventies, particularly with the very young. The two-stroke single-cylinders by the Austrian company KTM were among the most widely used. The 125 cc models started out with Sachs 6-speed engines delivering 19 HP at 8500 rpm, while the 175 cc models were given engines designed by KTM right from the start (23 HP at 8800 rpm in the first versions). This is the 175 model of 1974.

The first generation of very popular Cagiva bikes was derived from the Harley-Davidson two-stroke single-cylinders produced in Italy (at Schiranna near Varese). These models were built in 125, 175 (for a short time) and 250 cc versions. Cagiva bought the plant in 1978. This is a 250 from 1977.

Very popular in Italy and familiar in other countries as well, the Morini 3½ marked the return of medium-capacity longitudinal V-twins. The Turismo (Tourist) version appeared in 1972, followed two years later by the Sport version, which delivered 39 HP at 8500 rpm. This engine has a 62 mm bore, 57 mm stroke and push rod valve gear. This is one of the latest versions.

torque converter is found on the 1000 cc Moto Guzzi I Convert. Quite a few automatic belt drive systems are found on mopeds, and on a few scooters as well.

The age-old debate over the relative merits of chain versus shaft final drive, which has been going on ever since the pioneering days, is still far from over and the two systems coexist, each with its advantages and disadvantages. The chain is much simpler and smoother in operation but wears out more easily, although today's models with sealed lubricant last a very long time. The shaft with bevel gears is stronger, but sharper in transmitting the reactions of the engine. It is also harder to modify the transmission ratios; this is quite important for a sporting clientele like motorbike riders. The shaft is thus used for engines with a longitudinal axis (as is only logical) like the Moto Guzzi, BMW and Honda 1200, or on very powerful and prestigious models like the Kawasaki 1300, Suzuki 700, 1100 and 1200 and Yamaha 900 and 1200. There are also a few isolated examples of final drive by toothed belt: the Kawasaki 450 twin and a few models by Harley-Davidson. Finally, the Vespa (by Piaggio) has direct drive with the wheel mounted on the exit shaft of the gearbox.

One area which is developing faster than ever is that of frames,

The first modern motorcycle with a four-cylinder engine and double-camshaft valve gear of a higher displacement than the "classic" limit of 750 cc was the Kawasaki 900, which appeared in 1972. It delivered 82 HP at 8500 rpm. Bore and stroke = 66 × 66 mm. Five-speed gearbox.

BMW twin-cylinder "boxer" engines, which were completely redesigned at the end of the sixties (when the 5 series appeared in 500, 600 and 750 cc displacements) gave rise to many highly successful models such as the R 90 S, R 100 RS and R 80 GS. In 1979 models R 45 and R 65 (shown here) appeared, fitted with new 450 and 650 cc engines and very similar to the others in basic design. Since 1981 the higher-capacity model has delivered 50 HP at 7250 rpm. Bore and stroke = 82×61.5 mm. Push rod valve gear. Dry single-plate clutch and 5-speed gearbox. These bikes have aluminum alloy wheels, continuous tubular duplex cradle frames and shaft final drive.

The BMW K 100 is built on completely new lines: the 1000 cc (67×70 mm) engine with four cylinders in line is fitted longitudinally to the frame, the cylinders being completely horizontal. It has water cooling, chain-operated double-camshaft push rod valve gear and Bosch indirect fuel injection. The power is 90 HP at 8000 rpm. The cylinder head and block are of aluminum alloy. The cylinders have a thin coating of Nikasil rather than the usual cast iron liners. The bike has 5-speed gears, shaft final drive and triple disc brakes.

The Yamaha RD 350 LC has a water-cooled two-stroke twin-cylinder engine with a reed inlet valve and a partializing exhaust valve (YPVS). With a 64 mm bore and 54 mm stroke, this power unit delivers 59 HP at 9000 rpm.

The Honda VF 750 F made a great impact at its first showing in Cologne in 1982. The four-cylinder 90° V-type engine with double-camshaft valve gear with four valves per cylinder (bore and stroke = 70 × 48.6 mm) delivers no less than 90 HP at 10,000 rpm. It is water-cooled with a thermostatically controlled electric fan and a double radiator. It has chain final drive. The front wheel is 16 inches (40.64 cm) in diameter, the rear one 18 inches (45.72 cm) in diameter. Square section tubular steel frame; triple disc brakes.

The fully faired Kawasaki GPz 600 R, which came out in 1985, has a four-cylinder water-cooled engine with double-camshaft valve gear with four valves per cylinder. The bore and stroke measurements are 60 × 52.4 mm. Power delivery approximately 75 HP at 10,500 rpm.

where the search is always for maximum rigidity combined with light weight and economy of construction. Over the years people have tried replacing steel tubes derived from bicycles with backbone structures, still in tubing or in stamped plate, either of steel or light alloy, or aluminum castings (Rumi, Greeves), or mixed plate and tube arrangements, but without much success. Today, square section light alloy tubular frames are in vogue, being extremely light and easy to produce. The pattern most often followed today is the duplex cradle, or a cradle encircling the engine, with direct elements from the steering head to the rear fork joint – a design that is fifty years old (something very similar was used

on the prewar Gilera 500 four-cylinder) but which, apart from anything else, lends itself very well to mono shock absorber rear suspension.

While the most popular type of suspension is still the telescopic fork with hydraulic shock absorbers, often combined with pneumatic systems and antidive mechanisms to prevent a downward lurch on braking at the rear of the bike, the swinging fork with telescopic elements at the sides of the wheel has been replaced almost one hundred percent by designs which still have a swinging fork but with a single spring element fitted at an angle beneath the fuel tank (Yamaha Monocross) or vertically beneath the saddle. In the latter case it is

joined to the fork by more or less complex leverage designed to reduce oscillations. In this way, the wheel can move freely without deforming the spring unduly. In nearly all cases the spring load and damping are manually adjustable. Single-arm rear suspension systems are also found (e.g. BMW) which make it easier to remove the wheel, always a tricky business on old-fashioned bikes.

Road bikes normally have wheels with broad spokes cast in light alloy. These are more economical to produce and stronger than wheels with separate spokes. They enable tubeless tyres to be used and make it easier to fit disc brakes. Conventional spoked wheels are still used on off-road bikes, as they are better at

absorbing jolts without breaking.

Hydraulically actuated disc brakes are increasingly common. They are now normal at the front, even on low-speed models, and are fitted to the rear axle of all fast and heavy vehicles. Guzzi has developed a system whereby both brakes can be operated by a single control, and BMW has been researching anti-lock systems.

Tyres are also in a state of evolution. Radial carcasses and tubeless tyres have reached the motorcycling world too, as have plies in nylon or kevlar, the revolutionary high-technology synthetic fiber. Low-profile tyres are also frequently used now, rather than tyres of circular cross-section. "Slick" tyres are used only for circuit racing.

A typical example of the latest generation of low-powered Enduro bikes, this Cagiva Elephant 2 is driven by a two-stroke single-cylinder engine with reed valve induction. The displacement is 125 cc (bore and stroke = 56 × 50.6 mm); it is water-cooled and the cylinder barrel has a Nikasil lining.

The very recent Gilera Dakota 350 is driven by a single-cylinder, double-camshaft four-valve engine delivering 33 HP at 7500 rpm. The valve gear is operated by a toothed belt.

The very modern 1986 Gilera KZ 125 is an excellent representative of the latest generation of sports roadsters of this displacement. The two-stroke single-cylinder engine (bore and stroke = 56 × 50.5 mm) delivers 26 HP at 9250 rpm. It has reed valve induction, a 28 mm carburetor, water cooling and a 6-speed gearbox. The two front brake discs are 240 mm (9.4 in) in diameter. The maximum speed is approximately 150 km/h (93 mph).

The Suzuki GSX 1100 R, which went into production in 1986, has a top speed of about 260 km/h (162 mph). Bore and stroke = 76 × 58 mm, 5-speed gearbox, aluminum frame. Double-camshaft valve gear with four valves per cylinder. Weight 215 kg (474 lb).

▼

This is the very recent Ducati 750 F1. The 750 cc V-twin engine with desmodromic valve gear delivers about 75 HP. Weight 165 kg (364 lb).

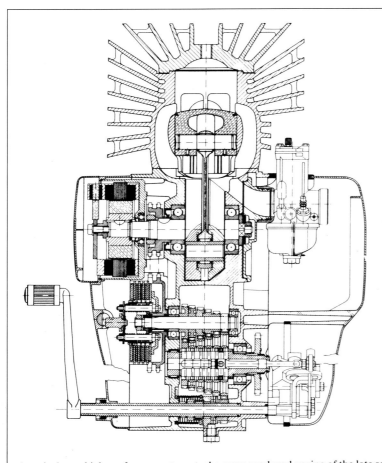

This is a (Suzuki) two-stroke motocross engine of the first half of the eighties. It has water cooling with forced circulation by means of a centrifugal pump. The inlet pipe divides in two below the carburetor, one branch ending in a port which opens into the cylinder wall (and is "controlled" by the piston) while the other opens into the crankcase and has a reed valve. The iron barrel is cast into the aluminum alloy cylinder. ▶

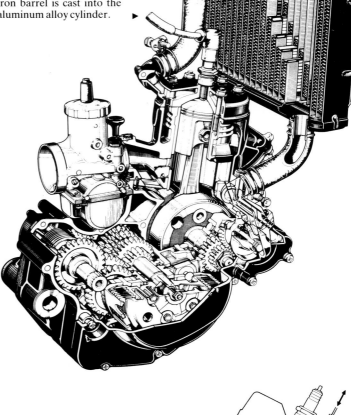

A typical very high-performance two-stroke mass-produced engine of the late seventies (designed for trail and motocross bikes) is this Maico single-cylinder with rotary disc induction and air cooling (note the fan-shaped finning on the cylinder head). The crankshaft turns on two large ball bearings. The piston has only one ring. The light alloy cylinder barrel has a Nikasil lining. The gearbox is of the sliding key type.

The engine of the Yamaha RD 350 LC (also produced in a 250 cc version) is very similar in design to the type used for years on the company's highly successful racing bikes, and at the same time extremely simple and rational. It is a water-cooled two-stroke twin-cylinder with reed inlet valves and partializing (YPVS) exhaust valves. According to the manufacturers, the final versions of this engine (bore and stroke = 64 × 54 mm) have a maximum power of 59 HP at 9000 rpm (1984).

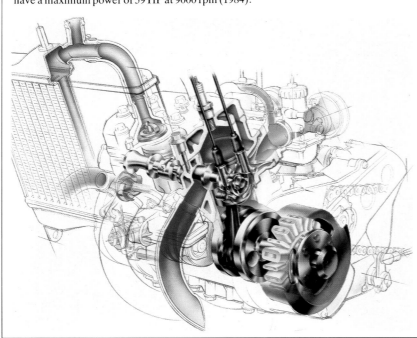

Yamaha was the first to develop valves which could vary the height of the exhaust port fully automatically to "adapt" the timing (for the exhaust stroke, of course) to the rpm. To begin with these valves were rotary type, but gate valves were later used as well. The mechanism can be operated by a centrifugal, electronic or even in some cases (e.g. a few Rotax engines) pneumatic device. The diagram shows the rotary valve used on the Yamaha RD 350 LC, known as YPVS. ▶

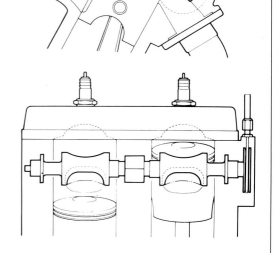

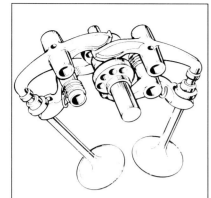

Ducati is the only company in the world to produce engines with desmodromic valve gear. This system employs two cams and two, two-armed rockers for each valve (one to open and one to close it). The results for both reliability and performance are excellent.

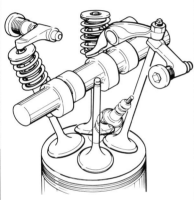

Honda has recently revived the use of four valves fitted radially for a few off-road single-cylinders. Rudge was famous for using this system back in 1920–1930 and it was later reintroduced by BMW on a few racing car engines after the mid sixties (the cylinder heads with radial valves were designed by L. Apfelbeck). Honda uses single-camshaft valve gear; each cam operates its respective valve by means of a two-armed rocker and a finger rocker. The combustion chamber is hemispherical.

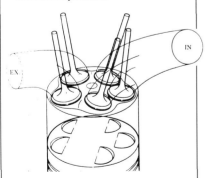

High-performance engines with four valves per cylinder are very common these days. Yamaha recently even made a 750 cc engine for its FZ model, with three inlet and two exhaust valves per cylinder.

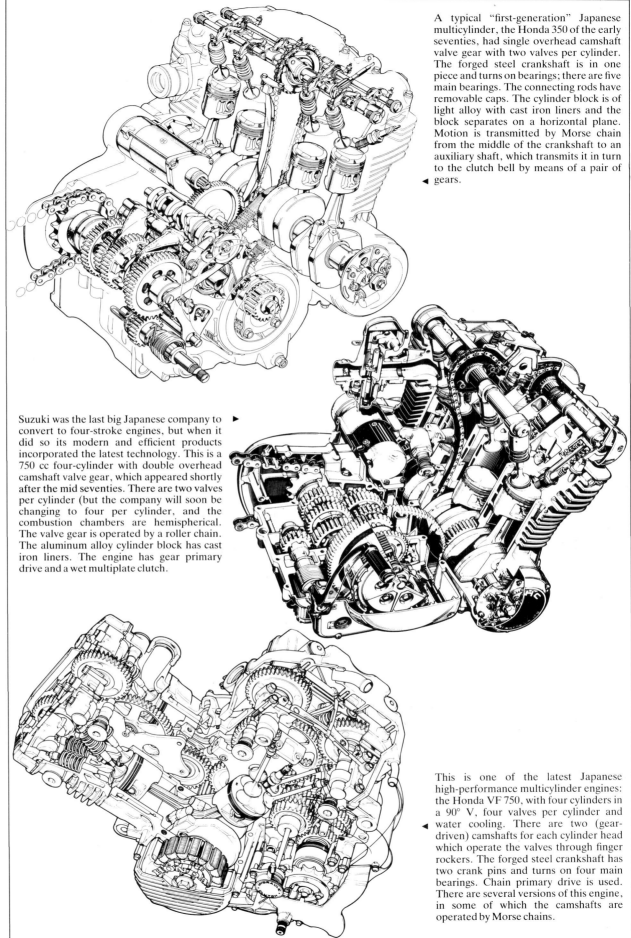

A typical "first-generation" Japanese multicylinder, the Honda 350 of the early seventies, had single overhead camshaft valve gear with two valves per cylinder. The forged steel crankshaft is in one piece and turns on bearings; there are five main bearings. The connecting rods have removable caps. The cylinder block is of light alloy with cast iron liners and the block separates on a horizontal plane. Motion is transmitted by Morse chain from the middle of the crankshaft to an auxiliary shaft, which transmits it in turn to the clutch bell by means of a pair of gears.

Suzuki was the last big Japanese company to convert to four-stroke engines, but when it did so its modern and efficient products incorporated the latest technology. This is a 750 cc four-cylinder with double overhead camshaft valve gear, which appeared shortly after the mid seventies. There are two valves per cylinder (but the company will soon be changing to four per cylinder, and the combustion chambers are hemispherical. The valve gear is operated by a roller chain. The aluminum alloy cylinder block has cast iron liners. The engine has gear primary drive and a wet multiplate clutch.

This is one of the latest Japanese high-performance multicylinder engines: the Honda VF 750, with four cylinders in a 90° V, four valves per cylinder and water cooling. There are two (geardriven) camshafts for each cylinder head which operate the valves through finger rockers. The forged steel crankshaft has two crank pins and turns on four main bearings. Chain primary drive is used. There are several versions of this engine, in some of which the camshafts are operated by Morse chains.

Despite the disasters of the war, Italy was one of the first European nations to resume motorcycle racing after 1945. A number of racers, having managed to save the bikes they had ridden up to 1939/1940, were able to put them to immediate use.

The best bikes available included the Moto Guzzi Albatross 250 and Condor 500, a few Benelli 250 single- and double-camshafts, the Gilera Otto Bulloni and Saturno 500 and a few British and German models, by Norton, Rudge, DKW, etc.

1946 was an important year, not only for being positively inundated by motorcycling events but also because it saw the resumption of the first international races abroad and the introduction of the drastic new regulations banning supercharged bikes. The last opportunity for an engine with a compressor to win a major competition was the Swiss Grand Prix, where Nello Pagani piloted to victory the supercharged Gilera four-cylinder which had won the European Championship with Dorino Serafini in 1939. As for Moto Guzzi, apart from their highly successful twin-cylinder – various details of which had been revised – they had already prepared the new single-cylinder Dondolino (derived from the Condor) and the splendid Gambalunga, which was fairly similar to the Dondolino from a mechanical point of view but much more "exclusive," being reserved for official racers.

Meanwhile the Tourist Trophy had also started up again, Norton and Velocette bikes winning the two higher displacements and the Moto Guzzis of Barrington and Cann taking the first two places in the 250 class.

The explosive period of technical development had not yet begun, the racing bikes of the time being basically updated or completely revised versions of existing models, but not innovatory in the true sense of the word. Moto Guzzi's big achievement was knowing how to make the best use of prewar material and creating new lightweight, easy-to-handle models that were very reliable.

1948 saw the affirmation in Italy of the 125, which was given its own championship for the first time, albeit of secondary status. This was prompted by a commercial reality: the rapid diffusion among a still poor group of users of economical machines like roller engines for bicycles (mainly Garelli Mosquito and Ducati Cucciolo), the Guzzino 65 and, as stated, lightweights.

The spread of utilitarian 125s soon led to transformations to increase their speed, followed by the production of special models designed for competitions. Together with the many victories achieved in the traditional 250 and 500 cc displacements in Italy and 350 cc abroad, there were increasing successes for new makes like MV Agusta and Morini (initially with two-stroke engines) and the Mondial four-stroke. But other marques

In 1947 Triumph produced this 500 cc twin-cylinder, derived from production models and capable of delivering about 40 HP at 7600 rpm.

RACING IN THE POSTWAR YEARS

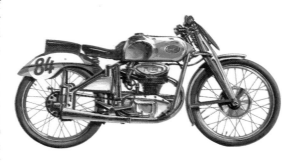

The Mondial 125 of 1949, powered by a single-cylinder engine with double overhead camshaft valve gear, developed about 12 HP at 9000 rpm. This bike (ridden by Nello Pagani) won the World Championship.

distinguished themselves in the various races in Italy and abroad: the Parilla 250 cc; the Benelli double-camshaft model entrusted to Dario Ambrosini; and the constantly improved Gilera four-cylinders and Sanremo model which, with 35 HP at 6000 rpm and a weight of 120 kg (265 lb), could do 180 km/h (112 mph).

In 1949 the World Championship finally got under way – a logical progression from the prewar European Championship that had drawn the crowds not just for its sporting contests, but because of the nationalist sentiments which the fans of each country attributed to those representing their flag.

The 125 class was disputed between Mondial, MV Agusta and Morini. Nello Pagani won with the Mondial double-camshaft, a handsome silver-blue machine delivering 12 HP at 9000 rpm, with a weight of 83 kg (183 lb) and speed of about 130 km/h (81 mph). It had a parallelogram front fork, as many other bikes of the same displacement and higher, still did, although with different structural features. The only ones with telehydraulic forks, which were later to be preferred, were by AJS, then Norton. Moto Guzzi, on the other hand, used its highly original system of swinging lower link rods, introduced on the 1946 Gambalunga then adapted for all subsequent bikes up to the last official models of 1957.

It was in fact a derivative of the Gambalunga, the Gambalunghino, which won the 250 World Championship with Bruno Ruffo, against the double-camshaft Benellis and a few Rudges. The 1949 Gambalunghino delivered 25 HP at 8000 rpm, weighed 122 kg (269 lb), had a top speed of 180 km/h (112 mph) and single-camshaft valve gear. Ambrosini's Benelli was a double-camshaft model of 28 HP at 10,000 rpm, weighing 115 kg (253 lb) and with a speed of about 175 km/h (109 mph). Both bikes (like most others except those of AJS and Norton again, which already had hydraulic rear shock absorbers) used rear suspension systems with friction shock absorbers.

The 350 was basically an all-British race, with just Norton, AJS and Velocette competing. The Velocette, with its 35 HP double-camshaft engine and speed of 180 km/h (112 mph), proved far superior, winning all five stages of the Championship with veteran Freddie Frith.

The 500 class was very interesting right from the start, because of the intense competition (which was to continue for years) between the agile Nortons and Velocettes and more powerful but less manageable Gilera four-cylinders. On the one hand, therefore, were the double-camshaft single-cylinder Nortons delivering about 40 HP at 7000 rpm with a speed of nearly 200 km/h (124 mph) and the highly original AJS Porcupine (so called because of the unusually shaped finning on the cylinder head) double-camshaft horizontal twin delivering 45 HP, ridden by that great champion Leslie Graham; on the other hand were the Gileras, which were more "generous" but not so versatile.

The Championship was very strongly contested. In the end victory went to Graham, who beat Nello Pagani by just one point.

All brands and all riders were after the title at the 1950 World Championship. The protagonists of the 125 class were almost the same as the previous year except for Pagani, who had chosen to concentrate on the 500 class. At the end of the three-stage event it was Ruffo who won with a Mondial, but Carlo Ubbiali also distinguished himself, going on to win the Ulster G.P. unexpectedly, also on a Mondial bike. An important point about the 125 class was that it was the first to use fairing (subsequently fitted to bikes of all displacements) to compensate for the bikes' low engine power by using aerodynamics. The first attempt was far from "timid," Mondial preparing a fully faired model for Monza on which Gianni Leoni beat Ubbiali.

In the 250 class there was a bitter contest between Moto Guzzi and Benelli. Ambrosini triumphed with the double-camshaft Benelli, which won at the TT and at Geneva (replacing Berne) and Monza, coming second behind Maurice Cann's Guzzi only at Ulster. Particularly significant was winning the Tourist Trophy after a relentless duel with Cann. With this success at the 42nd edition of the TT, Ambrosini became the second Italian to win the very hard British competition (425 km = 264 miles that year), the first being Tenni in 1937 with Moto Guzzi.

The 350 class was again won by Velocette, this time with Bob Foster: a far from easy victory, as he was competing against Norton and AJS. Together with established champions like Bell, Daniell, Graham, Lockett and Frend, excellent riders like Bill Lomas appeared, also on a Velocette, and above all Geoffrey Duke, with the Norton, who was to be the big discovery of those years and Gilera's most formidable adversary, until the Italian company hired him to represent their own colours.

An interesting event in 1950 was the first appearance among the 500s of the MV Agusta four-cylinder ridden by Arciso Artesiani, who achieved very good placings in a few races. This machine, designed by former Gilera engineer Pietro Remor, was mechanically similar to the Gilera but very different in a few details such as the four-speed gears, which were operated by two separate levers, one on either side of the bike according to whether the rider wanted to shift the gears up or down. It also had cardan shaft drive, torsion bar rear suspension and stamped plate front suspension, also with torsion bars. All in all not an

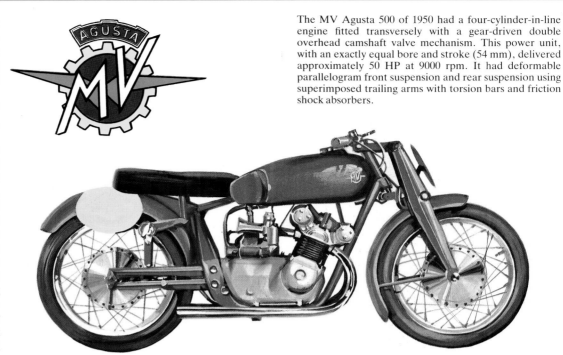

The MV Agusta 500 of 1950 had a four-cylinder-in-line engine fitted transversely with a gear-driven double overhead camshaft valve mechanism. This power unit, with an exactly equal bore and stroke (54 mm), delivered approximately 50 HP at 9000 rpm. It had deformable parallelogram front suspension and rear suspension using superimposed trailing arms with torsion bars and friction shock absorbers.

easy machine, but none the less promising with its 50 HP at 9000 rpm and speed of 200 km/h (124 mph), as was to be demonstrated after it was given telehydraulic suspension and four carburetors (initially there were only two).

The title in this class went to Umberto Masetti on a Gilera.

1950 marked the return of one of the top Italian motorcycling events: the Milan–Taranto race, which originated in 1919 as the Milan–Naples and was extended to Taranto from 1937, being held for the last time in 1940, just ten years before the first postwar edition.

It was a very rigorous test for both bikes and riders, covering 1280 km (795 miles) or 1400 km (870 miles), depending on which of two alternative routes was chosen (the first reached Florence from Bologna via the Futa Pass, the second went toward the Adriatic coast after Bologna), with no stops except for refuelling. The 1950 edition was won outright by Guido Leoni on the Moto Guzzi Dondolino, which covered the 1350-km (839-mile) route in 12 hours 59′ 09″, at an average of 102.033 km/h (63.400 mph).

1951 was one of the most dramatic years for accidents, despite earning Italy the world titles

This is the final version of the Moto Guzzi 500 twin-cylinder, which originated in the mid thirties but was gradually perfected and used for racing until 1951. By the end of its evolutionary period, the engine (bore and stroke = 68 × 68 mm) delivered 48 HP at 8000 rpm. The single overhead camshaft valve mechanism was operated by shaft and bevel gearing. The angle between the cylinders was 120°. The bike had a tubular duplex open cradle frame and swinging link front suspension.

Moto Guzzi won the world title in the 250 class in 1949, 1951 and 1952 with a fast, lightweight "Gambalunghino," with a single-cylinder engine and single-camshaft valve gear, of the same general design as other machines built by this company since 1926. The 1952 version delivered 27 HP at 8500 rpm; it had 5-speed gears.

The Moto Morini 125 single-camshaft was Mondial's strongest rival in the first World Championships. The engine could deliver 16 HP at 9500 rpm in the 1952 version.

in the 125 and 250 classes. There have been other particularly disastrous seasons in the history of motorcycling, but 1951 certainly made an enormous impression.

Ubbiali, after Pagani and Ruffo in the two previous years, continued Mondial's series of victories, winning the World Championship, which now had five stages compared with the previous three. However, the last stage of the program did not count for the final score, as only three riders completed it. Important events that year included the "purchase" of Leslie Graham by MV and the successful appearance of the Spanish two-strokes by Montesa, ridden moreover by Bultò, later the founder of Bultaco.

With the loss of Ambrosini at the third stage of the 250 Championship, after victory at Berne and second place behind Tommy Wood's Moto Guzzi at the TT, Benelli was out of the race and Ruffo, on the Guzzi Gambalunghino, regained the title he had won two years previously.

Geoffrey Duke put all his outstanding courage and skill into winning the 350 and 500 classes for Norton. Duke was the complete rider: lucid, intelligent, leaving nothing to chance; he was even responsible for introducing leather suits instead of the usual jacket and trousers, to improve aerodynamics.

With the 350 Duke won five of the eight competitions in the program including the TT, preceding in the final results Doran on an AJS, Lockett, Kavanagh and Brett all on Nortons, and Graham on the Velocette.

Duke, who was twenty-three at the time, also won the 500 title, thereby becoming the first rider in history to win both displacements. He won four of the eight contests with the 500, his strongest adversaries being Alfredo Milani and Masetti with the Gilera "four." Milani won two competitions – at Albi and Monza – whilst Masetti won only the opening event at Barcelona.

Fergus Anderson, on the renewed Moto Guzzi twin, was a clear winner at the Swiss G.P. at Berne, which took place in driving rain. It was the first time Moto Guzzi had won the 500 since the introduction of the World Championship. The MV Agusta four also did very well, with a team of riders composed of Graham, Bandirola, Bertacchini and Artesiani. Its best result of the season was the third place secured at Barcelona by Artesiani.

Germans also competed at the 1952 World Championship, with NSU, Horex and DKW

in the 250 and BMW in the 500 class. For the first time since the War, Germany also had her own championship at the Solitude circuit near Stuttgart. There were many important innovations to the engines, cycle parts and fairing, which was limited for the time being to the handlebar type, passing from the front numberplate to the sides of the fuel tank.

After Mondial's three-year supremacy in the 125 class, this time it was the double-camshaft MV Agusta ridden by Cecil Sandford which beat Ubbiali's Mondial and the new star Emilio Mendogni, who piloted the single-camshaft Morini to victory at Monza and Barcelona. The 1952 Mondial, which was similar to the 1949 version, delivered 15 HP at 10,000 rpm and could do 150 km/h (93 mph). The double-camshaft MV had the same power but 500 rpm more and was slightly faster than the Mondial, while the Morini, with a power of 16 HP at 9500 rpm, could do 155 km/h (96 mph). Sandford, who was hired at the last minute, won three races, Mendogni two and Werner Haas gave a glimpse of the future supremacy of NSU by unexpectedly winning the Solitude.

The 250 class was also a hive of activity, with Moto Guzzi, Benelli, Parilla, Velocette, Horex, DKW and NSU competing. The only two-stroke was the DKW twin-cylinder designed in 1951, in a rotary valve version and one with conventional induction using three ports and delivering 22 HP, which also won a national competition at the Solitude with Felgenheier. Of the other events, two were won by Fergus Anderson on a Moto Guzzi, one by Cann (Moto Guzzi) and one by Lorenzetti who, however, because of the uniformity of the placings, deservedly won the title with the more up-to-date version of the single-camshaft Moto Guzzi Gambalunghino, which was to be replaced by the double-camshaft the following year.

In the 350 class the Nortons with Duke (who won four out of eight races), Armstrong, Kavanagh and Amm (one victory each) beat the AJS bikes, the first of which came fourth in the final results with Rod Coleman. This was also the last year in which British bikes managed to win the World Championship. The era of Moto Guzzi followed by MV Agusta was about to begin.

In the 500 class, Umberto Masetti on the Gilera four-cylinder managed to snatch a very hard-fought title from Norton, winning in Holland and Belgium and coming second at Monza and Barcelona. Duke, after a few unlucky races, had a bad fall at the Solitude which put him out of action for some time. But Norton was well represented by Armstrong, who won the Tourist Trophy and German G.P., while Brett and AJS had an isolated victory at the opening race at Berne. Second place in the Championship went to Graham with MV Agusta, who won the last two races of

The AJS 500 twin-cylinder, piloted by Leslie Graham, won the first World Championship in 1949. The engine was designed before the F.I.M. banned supercharging. This bike was nicknamed "Porcupine" because of the curiously shaped finning on the cylinder head. It originally had horizontal cylinders but in 1952 was extensively modified, the cylinders being fitted at an angle of 45°. The exploded view shows the main characteristics of this engine: the two separate cylinders, the "cage" with cascaded gears which operated the double overhead camshaft valve gear, the single-piece crankshaft which turned on three main bearings and capped connecting rods. The final versions of this power unit delivered about 54 HP at 7500 rpm.

THE MOTOR CYCLE
COPYRIGHT

the season, at Monza and Barcelona.

The 1952 versions of the Norton delivered 49 HP at 7500 rpm (practically the power of the Italian multicylinders of a few years back), whilst the Gilera and MV bikes had 10 HP more and, despite being heavier, managed to show their mechanical superiority, thanks also to big improvements in the frames and suspension. MV was the last to bring itself up to date, completely transforming its machine, but the results were soon visible. Only Graham used an Earles front fork instead of the telescopic type.

Smith and Clements took over from Eric Oliver in the sidecar category, also on a Norton.

A wholly German revolution

There was total upheaval in all displacements at the 1953 World Championship, which saw the victory of NSU in the 125 and 250 classes, the advent of the Moto Guzzi 350 – which practically wiped British engines off the board – and the electrifying (and profitable) presence of Duke, competing for the first time on the Gilera four against his Norton "colleagues" of earlier seasons.

The season opened with the Tourist Trophy at which Graham piloted the MV to a stunning victory in the 125, beating Haas's NSU. Fergus Anderson beat the same German pair with the Moto Guzzi in the 250 class. Anderson also piloted the Moto Guzzi 317 on its first 350 class race. This was an enlargement of the Gambalungino 250, with curious-looking "duckbill" fairing and a single-camshaft

engine delivering 35 HP at 7800 rpm – a fortunate machine, introduced at the right moment, from which some prestigious bikes were to be developed.

The 500 class was a disaster for the Italians. Graham, who had injured his hand in a fall, left the road with the MV four-cylinder coming down Bray Hill, and was killed outright; Duke, on his first race for Gilera, fell at low speed, breaking the petrol tank, and was thus unable to continue. The winner was therefore the remarkable Ray Amm on a Norton, in front of his colleague Jack Brett and Armstrong's Gilera.

The 125 and 250 classes, despite being very strongly contested, were virtually monopolized by the single- and twin-cylinder NSUs of Werner Haas, who won both titles. The only sources of satisfaction to the Italians were victory in the 125 class at the German G.P. at Schotten for Ubbiali, who had passed from Mondial to MV Agusta, and at Barcelona for Copeta, still with the MV 125; and in the 250 the exploits of Lorenzetti at Monza and Barcelona, on the Moto Guzzi.

During the German competition the racers first protested strongly about the dangers of the track (similar episodes repeated elsewhere many years later resulted in the less suitable circuits being abolished), following which the 350 and 500 events there were scrapped.

In an effort to counter the supremacy of NSU, the MV 125 with six-speed gears was introduced at Ulster and the Guzzi 250 replaced the single-camshaft cylinder head of the Gambalunghino by a new, double-camshaft model which increased the power to

28 HP at 8000 rpm and the speed to 200 km/h (124 mph). But it was not enough. The NSU 125 single-cylinder, originally with a double camshaft then "reduced" to a single operated by shaft and bevel gears, delivered 15.5 HP at 10,000 rpm and, with a weight of 82 kg (180 lb), could do over 160 km/h (100 mph). The 250 was a technical masterpiece, with its twin-cylinder engine with a double camshaft operated by two shaft and bevel gears arranged in a V; it delivered 30 HP at 10,500 rpm and at 121 kg (267 lb) had very good acceleration, if not a top speed clearly superior to that of its competitors. The bike had good fairing, initially of the duckbill type, then enveloping the sides as well. Both the 125 Rennfox and 250 Rennmax had leading link forks like those of the Moto Guzzis, and the frames were largely made up of stamped elements.

Thanks to Lorenzetti on the Moto Guzzi, the 350 World Championship was won for the first time by an Italian bike and rider, at Assen. Lorenzetti also won at Monza.

Duke contributed greatly to the perfecting of the Gilera and – after his false start at the TT – won in Holland, in France at Rouen, at Berne and at Monza, while Alfredo Milani piloted the Gilera to victory in Belgium. At Ulster, Kavanagh managed to beat Duke's Gilera four with the Norton single once again. However, Duke was a clear winner of the 500 title, coming before Armstrong and Alfredo Milani with the Gileras, and Kavanagh and Amm with the Nortons.

An important competitor in the 500 class in 1953 was the revolutionary Moto Guzzi with

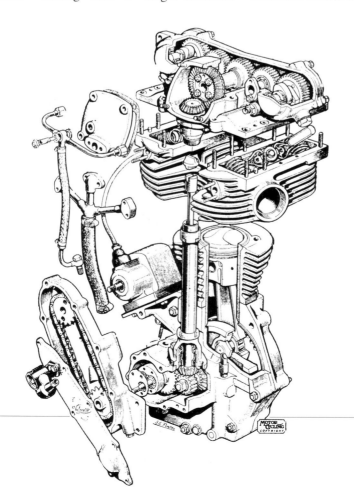

The Velocette 350 which took part in postwar Grands Prix was closely derived from the KTT of the late thirties. Obvious changes included the use of double overhead camshaft valve gear. This machine, which delivered approximately 35 HP at 7200 rpm, had the same size bore and stroke (78 × 81 mm) as the Velocette 350 of 1926. It won the world title in 1949 and 1950.

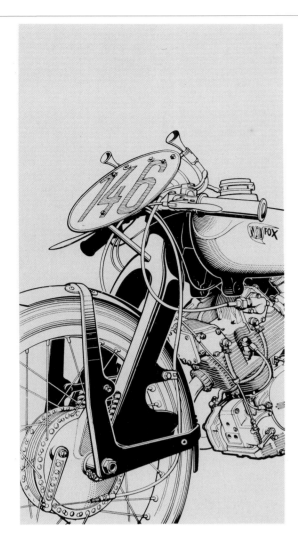

The arrival on the scene of the German company NSU revolutionized racing bike design. The "Rennfox" 125 Grand Prix model appeared in 1951. It had double-camshaft valve gear (operated by a shaft and bevel gearing on the right-hand side) and a power of 11 HP, increased to 13 the following year.

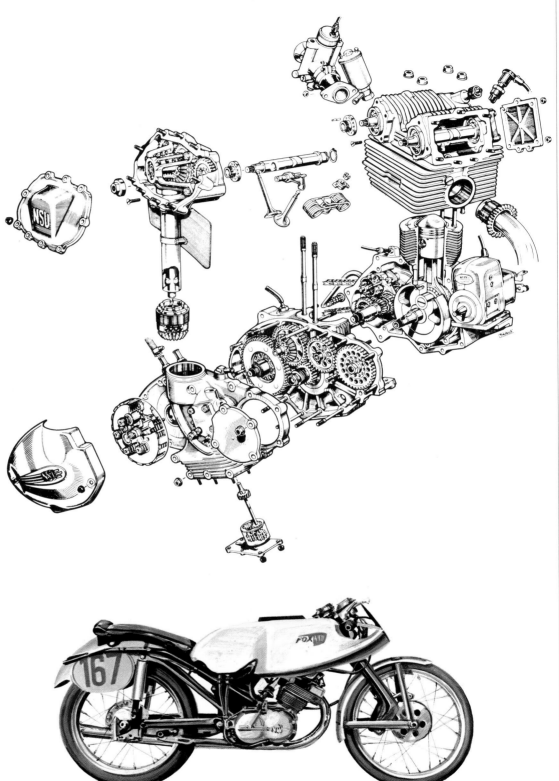

four cylinders in line, practically an automobile-type engine with water cooling, fuel injection, tubular lattice frame, cardan shaft drive and integral fairing. It delivered 54 HP at 9000 rpm, weighed 145 kg (320 lb) and had a speed of approximately 230 km/h (143 mph). This very interesting bike was successful at Monza, where it was piloted by Anderson.

The 1954 World Championship was almost a copy of the preceding one: NSUs dominated the 125 and 250 classes, with Hollaus in the 125 and Haas in the 250. In the 350 class, Fergus Anderson with Moto Guzzi beat Amm (Norton) and Coleman (AJS). Geoffrey Duke dominated the 500 class with an ever more efficient Gilera machine, beating Ray Amm's Norton and Kavanagh's Moto Guzzi.

These seemingly inevitable results do not mean that it was an uneventful season. 1954 was a year of great technical progress, with the appearance of new engines and other extensively revised ones and the widespread adoption of dustbin fairing (which was in fact abolished in 1957 as being far too dangerous).

In the 350 class the new MV four-cylinder engine, fitted to the frame of the company's 500 model, was introduced on an experimental basis, and progress was also seen in DKW

The engine was partially redesigned for the 1953 season, a single overhead camshaft being fitted and the shaft that worked it being moved to the left-hand side; the power was upped to over 15 HP at 10,000 rpm (and rose again to 17 in 1954). The frame was of pressed steel.

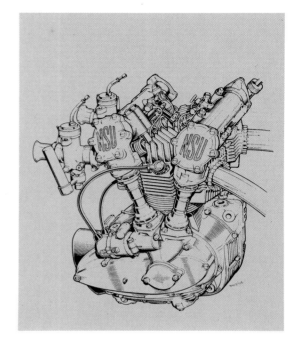

Parallel to the 125, NSU developed a hefty 250 twin-cylinder with double-camshaft valve gear which came out in 1952, with a power of 27.5 HP (increased to 30 the following year). Interesting features of this engine included the fact that each camshaft was operated by a shaft and bevel gears. The first versions had tubular, duplex crade frames and telescopic forks, but for 1953 these parts were replaced by pressed steel frames and forks with swinging link suspension.

triple-cylinder two-strokes, which had outstanding sprinting capabilities and were uncatchable in the early laps of races, thanks both to their 40 HP at 10,000 rpm and their modest weight of just 90 kg (198 lb). Norton also did well with their new engines with an external flywheel and five-speed gears and odd-looking "hammerhead" fairing, so called because the "nose" projected forward.

In the 500 class, the first Moto Guzzi single-cylinder of exactly 500 cc with double-camshaft valve gear, delivering 42 HP at 7000 rpm, featured prominently at the Dutch G.P.

Another marque won the sidecar category, after five years of success for Norton. This was BMW with Noll and Cron, who thus began many years of victory for German twin-cylinders.

The year ended with NSU's unexpected announcement that after two successful years the company was retiring from racing, the reason given being that none of its competitors was up to the standard of their machines.

Sadly, Ray Amm, who was enormously popular with motorcycling enthusiasts because of his outstanding courage, was killed in his first race on the MV 350 four-cylinder whilst competing for the Shell Gold Cup at Imola, which opened the season in April 1955.

Italian companies looked for foreign riders for all displacements at this period. In the 125 class, MV (not content with Ubbiali, Copeta and Venturi) engaged the Swiss Taveri; they also used Bill Lomas in both the 125 and 250 classes, "sharing" him with Moto Guzzi, who

had hired him for the 350.

In the absence of the official NSUs, MV regained the 125 title with Ubbiali, backed up by Taveri and Venturi. Mondial came fourth and sixth with Lattanzi and Ferri respectively.

The situation in the 250 class was particularly interesting. Now that the official Rennmax twin-cylinders had disappeared from the scene, NSU prepared the Sportmax single-cylinders derived from Max series models, which were made available to reliable racers and later sold in small numbers. The Sportmax had an overhead camshaft operated by an unusual system of link rods. The engine developed 29 HP at 9500 rpm (compared with the 39 HP at 11,500 rpm of the twin-cylinder). Thanks to excellent general qualities and a speed of approximately 200 km/h (125 mph), it even managed to win the title with Hermann Müller. This was the only instance of a bike derived from a production model winning a World Championship.

A new tendency with Italian companies was to derive a new generation of 250s from the 175s which were successful in Italian endurance and circuit races. The bikes thus obtained – designed according to the structural criteria of machines which were lighter than the conventional 250s – were "provisional" to begin with, but highly efficient later on. One such example was the MV Agusta 203, derived from the 175, which with a weight of 92 kg (203 lb), 27 HP at 11,000 rpm and the now standard dustbin fairing, could do 200 km/h (124 mph). With this bike Lomas won the TT, his first race

for MV. Taveri came first at Assen and Masetti, who had also been hired by MV, came third at Ulster. Two twin-cylinders were also ready for the closing race at Monza, produced by "joining" two 125s – but the single won, with Ubbiali. Twin-cylinders designed from scratch were preferred after that, but to begin with the most reliable was the single-cylinder version, increased to 249 cc with 32 HP at 11,000 rpm. Morini and Mondial also benefited from the 125 G.P. and 175 Formula Two experience in developing new models.

Norton had now surrendered arms honourably in the 350 and 500 classes, managing only some successes at the TT and Ulster with their Manx models, which were sold to privateers and soon became the most popular racing bikes on sale in the two higher displacements. All the victories therefore went to Moto Guzzi, who with the new arrival Bill Lomas, a great stylist and an indomitable fighter, won the title in the 350 class.

In the 500 class the front was divided between the Gilera team – Duke, Liberati, Armstrong, Alfredo Milani, Colnago, Valdinoci and Monneret – and the MV team with Masetti, Bandirola, Pagani and Forconi. Not to be underestimated either were sporadic appearances by Moto Guzzi who, while hard at work on the long-awaited eight-cylinder – which had already been seen on the Senigallia circuit – secured third place at the TT with their single-cylinder ridden by Kavanagh and even came first at Ulster, in front of Hartle's

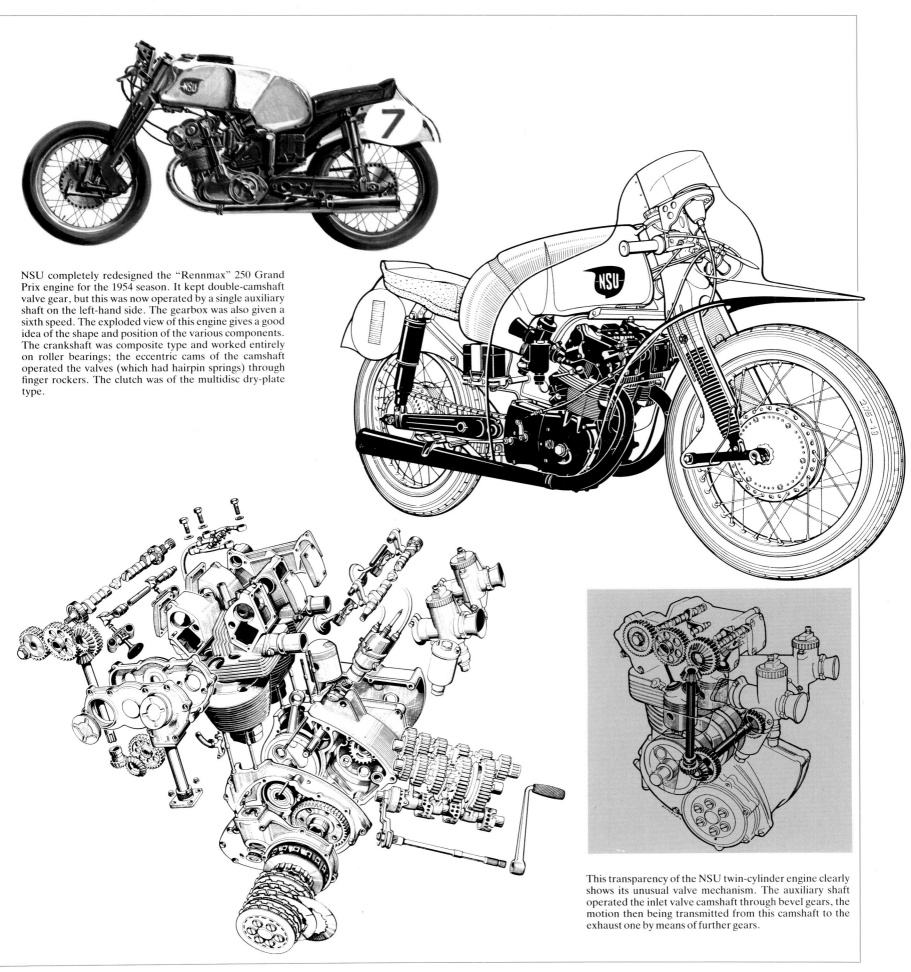

NSU completely redesigned the "Rennmax" 250 Grand Prix engine for the 1954 season. It kept double-camshaft valve gear, but this was now operated by a single auxiliary shaft on the left-hand side. The gearbox was also given a sixth speed. The exploded view of this engine gives a good idea of the shape and position of the various components. The crankshaft was composite type and worked entirely on roller bearings; the eccentric cams of the camshaft operated the valves (which had hairpin springs) through finger rockers. The clutch was of the multidisc dry-plate type.

This transparency of the NSU twin-cylinder engine clearly shows its unusual valve mechanism. The auxiliary shaft operated the inlet valve camshaft through bevel gears, the motion then being transmitted from this camshaft to the exhaust one by means of further gears.

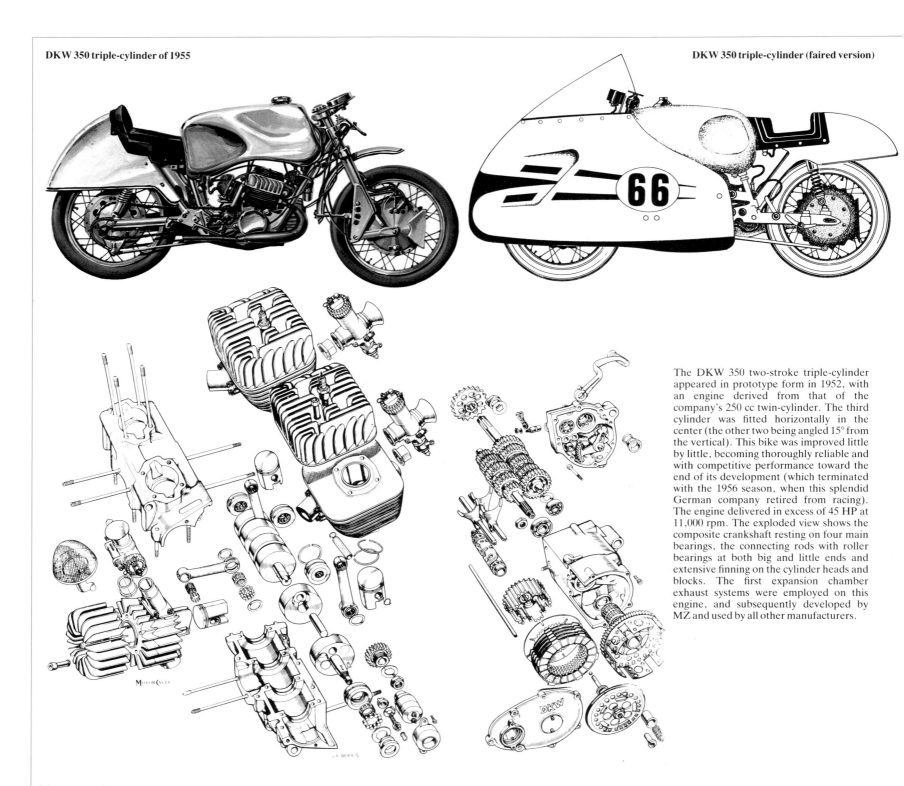

The DKW 350 two-stroke triple-cylinder appeared in prototype form in 1952, with an engine derived from that of the company's 250 cc twin-cylinder. The third cylinder was fitted horizontally in the center (the other two being angled 15° from the vertical). This bike was improved little by little, becoming thoroughly reliable and with competitive performance toward the end of its development (which terminated with the 1956 season, when this splendid German company retired from racing). The engine delivered in excess of 45 HP at 11,000 rpm. The exploded view shows the composite crankshaft resting on four main bearings, the connecting rods with roller bearings at both big and little ends and extensive finning on the cylinder heads and blocks. The first expansion chamber exhaust systems were employed on this engine, and subsequently developed by MZ and used by all other manufacturers.

Norton. The title went to Duke and Gilera once again, but the last test at Monza saw one of the greatest triumphs for Umberto Masetti, who won the race for MV, beating the Gileras of Armstrong, Duke, Colnago and Milani.

BMW won the sidecar category again, with Faust and Remmert.

The companies give up racing

In 1956, the World Championship was extremely interesting, with a wealth of new mechanical creations. The case of BMW speaks for them all. Fergus Anderson had gone over to BMW after a spell away from racing, during which he had concentrated on press relations and the technical side at Moto Guzzi. Feeling the desire to race again, he had persuaded BMW to develop a four-cylinder. However, this machine never saw the light, partly because Anderson was killed whilst competing against Lomas on the Floreffe international circuit during one of the first races with the twin-cylinder. BMW therefore raced only their twin-cylinders, entrusted to Zeller, Klinger and Riedelbanch, apart from competing in the sidecar class. The German twin had two horizontally opposed cylinders, cardan shaft drive and a front fork with long swinging arms and, despite some steering problems resulting from its shape and transverse direction of rotation, could do 240 km/h (149 mph) with a power of 60 HP at 9500 rpm and fuel injection (as an alternative to the carburetors preferred on mixed circuits).

The following were the most interesting bikes and events, class by class. In the 125 the title went to Ubbiali, who won five of the six competitions in the program with the MV. The new Gilera twin with Romolo Ferri won at the Solitude, after the same pair had scored a dramatic victory in their first race at the Italian Championship at Monza. The Gilera 125, nicknamed "the white fly" partly because of its rarity and partly because of the colour of the fairing, had beautifully light, clean lines. With its two cylinders side by side, double-camshaft valve gear, six-speed gears, 19 HP at 12,000 rpm and streamlined fairing at the front and rear, the "Gilly" (as it was known internationally) weighed 95 kg (209 lb) and could do 190 km/h (118 mph) with ease.

Other novelties in the 125 sector were the Spanish two-strokes by Montesa, already seen on previous occasions but highly efficient now, as demonstrated by second, third and fourth places in the Tourist Trophy. A completely new machine was the Ducati with desmodromic valve gear, derived from the single- and subsequent double-camshaft models. The Ducati Desmo, which would only become a real "threat" to MV in 1958, delivered 17 HP at 12,500 rpm in the first version, with a top speed of 180 km/h (112 mph).

Ubbiali, with the ultrafaired MV single-cylinder, was unrivalled in the 250 class. He won five competitions, being replaced by his fellow works rider Taveri only at Ulster.

There were no great technical innovations in the 250 class, although in the seclusion of racing departments people were hard at work

The Moto Guzzi 350 single-camshaft was derived from the 250 cc Gambalunghino model. It came out in 1953 and won the world title with F. Anderson. The engine (bore and stroke = 75 × 78 mm) delivered 35 HP at 7800 rpm.

on future machines. Mondial tried the twin-cylinder experiment by fitting two double-camshaft 125s together; the engine delivered the considerable power of 35 HP at 11,000 rpm, but the exorbitant weight of 140 kg (309 lb) advised them against using it.

There were more novelties in the 350 class. The Championship was still won by Bill Lomas and Moto Guzzi, but other machines were admired. The MV four-cylinder, which had been withdrawn the year before after the death of Amm, had now reappeared. Ridden by new arrival John Surtees it won the Belgian G.P., also obtaining other good placings. This bike, which was a smaller version of their 500 cc model, developed about 45 HP at 11,500 rpm, weighed about 150 kg (330 lb) and had a

top speed of 230 km/h (143 mph).

Gilera had also prepared a 350 version derived from their 500, which was an immediate success. Piloted by Libero Liberati, it won the G.P. des Nations at Monza, at an average speed 10 km (6.2 miles) higher than that of Dale the previous year. It developed 49 HP at 11,000 rpm, weighed 145 kg (320 lb) and could do approximately 235 km/h (146 mph).

DKW two-stroke three-cylinders with conventional valve gear had also made considerable progress in this class. They achieved good placings in various races, especially with Hobl and occasionally with Sandford, Bartl and Hoffmann. Their power was now 45 HP and their speed approximately 220 km/h (137 mph). After coming third in the 1956 World Championship with Hobl, DKW retired from racing for good.

The 500 class program started out with the triumphant debut of twenty-two-year-old John Surtees on the MV at the TT. He went on to win in Holland and Belgium, fell at the Solitude, but had gained enough points by then to win the title. He was helped in so doing by the absence of 17 riders, who had been disqualified for six months (starting from January 1956) following a strike called in protest at the low signing-on fees at the Dutch G.P. the year before. They included Duke, Milani, Colnago, Masetti and Armstrong. On his reappearance, Duke fell at Ulster but finished in magnificent style at Monza after

The Moto Guzzi double-camshaft won the rider world title in the 350 class for four consecutive years (1954–1957). This lightweight and reliable single-cylinder engine with two overhead camshafts operated by a shaft and bevel gears could deliver 38 HP at 8000 rpm in the final version, which unlike its predecessors had a long stroke (79 mm compared with the 75 mm bore). It had a wide range of use and high torque at medium-low speeds. The cylinder had a chromium-plated barrel. This incredibly lightweight bike (just 98 kg = 216 lb) was given streamlined dustbin fairing. The frame was lattice type with a big pipe at the top containing the oil for lubricating the engine.

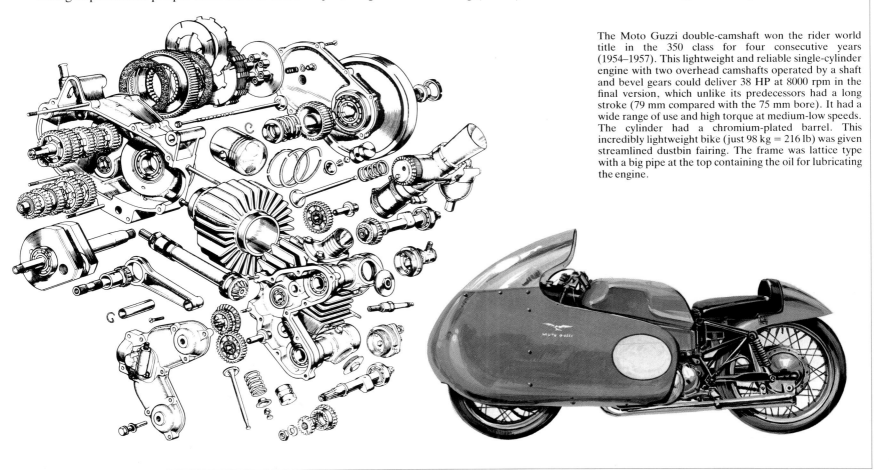

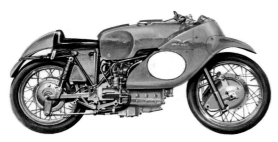

The Moto Guzzi 500, with four cylinders in line, water cooling, a tubular lattice frame and duckbill fairing, appeared in 1959 and took part in the World Championship for two years, but without any great success (54 HP at 9000 rpm).

The BMW 500 twin-cylinder of 1953–1958 with "split-single camshaft" valve gear was an excellent bike but could not match the performance of the Gilera and MV four-cylinders. This bike had a fuel injection system.

The MV Agusta 250 single-cylinder was built on similar lines to the 125 cc model. It had double overhead camshaft valve gear. It came out in 1955 and at the end of its development (1958) won the rider World Championship with Provini.

In 1953 the German company Horex, which had become popular for its excellent medium-powered production bikes, built this 350 cc double-camshaft four-stroke twin-cylinder, which was not a great success in competitions.

an epic duel with Liberati.

There were a few important episodes. MV Agusta won all four classes at the Belgian G.P. (Ubbiali two, Surtees two), showing a clear superiority. Norton tasted victory again at Ulster, thanks to John Hartle. Moto Guzzi took on a promising new racer, the Australian Keith Campbell, and finally brought out that mechanical prodigy, the eight-cylinder designed by Giulio Cesare Carcano. It was one of the most daring projects ever undertaken. The eight cylinders were arranged in two blocks of four in a 90° V, all the gears operating the camshafts were enclosed in a big lateral cartel and the eight 20 mm carburetors were interleaved at the center of the V. The bike had battery coil ignition and four-speed gears only. This machine was so complex that it was not always able to display its exuberance to the full. However, it did do well in a few races like the Shell Gold Cup at Imola and the Hockenheim international, at which Kavanagh averaged 199 km/h (124 mph).

In the sidecar category, Albino and Rossano Milano (brothers of Alfredo) obtained a four-cylinder model from Gilera with which they won the last stage of the Championship, which in fact went to Noll and Cron's BMW.

1957 was one of the most exciting seasons

for motorcycling, with very hard-fought competitions and enormous rivalry between riders (even of the same marque), with a very high technical standard. One of the most interesting confrontations was between Moto Guzzi and Gilera in the 350 class. Moto Guzzi pinned their hopes on the simplicity, light weight, aerodynamics and reliability of their double-camshaft horizontal single-cylinder, now delivering 38 HP at 8000 rpm (with a colossal carburetor 45 mm in diameter) which, at the "ridiculous" weight of just 98 kg (216 lb), could do over 230 km/h (143 mph). The Gilera machine had about 10 HP more, but was also about 30 kg (66 lb) heavier, which meant that its advantage in terms of speed was reduced to a few kilometers. They were well matched, as the final results show: Moto Guzzi won the rider World Championship with Keith Campbell while Gilera won the works title, thanks also to the considerable skill of Scottish racer Bob McIntyre.

In the two smaller displacements, MV's supremacy was ended by the highly efficient Mondials of Provini and Sandford, who won the 125 and 250 titles. The 125 developed 18 HP at 12,000 rpm with a speed of 190 km/h (118 mph), whereas the 250 (no longer an enlargement of the 175, but an original design) developed just under 30 HP at 10,800 rpm and could touch 220 km/h (137 mph). Their performance was roughly equal to that of the MV Agustas, but a fall by Ubbiali and the death of Roberto Colombo at Francorchamps made way for their competitors who, however, did not escape their share of accidents and setbacks.

The 500 class was also full of spectacular performances. A few riders distinguished themselves, then disappeared for some time because of falls. Others replaced them with equal success, the former then returning to try and recapture the points they had lost. MV, Moto Guzzi and Gilera contested the title. It went to Liberati on the Gilera bike; he closed the season with a superlative victory at Monza, coming before Duke, Milani, Surtees and Masetti. McIntyre, the most dangerous pretender to the title, was dissuaded from competing in the 500 after being taken ill at the end of the 350 (which he won), due to the after-effects of a bad fall at Assen. The Moto Guzzi eight-cylinder gave a clear indication of its potential when Campbell set a record lap speed at Francorchamps of 190.827 km/h (118.574 mph), which was to be unbeaten for several years. It also won the Shell Gold Cup at Imola with Dickie Dale, one of the hardest-fought competitions ever seen in any displacement, and the first stage of the Italian championship at Siracusa.

After such an eventful season it came as a big shock to learn that Moto Guzzi, Gilera and Mondial had decided to retire from racing, giving as their reasons a greater commitment

The Morini 175 Rebello, designed in 1955 for national competitions, had "split-single camshaft" valve gear; the famous Grand Prix single-cylinder 250s which appeared three years later were derived from it.

At the beginning of the fifties the Gilera Saturno 500, derived from a road model, was very popular with private racers. It had push rod valve gear. This is a 1953 version built for road racing.

For the 1954 season (the last in which it took part officially), Norton prepared a version of its 500 cc single-cylinder Grand Prix model with a very short stroke (bore and stroke = 90 × 78.4 mm) capable of 55 HP at 8200 rpm, on which the Rhodesian ace Ray Amm tried unsuccessfully to beat the Gilera four-cylinders. This bike, which had the famous Featherbed continuous duplex cradle frame, was exceptionally lightweight and maneuverable. For a few races, it was fitted with a curious type of fairing which projected a long way forward. ▶

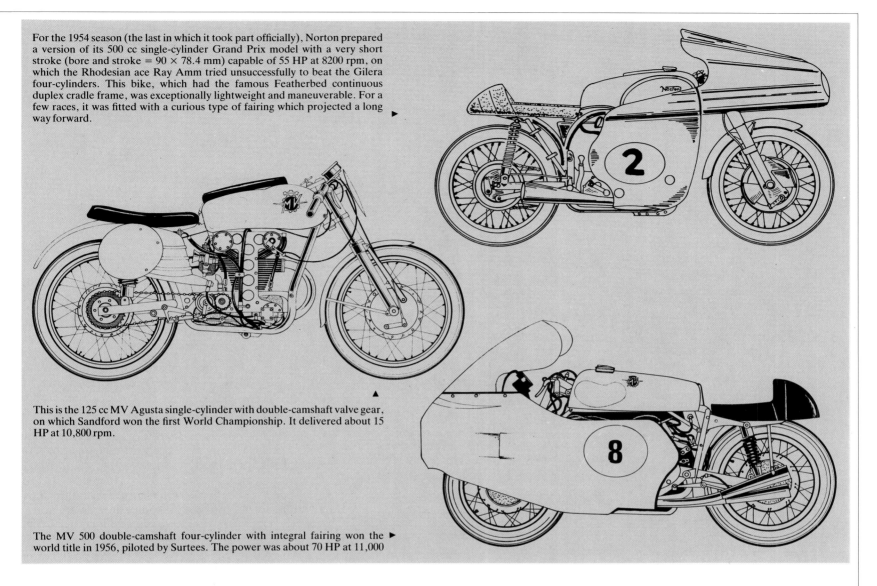

This is the 125 cc MV Agusta single-cylinder with double-camshaft valve gear, on which Sandford won the first World Championship. It delivered about 15 HP at 10,800 rpm.

The MV 500 double-camshaft four-cylinder with integral fairing won the ▶ world title in 1956, piloted by Surtees. The power was about 70 HP at 11,000

The NSU 250 single-cylinder – on which the German Müller won the rider World Championship in 1955 – was closely derived from the normal series "Max." The engine had an unusual system of link rods to operate the single overhead camshaft. The bore and stroke measurements were 69 × 66 mm, the top power being 29 HP at 9500 rpm. A pressed steel frame (a type much favoured by the engineers of this German company) was used here too: the bike had sprung wheel (swinging link) front suspension. The cutaway view of the engine clearly shows the main structural details: hairpin valve springs, gear primary drive on the left-hand side and a dry-plate clutch.

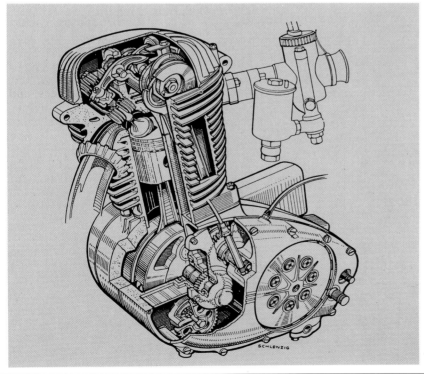

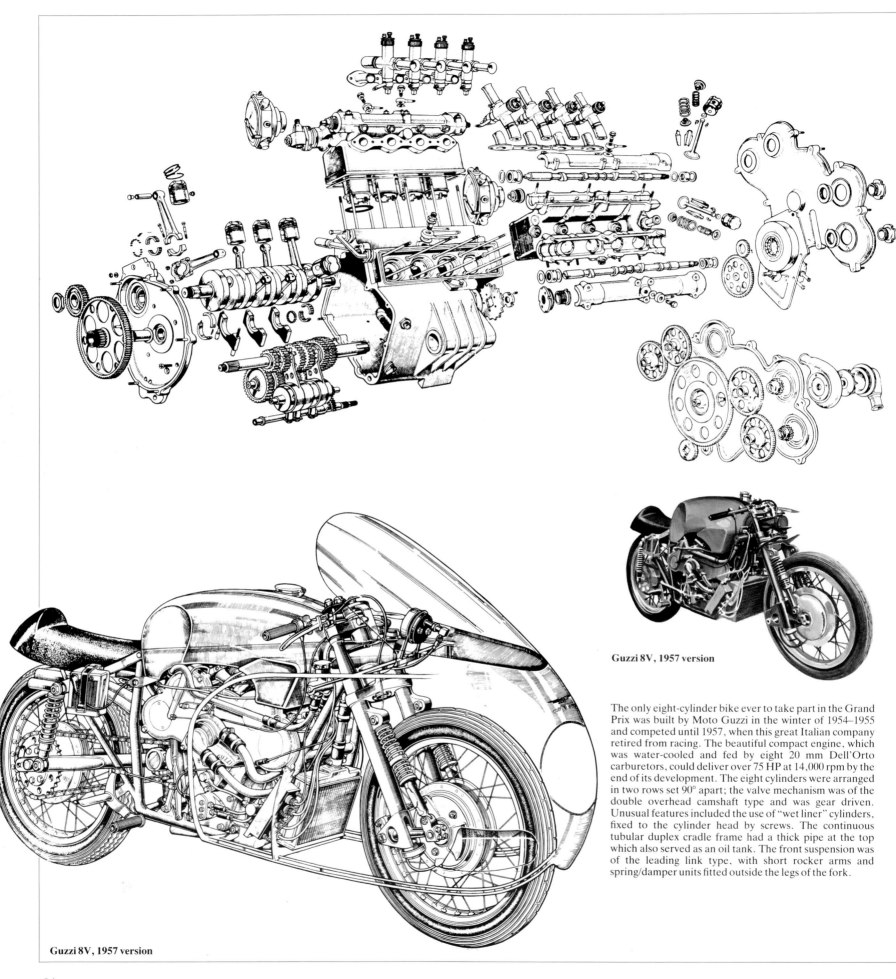

Guzzi 8V, 1957 version

Guzzi 8V, 1957 version

The only eight-cylinder bike ever to take part in the Grand Prix was built by Moto Guzzi in the winter of 1954–1955 and competed until 1957, when this great Italian company retired from racing. The beautiful compact engine, which was water-cooled and fed by eight 20 mm Dell'Orto carburetors, could deliver over 75 HP at 14,000 rpm by the end of its development. The eight cylinders were arranged in two rows set 90° apart; the valve mechanism was of the double overhead camshaft type and was gear driven. Unusual features included the use of "wet liner" cylinders, fixed to the cylinder head by screws. The continuous tubular duplex cradle frame had a thick pipe at the top which also served as an oil tank. The front suspension was of the leading link type, with short rocker arms and spring/damper units fitted outside the legs of the fork.

Gilera 500, 1956 version

Few racing bikes have been as famous as the Gilera four-cylinder, which dominated the 500 class in the fifties, winning no fewer than six rider world titles. Designed immediately after the War, the double-camshaft engine delivered about 50 HP at 8500 rpm in the initial (1948) version – but these figures were steadily increased as the bike was improved year after year. By 1971 it delivered nearly 70 HP at 10,500 rpm. The two camshafts were driven by cascaded gears positioned between the two central cylinders. It also had gear primary drive.

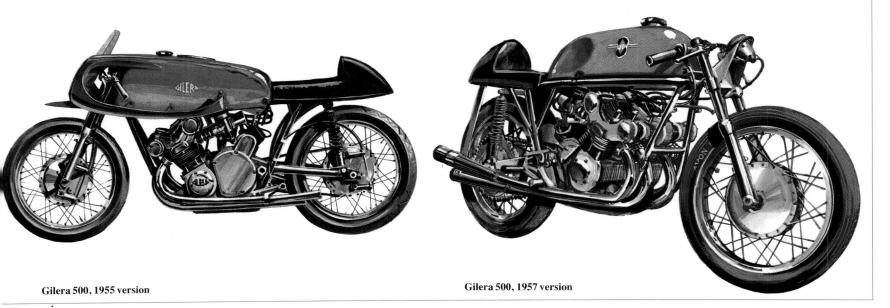

Gilera 500, 1955 version

Gilera 500, 1957 version

Norton Manx, 1957 version

The Norton "Manx" was the favourite steed of privateer racers in the 500 class for very many years. The classic single-cylinder engine (with a double camshaft operated by a vertical shaft and bevel gears) was derived from the single-camshaft version used before the War. The "Featherbed" continuous duplex cradle frame was used from 1951 (i.e. a year after it was used on the official 500s). The exploded view shows the main structural features of the engine. The two drawings of the complete bike refer to the 1957 version, which had a bore and stroke of 86.1 × 85.6 mm and delivered approximately 51 HP at 7200 rpm. These bikes were also available in a 350 cc version.

to series production and the lack of foreign competitors.

1958, 1959 and 1960 were to some extent similar in that MV Agusta were undisputed leaders in all displacements, with John Surtees in the 350 and 500 classes, virtually unrivalled except by his team mates John Hartle and Remo Venturi, occasionally joined by Emilio Mendogni. However, there were a few skirmishes and a few very good performances by private racers with the Norton Manx, above all "ex official" riders Geoffrey Duke (who was also to have an unsuccessful experience with BMW), Bob McIntyre, Dickie Dale and Keith Campbell. Once again the Norton bikes trained new riders who were shortly to become famous, like Gary Hocking (hired by MV in 1960), Jim Redman, Derek Minter, Terry Shepherd, Bob Anderson and Mike Hailwood.

Thanks to the initiative of various engineers who had developed six-speed gears and improved the standard engine, the Norton Manx 350 delivered 37 HP at 7800 rpm and the 500 51–52 HP at 7200 rpm, having speeds of about 208 and 220 km/h (129 and 137 mph) respectively, with the new, partial fairings.

The situation in the 125 and 250 classes was different. In these MV, even if they were to win in the end, were up against some powerful adversaries, particularly Ducati and MZ, and some fleeting appearances by Morini and the first glimpses of the yellow peril, represented by Honda only in 1960. In those three years, MV entered the single-cylinder 125 – which, with improvements to the cycle parts and a reduction in weight, developed 20 HP at 12,000 rpm and could do 190 km/h (118 mph) with partial fairing – and the twin-cylinder 250 (nothing to do with earlier attempts) prepared in 1959 and capable of 37 HP at 12,500 rpm, with a speed of 220 km/h (137 mph). In 1960 Hocking won the 350 at Clermont-Ferrand on an "enlargement" of this machine, built on an experimental basis.

On the opposing front were the desmodromic Ducati 125s with a team made up of Gandossi, Ferri, Taveri, Chadwick, Miller, Francesco Villa, and subsequently Spaggiari,

The AJS 350 7R "Boy Racer" single-cylinder with (chain-driven) single-camshaft valve gear was very popular for a long time with private riders competing for the World Championship. With a bore and stroke of 75.5 × 78 mm, this engine could deliver 39 HP at 7750 rpm (1958 version).

Hailwood and Kavanagh as well. These bikes could deliver 19 HP at 13,000 rpm, with a generous margin for overrevving safely, thanks to the desmodromic control which prevented "valve float," something the riders took undue advantage of, particularly at the start of races. But the 1959 twin-cylinder version was to be still more powerful, with 22.5 HP at 14,000 rpm (this could even be taken to 17,000) and a speed of 190 km/h (118 mph). However, it was the 1958 single-cylinder edition which very nearly stole the title from MV. It failed to do so only because Gandossi fell when he was strongly in command at Ulster. Proof of the efficiency of this bike were two victories by Gandossi and one by Spaggiari in 1958, followed by Hailwood in 1959. A 250 "ordered" by Mike Hailwood's wealthy father was built on similar lines to the twin-cylinder. On it, young Mike (who had acquired a Paton 125 and Mondial 250) was to

achieve some good placings. But the threat to MV did not come only from Ducati. The East German company MZ, with their original single-cylinder 125 and twin-cylinder 250 two-stroke rotary disc valve machines designed by engineer Kaaden – which had already been seen but not perfected to the same extent – managed to achieve some good placings and even a few victories in the hands of Degner, Fugner and the occasional but highly efficient reserve, Gary Hocking. The 1958 MZ 125 delivered about 20 HP at 10,000 rpm; the 250, 36 HP at 9800 rpm. They were both fast, with rapid sprint, but difficult to handle, particularly the 250. They may both be regarded as forerunners of the Grand Prix two-strokes of the modern school, which were subsequently developed by the Japanese in large displacements too.

From 1961, the World Championship

The MV Agusta 125, successive version of which won six World Championships (this one is from 1958), was powered by a single-cylinder engine with (gear-driven) double-camshaft valve gear and dry-sump lubrication. In the final versions, the power was approximately 20 HP at 12,000 rpm.

The Gilera 125 twin-cylinder came out in 1956. The double overhead camshaft engine delivered 19 HP at 12,000 rpm.

The Mondial 250 double-camshaft single-cylinder won the world title with Sandford in 1957. The engine (bore and stroke = 75 × 56.4 mm) delivered about 29 HP at 10,800 rpm.

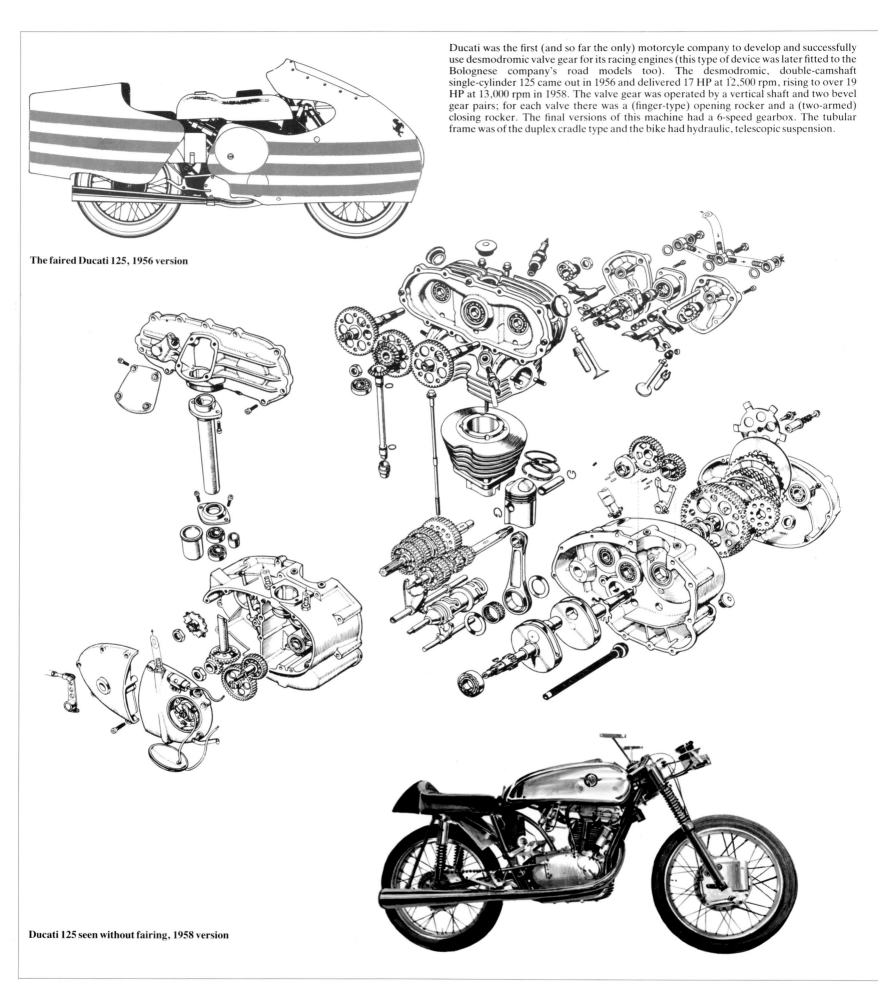

Ducati was the first (and so far the only) motorcyle company to develop and successfully use desmodromic valve gear for its racing engines (this type of device was later fitted to the Bolognese company's road models too). The desmodromic, double-camshaft single-cylinder 125 came out in 1956 and delivered 17 HP at 12,500 rpm, rising to over 19 HP at 13,000 rpm in 1958. The valve gear was operated by a vertical shaft and two bevel gear pairs; for each valve there was a (finger-type) opening rocker and a (two-armed) closing rocker. The final versions of this machine had a 6-speed gearbox. The tubular frame was of the duplex cradle type and the bike had hydraulic, telescopic suspension.

The faired Ducati 125, 1956 version

Ducati 125 seen without fairing, 1958 version

98

The Matchless G 50 produced from 1959 was a bigger version of the AJS 350 "Boy Racer" and soon became very popular with privateers the world over. With a 90 mm bore and 78 mm stroke, the single-cylinder double-camshaft engine could deliver over 50 HP at 7200 rpm. The tubular frame was duplex cradle type and the gearbox (which was separate, as with most bikes of the British school) had four gear ratios. Interesting technical features included operation of the camshaft by a roller chain on the right-hand side, two-armed rockers with a pin, and hairpin valve springs. The cylinder was of light alloy with a cast iron barrel lining and the (three-piece) crankshaft worked entirely on roller bearings.

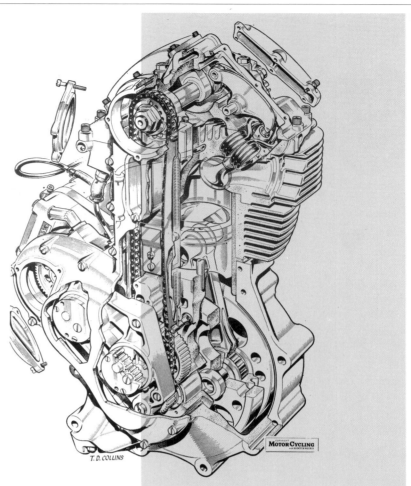

The German company MZ was undoubtedly responsible for the very successful relaunch of two-stroke engines in the racing sector. Toward the end of the fifties this company produced 125 and 250 cc racing bikes with rotary disc inlet valves and expansion chamber exhaust systems, capable of competing on equal terms with four-stroke engines of the same displacement and number of cylinders. In 1958 the 125 cc single-cylinder delivered over 20 HP at 10,000 rpm, but this was to rise to 25 HP at 10,500 rpm in the 1960 version. The bore and stroke measurements were 54 × 54 mm. The exploded view clearly illustrates the main technical features: the rotary disc which controlled induction, gear primary drive and a "semi-unit construction" gearbox.

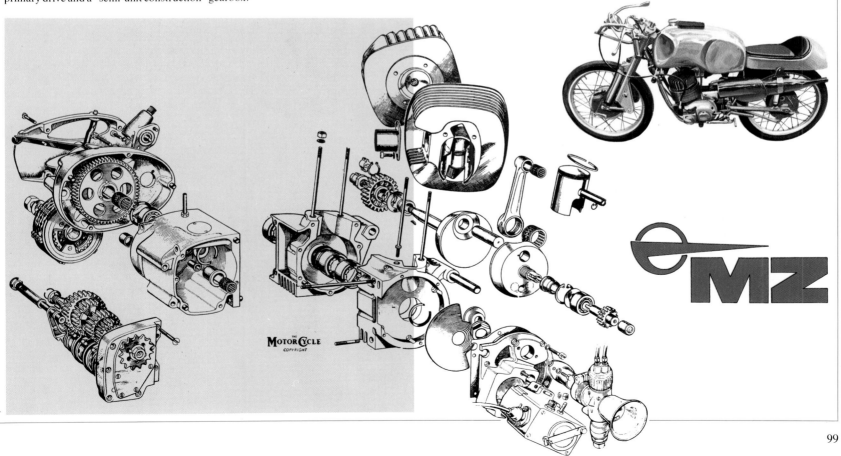

For 1960, Ducati produced two twin-cylinders with desmodromic valve gear for Mike Hailwood. The 250 (bore and stroke = 55.3 × 52 mm) delivered 43 HP at 11,600 rpm and the 350, about 10 HP more.

The EMC was craftsman-built in Britain in 1960. The 125 cc two-stroke single-cylinder engine (bore and stroke = 54 × 54 mm) delivered 21.2 HP at 10,400 rpm.

The Jawa 350, which came out in 1960, could develop 46 HP at 10,200 rpm by the following year. A 250 was built to a similar general design (twin-cylinder with dohc valve gear).

changed direction. MV Agusta decided to retire for a while, leaving Gary Hocking and just one engineer more or less "in charge" of the four-cylinder 350s and 500s, under the conspicuous trademark "MV-Privat."

This great Rhodesian rider had little difficulty in winning both displacements in the 1961 season, but left MV after the TT in 1962 and took up automobile racing.

Japanese rule

In the lower displacements, the era of Japanese supremacy began. First, there was Honda with a large team composed of Tom Phillis, Jim Redman, Luigi Taveri, Mike Hailwood, Bob McIntyre and Tommy Robb, with the Japanese riders Takahashi and Shimazaki. Honda was soon joined by Yamaha and Suzuki, who began several years of violent competition, mobilizing all the best riders available. The Japanese competed in all displacements, from 50 (included in the World Championships from 1962) to 500 cc (from 1966).

As for the Italians, Benelli attempted to re-enter the 250 class with a renewed edition of their double-camshaft single-cylinder (dif-

The Yugoslav Tomos, built for the 50 class European Championship introduced in 1962 (and replaced the following year by the World Championship) was an interesting two-stroke single-cylinder delivering 8 HP at 11,000 rpm.

The German Kreidler, derived from a mass-produced moped, had a horizontal two-stroke engine and made its mark at the 50 class European Championship in 1962. The power was about 8 HP at 12,000 rpm.

ferent from that of Ambrosini) entrusted to Duke and Grassetti, then with a completely new four-cylinder. The Morini 250 double-camshaft took part occasionally with Provini, while Bianchi, with their handsome twin-cylinder designed by Lino Tonti, figured prominently in the 350 class and later the 500 as well with Bob McIntyre, Alistair King, Ernesto Brambilla, Alan Shepherd and subsequently Silvio Grassetti and Remo Venturi. Aermacchi also appeared with Alberto Pagani, son of Nello, encouraging the Varese company to produce the 250 and 350s (in addition to a few enlarged versions for 500 class races) which were soon to be virtually the only bikes available to private racers after the progressive disappearance of the British single-cylinders.

The 1961 125 class title went to the Honda of the young Australian Tom Phillis, who preceded Degner's MZ. The double-camshaft twin-cylinder engine of the former delivered 20 HP at 13,500 rpm and weighed 80 kg (176 lb). Hailwood won the 250 title with an updated version of the Honda four which had already proved a force to be reckoned with in 1960.

In the 350 class, the Bianchi bike (derived from a less successful 250) with 50 HP at 11,000 rpm distinguished itself. The Czech Jawa twin, delivering 46 HP at 10,200 rpm, also did well, coming second in the World Championship with Stastny.

In 1962, the men but not the machines changed at the top of the 125 and 250 classes, which were won by the Hondas of Taveri and Redman, respectively. Redman also won the 350 with the Honda "four" of 50 HP at 12,500

MV Agusta replaced their 250 cc single-cylinder machine by this handsome double-camshaft model, which won the world title in 1959 and 1960. The bore and stroke measurements were 53 × 56 mm and the power in the final version was 37 HP at 12,500 rpm.

rpm, with a speed of over 230 km/h (143 mph). In the 500 Hailwood took over from Hocking with the MV, while in the new 50 class there was a bitter struggle between the Honda double-camshaft single-cylinder (10 HP at 14,000 rpm, speed 140 km/h = 87 mph), the Suzuki rotary-disc two-stroke (11 HP at 13,000 rpm, speed 145 km/h = 90 mph) and the German Kreidler two-stroke with Huberts and Anscheidt (8 HP at 12,000 rpm, speed over 145 km/h = 90+ mph). In the years to come the 50s – to which the Spanish Derbi and Dutch Jamathi were to be added – became over-engineered. They were given 12- and 14-speed gears, twin-cylinder engines (Suzuki even prepared a triple-cylinder which was not in fact raced), anything up to 20,000 rpm, speeds of nearly 190 km/h (118 mph), 16–17 HP and a weight of approximately 60 kg (132 lb). The first 50 World Championship went to Degner with Suzuki, the promising new Japanese marque which was to win the same class again in 1963 with Hugh Anderson, and the 125. But it was Redman who won the 250 and 350 classes with the Honda "four," having the satisfaction of beating Hailwood (on an MV Agusta) in the 350 and a fantastic Provini (on a Morini) in the 250 class. It was very interesting to compare the two machines: on the one hand the slimline, double-camshaft Morini which handled beautifully and now had a power of 37 HP at 10,500 rpm, with a weight of 105 kg (231 lb); on the other the Honda with about 10 HP more, but heavier too and less manageable. To add to the tension, there was another disparity of strength: Provini was completely on his own against the big Honda team. The title was contested to the final stage in Japan and won by Redman, because

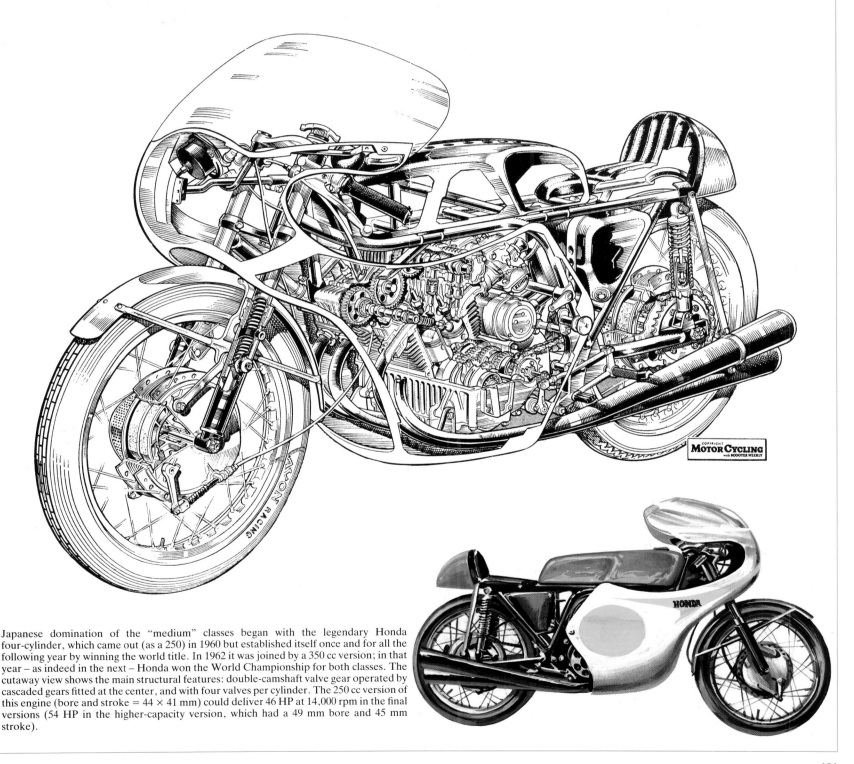

Japanese domination of the "medium" classes began with the legendary Honda four-cylinder, which came out (as a 250) in 1960 but established itself once and for all the following year by winning the world title. In 1962 it was joined by a 350 cc version; in that year – as indeed in the next – Honda won the World Championship for both classes. The cutaway view shows the main structural features: double-camshaft valve gear operated by cascaded gears fitted at the center, and with four valves per cylinder. The 250 cc version of this engine (bore and stroke = 44 × 41 mm) could deliver 46 HP at 14,000 rpm in the final versions (54 HP in the higher-capacity version, which had a 49 mm bore and 45 mm stroke).

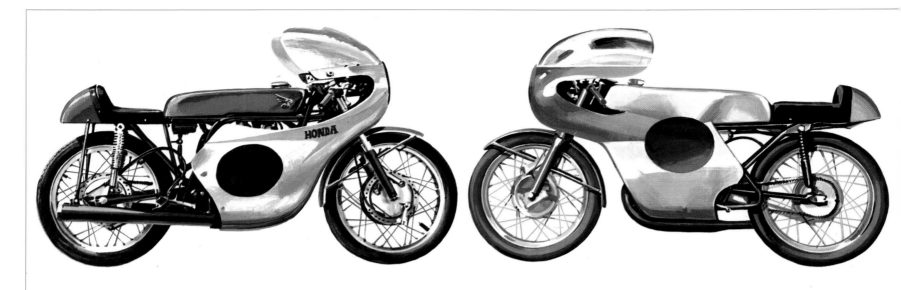

The Honda 125 twin-cylinder won the World Championship in 1961 and 1962. It had the same technical features and bore and stroke measurements as the 250 cc four-cylinder model; the power in 1962 was 24 HP at 14,000 rpm.

The first 50 class World Championship was won by Suzuki, who entered a handsome two-stroke single-cylinder capable of delivering 11 HP at 13,000 rpm (bore and stroke = 40 × 39 mm). This bike won the title in the following two years as well.

the Italian champion was ill.

The 1963 500 title went to Hailwood's MV. That year Gilera reappeared, having agreed to hand over to the Duke stable – run by the great former ace – their magnificent four-cylinders which had some good results with Hartle, Read and Minter, including victory for Hartle at Assen and Minter at Imola, but some disappointing ones too, so that the experiment was short-lived.

At the 1964 World Championship – after the usual bitter contests in the lower displacements – Anderson with Suzuki beat Bryans with Honda in the 50 class, while in the 125 class Taveri, armed with the new Honda four-cylinder, got the better of Redman and Anderson. This new Japanese creation developed 25 HP at 16,000 rpm, had 8 gear ratios, weighed 95 kg (209 lb) and could easily do 200 km/h (124 mph).

There were new protagonists in the 250 class as well. Apart from MZ, who won at Daytona thanks to Alan Shepherd, Yamaha was present in force with their lightweight two-stroke twins (47 HP at 13,000 rpm, speed over 230 km/h = 143 mph), entrusted to the Canadian Mike Duff and Phil Read. Read won the title, preceding Redman. The fully modernized version of the Benelli four, which Provini was perfecting, having left Morini, young Agostini also raced for the first time. The Benelli of that year developed about 40 HP at 13,000 rpm and scored an amazing victory at the Barcelona G.P. on the tortuous Montjuich, which seemed tailor-made for Provini. But competition was stiff because Honda, feeling themselves weak compared with Yamaha, brought out the new six-cylinder 250 in time for the final stage of the championship at Suzuka. This was another mechanical masterpiece: 54 HP at 17,000 rpm with a top speed of 240 km/h (149 mph). From it, in 1967

the 350 was derived: with 64 HP at 17,000 rpm and a speed of 255 km/h (158 mph). In the 350 class, Redman won with Honda. In the 500 Hailwood had no difficulty with the MV four to the extent that he skipped Ulster and the Finnish G.P., giving Norton a taste of victory again with Read and Ahearn.

There was considerable excitement in 1965. In the 50 class Bryans's Honda stole the title from Anderson (on the Suzuki), who in turn carried it away from Taveri in the 125 class. In the 250 class Read won with the Yamaha twin-cylinder, but by the end of the season he was already testing the complex rotary-disc V-four at Monza, with a power of 58 HP at 14,000 rpm, weight of 135 kg (297 lb) and speed of over 245 km/h (152 mph). At the G.P. des Nations held in rain at Monza, Read and his sophisticated machine were outclassed by Provini with the Benelli.

Amid all this technical extravagance a brave Spanish racer, Ramon Torras, distinguished himself on a number of occasions with the Bultaco single-cylinder two-stroke (30 HP at 10,000 rpm), but perished in a race in Spain the same year.

In the 350 class, Redman seemed to be losing his touch. He won the title again with the Honda six, but had a hard battle against the MVs of Hailwood and the new star, Agostini. The latter had piloted to success, on his first race at Nürburgring, the new triple-cylinder which was to be his favourite bike for years. The 350 cc MV three-cylinder was the ideal machine for Agostini's build and riding style. It was more stable and lighter than the four and delivered about 54 HP at 13,000 rpm (later increased to 63 at 13,500, with a speed of 265 km/h = 165 mph).

The 500 title went to Hailwood and MV Agusta again.

In 1966 Anscheidt, after a year's absence

due to the retirement of Kreidler at the end of 1964, raced a Suzuki to victory in the 50 class. In the 125 class Taveri won on the Honda five-cylinder, in front of Bill Ivy's Yamaha. In the 250 and 350 classes Hailwood did not disappoint Honda, coming before Read with the Yamaha in the 250 and Agostini in the 350. Renzo Pasolini came third in this class, with the push rod-operated horizontal-cylinder Aermacchi which, with its 37 HP at 8200 rpm (32 HP at 10,500 rpm for the 250) was above all very simple and strong.

In 1966, for the first time, Honda competed in the 500 class as well with a powerful four-cylinder which only Hailwood managed to master, as it was rather awkward to handle. The engine had four valves per cylinder and developed 85 HP at 12,000 rpm. The machine weighed 135 kg (298 lb) and could do 270 km/h (168 mph). MV had also replaced their four-cylinder in this class by a "three" which, although a lot less powerful than its opponents, was a bit lighter and certainly much easier to handle. The title went to the Italian duo MV and Agostini in the final, decisive contest at Monza from which Honda retired, following a mechanical failure.

1967 was almost an exact copy, Anscheidt winning again with the Suzuki 50 and Hailwood winning the 250 and 350 with the Honda, before Read (Yamaha) and Agostini (MV) respectively. Agostini also won the 500 again, thanks to the perfect efficiency of his MV, compared with the inexplicable state of neglect in which the Honda was left by the end of the season. The only novelty was victory in the 125 class for small, highly strung Bill Ivy on the Yamaha four-cylinder (250 type) which, with 9 gear ratios and 35 HP at 18,000 rpm, could exceed 210 km/h (130 mph). Read completed their success, coming second with the same bike.

The 350 cc Bianchi twin-cylinder was built in 1960 and, constantly updated and improved, continued racing until 1964 (when the company retired from racing). The final versions of this double-camshaft twin-cylinder (bore and stroke = 70 × 59 mm) delivered about 50 HP at 11,000 rpm.

The Yamaha 250 twin-cylinder two-stroke with rotary disc valve induction won the world title in 1964 and 1965. It developed 47 HP at 13,000 rpm.

The Honda 50 double-camshaft single-cylinder (10 HP at 14,000 rpm) could not compete with other two-stroke machines in 1962 and was replaced by a twin-cylinder model.

The Moto Morini double-camshaft single-cylinder missed the 250 class world title in 1963 by just two points. Bore and stroke = 72 × 61 mm; 37 HP at 10,500 rpm.

The CZ 125 double-camshaft twin-cylinder, which in 1964 delivered a power of 24 HP at 15,000 rpm, was not a success. The bore and stroke measurements were 45 and 39.2 mm respectively.

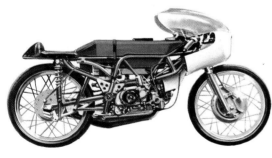

Kreidler tried unsuccessfully to oppose the all-powerful Japanese in the 50 class with this two-stroke single-cylinder. The 1964 version (shown here) delivered 14 HP. It had 12 gear ratios.

The revolutionary Suzuki 250 with four cylinders in a square appeared in 1963. By the end of 1965 this rotary disc valve two-stroke engine could deliver over 55 HP.

The Honda 125 four-cylinder (25 HP at 16,000 rpm). It had double-camshaft valve gear with four valves per cylinder.

MZ continued to improve their two-stroke engines with rotary disc valve induction in the sixties. This is the 1965 water-cooled 125 single-cylinder (28 HP at 12,000 rpm).

In 1965 the 125 class World Championship was won by Suzuki with this rotary disc valve two-stroke twin-cylinder (30 HP at 14,000 rpm; bore and stroke = 43 × 42.6 mm).

The Honda 50 double-camshaft twin-cylinder (15 HP at 20,000 rpm; bore and stroke = 33 × 29 mm).

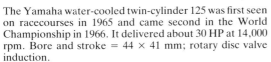

The Yamaha water-cooled twin-cylinder 125 was first seen on racecourses in 1965 and came second in the World Championship in 1966. It delivered about 30 HP at 14,000 rpm. Bore and stroke = 44 × 41 mm; rotary disc valve induction.

Toward the mid-sixties the 125 cc Bultaco single-cylinder was widely used by privateers. The engine was originally air-cooled, but was soon given water cooling. It delivered 27 HP at 11,500 rpm.

In 1967 Montesa, assisted by engineer F. Villa, built this interesting 250 cc twin-cylinder delivering about 44 HP at 9800 rpm. Induction was controlled by rotary disc valves; it had "mixed" cooling (air for the cylinder heads and water for the cylinders).

In 1968, Honda and Suzuki retired from racing. MV had reclaimed Hailwood, with the idea of putting on a magnificent show with him and Agostini. But when the British rider learned that he was not free to run the race as he wished he accepted an invitation from Benelli, with whom he distinguished himself in a few, desperate laps hard on the heels of Agostini's MV – a clearly superior bike – before ending with a spectacular breakaway at the Parabolica. Agostini won the 500 Championship with ease. He also won the 350, but with more "modern" machines hard behind him such as Pasolini's Benelli, Carruthers's Aermacchi and Rosner's MZ.

In the 50 class Anscheidt won the title with the Suzuki for the third time running, while the two Yamaha racers Ivy and Read distinguished themselves in the 125 and 250 classes. Read won both titles, although he managed to secure the 250 only by totalling the shortest time over all the competitions that year.

BMW's unbroken supremacy in the sidecar category was interrupted for the first time by the URS four-cylinder built and ridden by the indomitable Helmuth Fath (with Kallaugh as passenger) at a time when he should have retired from racing following an accident in 1961 in which he had lost a leg.

There were many novelties in 1969, the final year in which bikes with a large number of cylinders could compete. From 1970, in fact, a new formula was imposed, prescribing single-cylinders for 50 cc bikes, twins for 125s and 250s and a maximum of four cylinders for 350s and 500s, with no more than six gear speeds for all classes.

At last there was a new name in the 50 class: the Spaniard Angel Nieto, who won on the Derbi (17 HP at 193 km/h = 120 mph), after a championship strongly contested with Kreidler and Jamathi. In the 125 class, the British rider Dave Simmonds with the Kawasaki two-stroke twin (32 HP at 14,000 rpm) won 8 of the 11 competitions in the program, beating the private Suzukis of Braun and Van Dongen.

In the 250 class, the last twelve events of the season were contested by Carruthers's Benelli four-cylinder (50 HP at 16,000 rpm, weight 115 kg = 254 lb, speed 240 km/h = 149 mph), Santiago Herrero's Spanish Ossa single-cylinder (two-stroke rotary disc, aluminum box section element frame, 45 HP at 11,000 rpm, weight 90 kg = 198 lb, speed 230 = 143 mph) and Kent Anderson's Yamaha two-stroke twin.

Victory went to Carruthers and to Benelli, who thus became world champion again, 19 years after Ambrosini had won the title. The 350 went to MV and Agostini, who fought Bill Ivy with the new Czech Jawa water-cooled rotary-disc two-stroke four-cylinder, delivering 60 HP at 13,000 rpm. However, Ivy fell because of an engine seizure and was killed at the Sachsenring. After that, the only racer who had the courage to ride this fast but dangerous bike was the Italian Silvio Grassetti, who came second at Imola (where the G.P. des Nations was held for the first time, instead of at Monza) and achieved other good placings the following year. In the 500 class, Agostini

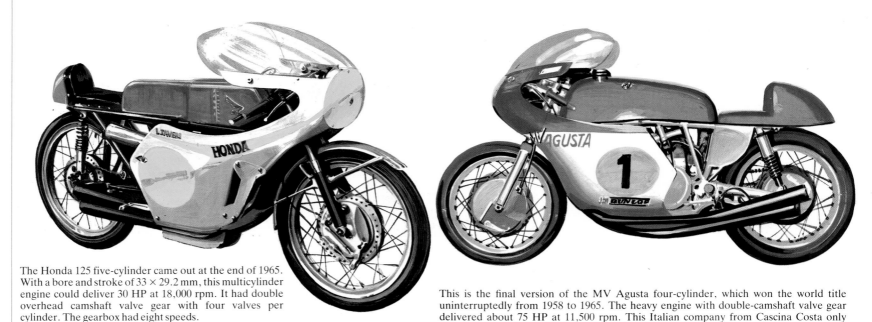

The Honda 125 five-cylinder came out at the end of 1965. With a bore and stroke of 33 × 29.2 mm, this multicylinder engine could deliver 30 HP at 18,000 rpm. It had double overhead camshaft valve gear with four valves per cylinder. The gearbox had eight speeds.

This is the final version of the MV Agusta four-cylinder, which won the world title uninterruptedly from 1958 to 1965. The heavy engine with double-camshaft valve gear delivered about 75 HP at 11,500 rpm. This Italian company from Cascina Costa only reverted to the use of four-cylinders, but with a new engine design, only in 1972.

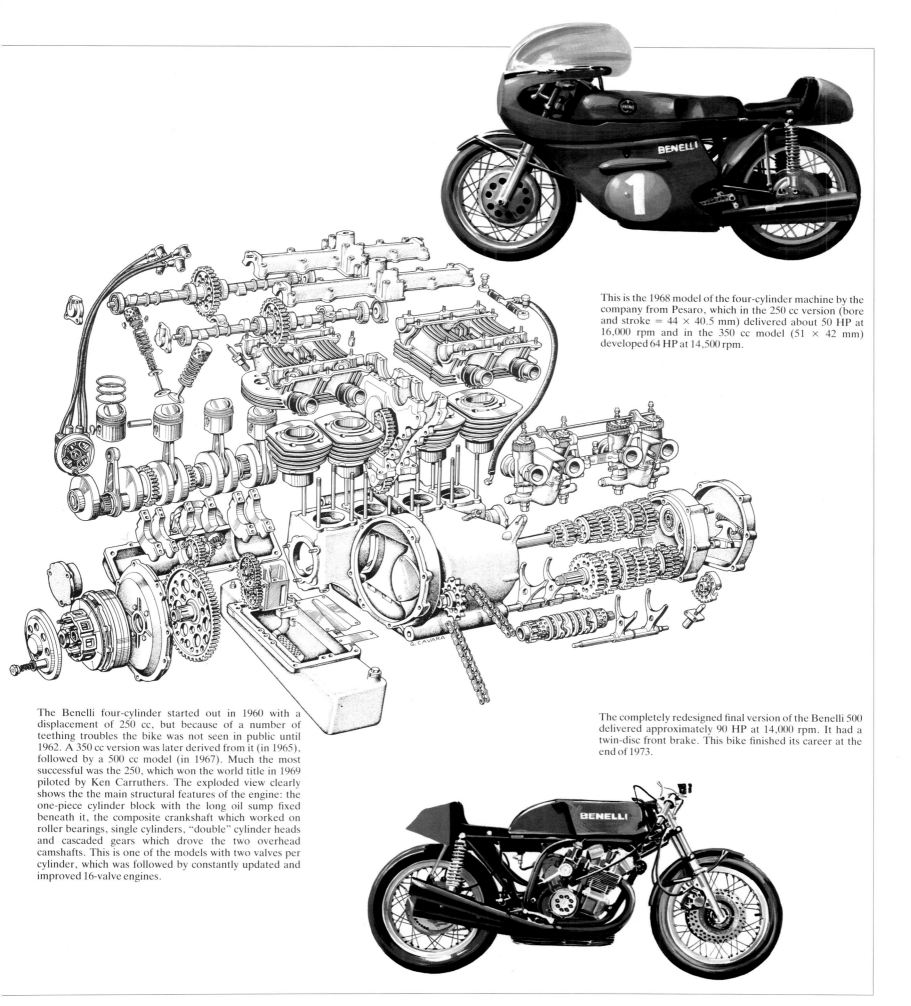

This is the 1968 model of the four-cylinder machine by the company from Pesaro, which in the 250 cc version (bore and stroke = 44 × 40.5 mm) delivered about 50 HP at 16,000 rpm and in the 350 cc model (51 × 42 mm) developed 64 HP at 14,500 rpm.

The Benelli four-cylinder started out in 1960 with a displacement of 250 cc, but because of a number of teething troubles the bike was not seen in public until 1962. A 350 cc version was later derived from it (in 1965), followed by a 500 cc model (in 1967). Much the most successful was the 250, which won the world title in 1969 piloted by Ken Carruthers. The exploded view clearly shows the the main structural features of the engine: the one-piece cylinder block with the long oil sump fixed beneath it, the composite crankshaft which worked on roller bearings, single cylinders, "double" cylinder heads and cascaded gears which drove the two overhead camshafts. This is one of the models with two valves per cylinder, which was followed by constantly updated and improved 16-valve engines.

The completely redesigned final version of the Benelli 500 delivered approximately 90 HP at 14,000 rpm. It had a twin-disc front brake. This bike finished its career at the end of 1973.

The Tomos 50 from the late sixties, with a two-stroke single-cylinder water-cooled engine and "old-style" (i.e. piston-controlled) induction. It delivered about 12 HP at 12,000 rpm.

The Jamathi 50 was craftsman-built in Holland. It won a few World Championship trials in 1968 and 1969. The two-stroke single-cylinder engine with rotary disc valve induction delivered 14 HP at 13,500 rpm.

In 1968 the 500 cc Linto twin appeared, obtained by combining two 250 cc Aermacchi "Ala d'Oro" (Gold Wing) single-cylinders; it became quite popular with privateers.

The Spaniard Santiago Herrero raced this Ossa two-stroke single with a sheet aluminum unitized body in 1969. It delivered over 45 HP at 11,000 rpm.

From 1968 to 1970, the Bultaco 250 water-cooled single-cylinder was popular with unofficial riders. The maximum power was about 39 HP at 9500 rpm.

For a number of years the Aermacchi "Ala d'Oro" (Gold Wing), built first in a 250 cc and then in a 350 cc version (but derived from a 175 cc model of 1957), was very popular with privateers. The one above is the 250 of 1957, delivering 32 HP at 10,000 rpm. The horizontal single-cylinder engine had push rod valve gear. The bore and stroke measurements were 72×61 mm for the 250 and 77×75 mm for the 350 (which delivered 42 HP). At the end of the sixties Aermacchi built a two-stroke single-cylinder of 125 cc displacement (below).

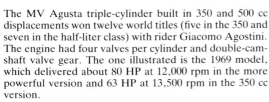

The CZ 350 seen on racecourses in 1969 had an air-cooled V-four engine with double-camshaft valve gear with four valves per cylinder.

The MV Agusta triple-cylinder built in 350 and 500 cc displacements won twelve world titles (five in the 350 and seven in the half-liter class) with rider Giacomo Agostini. The engine had four valves per cylinder and double-camshaft valve gear. The one illustrated is the 1969 model, which delivered about 80 HP at 12,000 rpm in the more powerful version and 63 HP at 13,500 rpm in the 350 cc version.

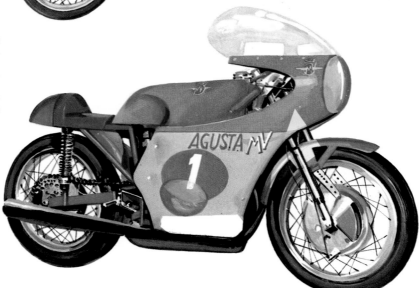

One of the most outstanding 750s derived from production models in the seventies was the Triumph/BSA (the engine was the same) triple-cylinder with push rod valve gear. With this bike, which delivered about 84 HP at 8200 rpm, Mann won the 200-mile Daytona race in 1971.

The 750 cc Ducati twin got off to a magnificent start by winning the 200-mile Imola race in 1972, taking first place with Smart and second with Spaggiari. The 90° V-twin engine with desmodromic valve gear (bore and stroke = 80 × 74.4 mm) delivered over 85 HP at 9200 rpm.

▼

750 CLASS

From 1973 to 1976 the International Motorcycling Federation, or F.I.M. (for Fédération Internationale Motocycliste) established a special trophy for 750 cc racing bikes, which was transformed into the World Championship for 1977 to 1979. Bikes of this displacement had in fact been popular ever since the early seventies, thanks to the 200-mile Daytona (a classic American race contsted since 1937) and then the 200-mile Imola race (introduced in 1972). Originally derived from production machines, these bikes of the 750 class were later built specially for these races and became increasingly like the Grand Prix models. But their popularity at an international level diminished and the F.I.M. abolished this world championship at the end of 1979.

The Honda 750 four-cylinder came out in 1970, winning the 200-mile Daytona race. The engine, with single-camshaft valve gear, delivered about 90 HP, but it was heavy and its road performance was unsatisfactory.

One of the 750 cc four-stroke engines which fought against two-strokes to the bitter end was the beautiful Harley-Davidson V-twin with push rod valve gear. This is the 1972 version (over 80 HP at 8000 rpm).

Norton also tried opposing the more powerful two-strokes with slimline, easy-to-handle twin-cylinder models with push rod valve gear. This is the 1973 version, which delivered about 80 HP.

The Suzuki triple-cylinder two-stroke was derived from a production model. The first version (bore and stroke = 70 × 64 mm) delivered about 100 HP, but presented serious steering problems (1972).

The Yamaha 750 four-cylinder with reed valve induction was unbeatable in 750 class events for a number of years. This is the 1976 version, which delivered about 140 HP.

Kawasaki was not successful in 750 races, despite entering some interesting two-stroke triple-cylinders – first with air, then with water cooling systems.

ENDURANCE CHAMPIONSHIP

The Endurance Championship originated in 1975 as the "Coupe Europe" and was transformed into the World Championship in 1980. Long-distance races held on circuits using bikes derived from production models had been popular ever since the late sixties (Bol d'Or, 24-hour Barcelona, 500-mile Thruxton). National championships for high-powered motorbikes identical to those used in endurance contests developed parallel to these in many countries.

In contrast to what happens in pure speed races, four-stroke engines are the undisputed leaders in endurance competitions, mainly because they are more reliable and durable than two-strokes.

Much the most famous endurance race is the 24-hour Bol d'Or, which has been held since 1922 (apart from two brief interruptions during the war and in the sixties).

The single-camshaft Laverda "SFC" twin-cylinder was popular in the early seventies, being freely available and usable as a road bike as well (the exhaust silencers are visible on this model from 1973).

Despite its less powerful engine, the Ducati 860 twin-cylinder had such good steering and roadholding that it often managed to outshine the Japanese multicylinder machines on tortuous circuits.

The Kawasaki 1000 double-camshaft four-cylinder was one of the great protagonists of endurance competitions for many years thanks to its exceptional strength and reliability, combined with high power.

One of the most interesting bikes which has been most successful in endurance competitions in recent years is the Honda 750 90° V-four with an aluminum frame. Its power is seemingly in excess of 120 HP.

Honda also won a lot of endurance races with their four-cylinder-in-line machines, fitted with single-, then with double-camshaft valve gear, with four valves per cylinder. This is the 1976 version, delivering about 115 HP at 9000 rpm.

and MV won all the competitions in which they took part.

New formulae and new champions

A chapter in the history of international motorcycling ended with the sixties. The technical regulations were in fact changed, with the result that from 1970 there were big variations in the bikes competing and the types of engineering chosen by their manufacturers. According to the new regulations, bikes could not be given more than six speeds; the number of engine cylinders was not to exceed two for the 125 and (later) 250 classes and four for the 350 and 500 classes. New limits were also imposed regarding minimum weight. The 50s had to be single-cylinders. This led to the disappearance of multicylinder four-strokes in the 250 class (like the Benelli four, which could not defend the title won in 1969) and dealt a bitter blow to four-stroke engines in general, whose one defense against the ever more powerful two-strokes was adding more cylinders.

At the beginning of the seventies the companies officially involved in the World Championship were the Italians – with MV and Agusta at the top of the list – the Spanish Derbi and Bultaco, the German MZ and Kreidler and the Czech Jawa and CZ. Of the big Japanese companies, only Yamaha was more or less officially involved, whilst Kawasaki and Suzuki participated ony indirectly. But this situation was not to last for long. In 1970, the world titles went to Derbi in the 50 class (the Spanish company repeating its success of the previous year, also with Nieto), to the Suzuki twin-cylinder (piloted by D. Braun) in the 125 and to the Yamaha in the 250. This bike, which was closely related to a series model, was driven by an air-cooled two-stroke twin delivering about 45 HP at 12,000 rpm in the customer version and just 50 HP in the official version, which won the title with Gould.

The two bigger classes were won by the "usual" Agostini on the "usual" MV Agusta three-cylinders. The 350 cc Benelli four-cylinder ridden by Pasolini made a very good impression during the year and the Jawas (two-stroke four-cylinder, approximately 70 HP at 13,500 rpm), CZ (four-stroke four, just under 60 HP at 13,500 rpm) and MZ (300 cc two-stroke twin, delivering 64 HP) also performed well.

It began to become clear what the main technical innovations of the seventies, shortly to be used by all manufacturers, would be: magnesium alloy integral-spoked wheels and hydraulically actuated disc brakes. Slick tyres were to appear in 1973, soon becoming popular.

In 1971, while Agostini with MV Agusta continued to dominate the 350 and 500 classes,

Nieto won the world title in 1972 with this Derbi 125. The two-stroke twin-cylinder engine with rotary disc valve induction delivered over 35 HP at 14,000 rpm.

In 1972 the Derbi 250 two-stroke twin won the Austrian Grand Prix, piloted by Jansson. It delivered somewhere in excess of 55 HP at 12,500 rpm. As with the less powerful model, fuel induction was controlled by rotary disc valve.

The last Yamaha air-cooled twin-cylinders were sold to privateers in 1972 (by which time the official bikes had water cooling systems). This is the 250, delivering nearly 50 HP at 11,000 rpm.

The Derbi 50 of 1972 had a two-stroke water-cooled engine with rotary disc valve induction. It delivered about 17 HP at 16,000 rpm.

This is the air-cooled Aermacchi Harley-Davidson 250 twin-cylinder on which Pasolini lost the world title in 1972 by just one point. Power approx. 50 HP at 11,400 rpm.

One of the last four-stroke Grand Prix racing models, the Paton twin-cylinder, was hand-built by Giuseppe Pattoni in Milan. This is the 500 of 1974, delivering about 65 HP.

The great novelty of the 1973 season was the Yamaha 500 water-cooled four-cylinder, which won the title two years later, with Agostini. It delivered about 100 HP at 10,000 rpm. Bore and stroke 56 × 50 mm.

The MV Agusta 350 four-cylinder replaced the highly successful triple-cylinder of 1972, enabling Agostini to win the world title. It delivered about 70 HP at 14,800 rpm. ▶

The Morbidelli twin-cylinder which won the world title in 1975, 1976 and 1977 was designed by German engineer Jorg Möller. The water-cooled engine, which had a 43.9 mm bore and 41 mm stroke and two rotary disc valves, delivered about 40 HP at 14,000 rpm.

The Harley-Davidson two-stroke twin-cylinder, produced in 250 and 350 cc versions, was made near Varese in Italy. This bike won three world titles in the lower class (1974, 1975, 1976) and one in the higher class (1976), the rider in all cases being W. Villa. The 250 delivered about 58 HP and the 350 about 70. It had piston-controlled fuel induction and water cooling.

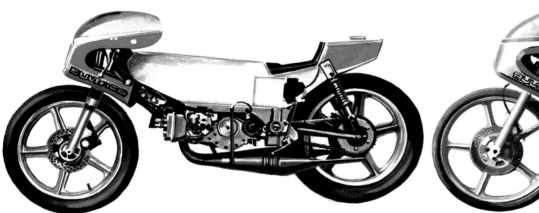

At the end of 1975 Bultaco bought up the entire Piovaticci stable at Pesaro (bikes and designers), thus providing itself – after only slight modifications – with some highly competitive machines for the World Championship, such as this 125 twin-cylinder delivering over 35 HP at 14,000 rpm. Fuel induction was controlled by rotary disc valves.

In 1976 Nieto won the 50 class world title with this slimline Bultaco (ex-Piovaticci) single-cylinder. It had a unitized body. The water-cooled engine with rotary disc valve induction delivered about 18 HP at 16,000 rpm.

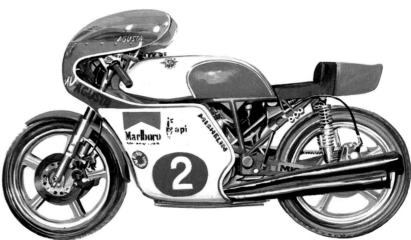

1976 was the last year of racing for one of the most famous companies of all time: MV Agusta. Agostini tried in vain to oppose the superlative strength of the Japanese two-strokes with the company's four-stroke four-cylinders (which had double-camshaft valve gear with four valves per cylinder). The 500 (bore and stroke = 57 × 49 mm) could deliver over 95 HP at 14,000 rpm.

This is the final version (1976) of the MV Agusta 350 four-cylinder. The two overhead camshafts were operated by cascaded gears. The engine, with a bore and stroke of 53 × 39.5 mm, delivered about 75 HP at 15,000 rpm (unit construction 6-speed gearbox; triple disc brakes; magnesium alloy wheels).

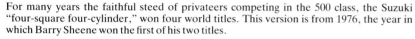

After an uneventful start, the Kawasaki "tandem" twin-cylinders dominated the 250 and 350 classes for years, winning no fewer than eight world titles from 1978 to 1982 with riders Ballington and Mang. The bikes were water-cooled and fuel induction was controlled by rotary disc valves.

For many years the faithful steed of privateers competing in the 500 class, the Suzuki "four-square four-cylinder," won four world titles. This version is from 1976, the year in which Barry Sheene won the first of his two titles.

The Yamaha 250 and 350 cc twin-cylinders were for very many years the best bikes in their class available to privateers (each year, this Japanese company produced bikes that were virtually the same as the official ones of the previous year). The final versions of these bikes were given aluminum frames.

▼

the 250 title went to a great rider on a wholly private machine: Phil Read on the Yamaha twin-cylinder. The 125 went to Nieto on the Derbi and the 50 to De Vries on the Kreidler.

The pattern was much the same the following year. Two more titles were added to those already won by Agostini and MV Agusta in the 350 and 500 classes. In the 250 the Yamaha twin-cylinder prevailed again, ridden by rising star Jarno Saarinen, while Nieto won the 125 and 50 titles with the Derbi.

While all this was happening, big changes were taking place. In the 250 and 350 classes the Harley-Davidsons, designed and built at the (ex Aermacchi) plant at Schiranna near Varese, were becoming increasingly efficient, while in the 125 class the Morbidelli twin-cylinder was also coming on well. Furthermore, unbeknown to all concerned, Yamaha was developing a 500 cc water-cooled two-stroke four-cylinder. This machine, delivering 80 HP, began its career at the French Grand Prix in 1973, ridden by Saarinen. While the year promised to be outstanding from a sporting and technical point of view, tragedy struck on 20 May on the Monza circuit. On the first lap of the 250 race a very serious accident

occurred in which two of the best-loved riders of all time, Renzo Pasolini and Jarno Saarinen, lost their lives. Parlotti was also killed at the TT shortly afterward, whilst in command of the race on the Morbidelli 125.

At the end of the one of the blackest years in the history of motorcycling, De Vries became world champion on the Kreidler in the 50 class, Anderson on the Yamaha in the 125, Braun on the Yamaha in the 250 and Agostini on the MV Agusta in the 500. The company in Gallarate had already replaced its magnificent three-cylinders by much more up-to-date fours the year before, but now the threat from two-stroke engines was even greater. While the Yamaha bike was becoming ever more competitive in the 350 class – together with the Harley-Davidson twin-cylinder – in the 500 the four-cylinder-in-line Yamaha was joined in 1974 by the new Suzuki square four with rotary disc valve induction, delivering over 90 HP.

In 1974 Agostini, who had left MV Agusta to go and defend the colours of Yamaha, won the title in the 350 class, while he was unable to stop Read winning the 500 with the MV Agusta. The 250 was won by Walter Villa with

the Harley-Davidson water-cooled twin, the 125 by Anderson on the Yamaha and the 50 by Van Kessel on the Kreidler. Meanwhile Morbidelli had taken on the German engineer Georg Möller, who designed a 125 water-cooled twin with rotary disc induction, which was to dominate the international scene for some years.

In 1975 the sun set for good on four-stroke engines, slain by an iniquitous regulation according to which their displacement was equated with that of two-strokes (which, apart from anything else, can make far greater use of exhaust resonance). MV Agusta in fact disappeared from the list of world title holders even in the 500 class, which was won by Agostini on the Yamaha (this was to be the last world title for the champion from Bergamo). The Suzuki RG began to show its potential, winning two Grands Prix in this class.

The 350 was won by the very youthful Venezuelan ace Johnny Cecotto on the Yamaha twin-cylinder, while in the 250 Villa, with the Harley-Davidson, repeated his success of the previous year. Making its debut in this class was the new Kawasaki tandem twin-cylinder with rotary disc valve induction,

For three consecutive years (1978–1980) the American Kenny Roberts monopolized the 500 class World Championship with his Yamaha bike, winning the world title with apparent ease. This machine had a four-cylinder-in-line engine with piston-controlled induction and a bore and stroke of 56 × 50 mm. A partializing exhaust valve was fitted in 1979. The version shown (from 1979) had twin disc brakes at the front, 295 mm in diameter, and magnesium alloy spoked wheels. The power was estimated at 120 HP and the weight at 130 kg (287 lb).

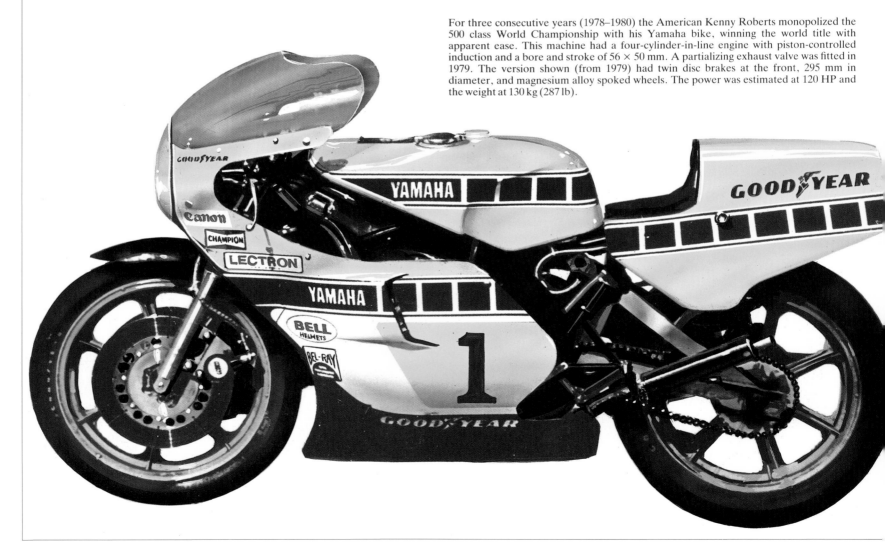

which took part in the Dutch and Belgian Grands Prix only.

The 125 was won by Pilera on the Morbidelli, which delivered about 40 HP at 14,000 rpm. Nieto won the 50 again with the Kreidler. At the end of the season, the glorious MV Agusta retired from racing. Just to deliver the *coup de grâce* to four-stroke engines, the F.I.M. decided that from 1976 Grand Prix motorcycles were to be fitted with exhaust systems which would reduce noise levels to set values, which in time were to become practically the same as those for normal road traffic. Needless to say, this obtuse measure has never been applied to other motor sports (such as power-boat and automobile racing).

In 1976 Nieto, who had passed to Bultaco, won back the 50 class world title, while Morbidelli reclaimed the 125 (this time with Bianchi). Harley-Davidson won both the 250 and 350 with Villa, while Barry Sheene took the 500 title with the Suzuki RG of over 110 HP at 11,000 rpm.

This British rider was to win the 500 title the following year too, still with the Suzuki four-cylinder (whose power had risen in the meantime to nearly 120 HP), while Yamaha was looming on the horizon again, with the new four-cylinder-in-line OW 35. In the 350 the title went to the Japanese Katayama on the Yamaha, while in the 250 (rejoined by the tandem cylinder Kawasakis, which won two trials) Lega won on the Morbidelli. The 125 was won by Bianchi again on the Morbidelli and the 50 by Nieto on the Bultaco.

With 1978, the Roberts era began. This superlative Californian rider won the 500 by a very big margin, far outclassing all his opponents. The same thing happened in the 250 and 350 classes, with Kawasaki and Ballington. Lazzarini won the 125 with the MBA (closely related to the Morbidelli) and the Spaniard Tormo won the 50, with the Bultaco bike.

The Kawasaki machines, which were to win the title the following year too – still with the South African Ballington – had a power of 60 HP at 12,000 rpm and 75 HP at 11,800 rpm in the 250 cc (bore and stroke = 54×54 mm) and 350 cc (64×54 mm) versions respectively. Kenny Roberts on the Yamaha also won the title again in 1979, while in the 125 the new Minarelli designed by the German Georg Möller triumphed with Nieto and in the 50 class, the Kreidler with Lazzarini.

The eighties began with Roberts winning the 500 again on the Yamaha (now with a partializing exhaust valve and a new square section, tubular aluminum frame). Eckerold on the Bimota-Yamaha won the 350, while the German Mang took the 250 with the Kawasaki. Meanwhile Möller had left Minarelli as well and his place had been taken by the Dutch engineer Jan Thiel. The latter – who, after producing the 50 cc Jamathi, had passed first to the Italian firm Piovaticci, then to the Spanish Bultaco – did not have time to complete the new Bolognese 125. The title therefore went to Bianchi on the MBA. Lazzarini won the 50 class again with the Kreidler-Iprem.

The Minarelli 125, with a new unitized body, won the title the following year with Nieto, while Bultaco secured the 50 class title with Tormo. Kawasaki triumphed in both the 250 and 350 classes, thanks to Mang. In the 500, at the end of a bitterly contested season, Lucchinelli won with the Suzuki RG Gamma of no less than 130 HP at 11,000 rpm. The great Roberts and Sheene were defeated with their

The Minarelli 125 was very similar to the Morbidelli. The two bikes were in fact designed by the same person (the German Möller). This machine won the world title in 1979 and 1981, piloted on both occasions by Nieto. The two-stroke twin-cylinder engine with rotary disc valve induction (bore and stroke = 44×41 mm) delivered over 40 HP. The fuel was supplied by two 29 mm Dell'Orto carburetors.

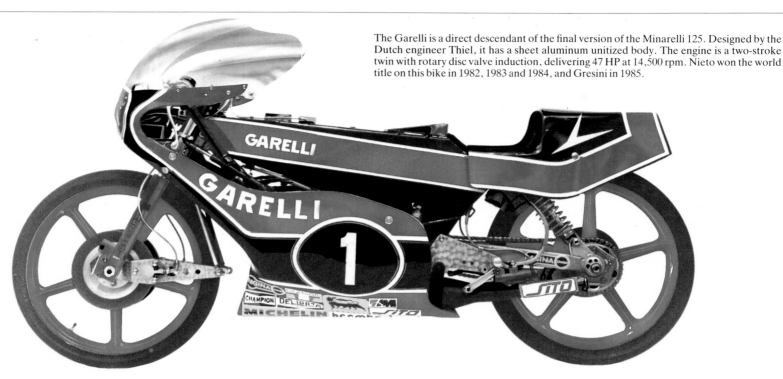

The Garelli is a direct descendant of the final version of the Minarelli 125. Designed by the Dutch engineer Thiel, it has a sheet aluminum unitized body. The engine is a two-stroke twin with rotary disc valve induction, delivering 47 HP at 14,500 rpm. Nieto won the world title on this bike in 1982, 1983 and 1984, and Gresini in 1985.

rotary-disc Yamaha square fours, which suffered from major steering and roadholding problems. Suzuki won back the 500 title in 1982 with Franco Uncini, while Roberts's new Yamaha OW 61 still failed to live up to expectations. In the meantime the Honda NS, driven by a compact and powerful triple-cylinder V-type engine with reed valve induction, had appeared. The design chosen (two vertical cylinders with a third in the center, angled 20° downward) was similar to that of German DKWs of the fifties.

Kawasaki won the 350 class again with Mang, but left the 250 title to the Frenchman Tournadre with the Yamaha bike. The 125 was claimed by Nieto with the Garelli and the 50 by Dorflinger on the Kreidler.

1982 saw the triumph of Freddie Spencer with the Honda NS (over 130 HP, weight less than 120 kg = 264 lb) over the unfortunate

Roberts, who was trying to get to grips with the Yamaha OW 70, which experienced a lot of teething troubles. At the end of the season, the two riders were separated by just two points.

After the F.I.M. abolished the 350 class, the 250 was won by the Venezuelan Lavado with the Yamaha, while Nieto won the 125 again on the Garelli, and Dorflinger the 50 on the Krauser-Kreidler. The Spanish champion, with his Garelli 125 – now delivering about 47

At the beginning of the eighties Honda made a dramatic comeback, first in the 500 class alone and then in the 250 as well (in 1985). For the higher-capacity event the company entered a very interesting triple-cylinder with the cylinders arranged in a V, according to a scheme very similar to that of DKW bikes of the fifties, followed by a four-cylinder V-type model, shown here. Spencer won the 500 class world title with this machine in 1985 (he had already won one with the triple-cylinder in 1983). The bike has an aluminum frame with square section elements. The engine power is approximately 140 HP.

HP at 14,500 (bore and stroke = 44 × 41 mm) – won again in 1984, when the 250 title went to Frenchman Christian Sarron with the Yamaha and the 500 to Eddie Lawson on the Yamaha OW 76 V-four, with two parallel crankshafts and reed valve induction (power approximately 140 HP).

In 1985 Garelli also won the 125 class with Fausto Gresini, while in the 250 and 500 Freddie Spencer scored a spectacular victory on the Honda.

Yamaha won the 500 class world title with rider Lawson in 1984, on a V-four with two crankshafts and reed valve induction. This machine delivers about 140 HP and also has a partializing valve over the exhaust port. The aluminum frame is made of box section elements welded together.

In 1985 the Italian company Aprilia entered a fantastic bike with sheet aluminum box section elements in the 250 class. The engine is a Rotax twin-cylinder delivering about 80 HP at 12,500 rpm. The cylinders are arranged "in tandem" and induction is controlled by rotary disc valves. A special, pneumatically controlled partializing exhaust valve is used. Bore and stroke 54 × 54 mm; 38 mm carburetors; weight 90 kg (198 lb). The 1986 version is shown here.

ENDURO

In 1913 the British Cycle and Motorcycle Manufacturers and Traders' Union Ltd. decided to offer the F.I.M. (International Motorcycling Federation established shortly before to bring together the various national federations) a trophy to be awarded to the winner of an important competition designed to test the strength and endurance of bikes on mixed courses, together with the skill of the riders. The Six Days Trial thus came into being, and with it "enduro." The word "enduro" (directly derived from the American endurance competitions) was in fact coined in 1981, when the Six Days Trial was given World Championship status for national teams. Before that this specialty was called "Regolarità" (Reliability trials – using trail bikes) in Italy, "Todo Terreno" in Spain, "Gelande Sport" in Germany and "Tout Terrain" in France. In Eastern bloc countries it was identified with "classic" races like the various international competitions of Zakopane, the Tatra Mountains, Zilina, and so forth. In those days, the sport was practiced by only a small minority of people.

Enduro (trail bike) engines have always been divided into two- and four-strokes. Before the introduction of the European Championship in 1968 – in response to pressure from manufacturers like Zündapp, then Puch, KTM and Jawa and Simson – most of the Western bikes had four-stroke engines, and the international scene was dominated by East European riders with powerful two-strokes by MZ, Jawa and CZ. Duplex cradle frames and drum brakes were common to more or less all of the bikes, which had forks and dampers with a long stroke to help cope with the uneven ground.

As two-stroke technology evolved, bikes switched from classic types of fuel induction to rotary disc valve engines (Austrian Rotax engines are still famous today) and finally, machines with reed valve induction and sophisticated electrtonic ignition systems. As far as suspension is concerned, forks with combined air/oil operation are now found, while the rear mono shock absorber fitted to various different types of fork leverage has now done away with the traditional twin dampers with helical springs. Two-stroke engines have changed a great deal over the years, with the result that for high-powered bikes better torque distribution is preferable, to get the best performance out of the vehicle at all rpm.

Enduro is divided into three different schools: Czech, German and Italian, with France and Sweden now developing schools in their own right.

Enduro competitions are mainly off-road events, on a circuit of about 50 km (31 miles), to be repeated several times, along which there are various checkpoints to establish the exact minute and second at which each rider passes. The basic rule is observance of a given speed. Every minute's delay is penalized by 60 points, while a contestant running a minute fast is more heavily penalized. To determine the placings for riders with the same number of penalties special trials are held both over fields, where the course is marked out by strips

THE SIX DAYS TRIAL

More than a sporting challenge, the Six Days Trial is an opportunity for riders the world over to meet, but perhaps still more an exhibition of friendship and brotherhood which breaks down traditional barriers, uniting Eastern champions and Western athletes in a common purpose. Such is the spirit in which this contest, which has justifiably been called the "Cross-country Olympics," is renewed each year. The Six Days Trial does in fact have a lot in common with the most famous world sporting event of all – from the number of different nations taking part to the huge influx of competitors, the lure of the crowd, the intermingling of different languages and dialects and sampling of the traditions and lifestyle of the host country.

The most famous brands of motorcycle have taken part in the Six Days Trial, from British to German, to those of Eastern bloc countries like Czechoslovakia, Poland and East Germany, then Spain and finally, nowadays, Japan, Sweden, Austria and Italy.

In 1913 the competitors in what was to be the first edition of the Six Days Trial assembled on the starting line at Carlisle in the North of England. The winner was the British team, captained by one Charlie Collier, whose father founded the legendary Matchless marque.

Over the years the rules governing the Six Days Trial have been streamlined and adapted to suit the times and the evolution of motorbikes, although constant technical progress and ever keener competition will no doubt bring further changes to make the contest still more exciting. The national teams competing for the Trophy (which has been recognized as a World Championship for national teams since 1981) are composed of six riders with bikes of various makes, but subdivided into at least four different displacements. Competing for the Silver Vase (which has qualified for the "Under 21" World Championship since 1985) are four young riders with bikes subdivided into at least two different displacements. All the other riders enrolled can take part in club formation or individually, competing for the title in each of the five displacements. The displacements allowed are the same as for the Italian and European Championships: 80; 125; 250; 500 and over 500 cc, the latter being reserved for bikes with four-stroke engines.

In the Six Days Trial, the results are based on individual grades. At the end of each stage each competitor is given a mark, based on the penalties received at time checks, in special trials and for breaches of regulations. The rider with the lowest number of points for his displacement is the winner and is given the "rating" zero. Apart from the overall number of points, those following him have as team points the difference obtained by subtracting the figure for the first classification from the actual number of points. The sum of the team points of each member determines the team placings for the World Championship Trophy and Silver Vase. In deciding the final results, credit is given to teams which have completed the contest with at least one competitor arriving according to the rules. For each stage of the contest, any rider who withdraws is penalized by 15,000 points. All riders who finish the Six Days Trial properly are entitled to an individual medal. The gold medal is given to those who end the trial with points not more than 10% higher than the first classification, the silver to those who do not go more than 40% above it, and the bronze to all the rest.

of plastic, and along bridleways or on ploughed land. The length of a special trial varies, but is in most cases between 3 and 5 kilometers (2–3 miles). Obviously, the winner is the one who takes the shortest time. Apart from the special trials at the European Championship and Six Days Trial there is also an acceleration test, where victory is determined by a system of points, which multiplies the seconds taken by the riders to cover the 200-meter (218-yard) course.

From 1972 to 1981 there was a tremendous boom in enduro (trail) bike sales, as these bikes could be used to go to school or work on, as well as for "reliability trials" at the weekend. But as technical expertise has grown, the bikes have been increasingly adapted to cross-country routes so that they are now very much like motorcross bikes; this has of course limited their use in towns, drastically reducing sales.

MOTOCROSS

Unlike enduro and trial biking, motocross is a real speed contest which does not take place on asphalted roads but on rough terrain, with holes, jumps, gradients and various other natural obstacles. Nowadays such competitions are also held in stadia, where dug earth is made to mimic natural features, so that the sport loses none of its spectacular qualities.

It is certainly easier to run a race of this type with the bikes available today, thanks to better suspension systems, engines, tyres, frames and disc brakes. But one must not forget that it is always the rider who steers a bike to victory, and he must possess exceptional courage and physical strength combined with a riding technique good enough to tackle all different situations. That is why motocross champions are veritable athletes, to the extent of performing all kinds of acrobatics in the saddle, which is what makes this sport so spectacular. The most breathtaking examples of motocross riding are undoubtedly to be seen at the American "Supercross" Championship events. All seven stages of the program take place in enormous football stadia with the riders travelling at breakneck speed, thrilling the audience with the numerous different heats and recoveries. The best of them take part in the final, where thousands of dollars are at stake; this is held in the famous Coliseum at Los Angeles in front of more than 100,000 spectators.

The history of motocross is also divided into different schools which have come to the fore as technical progress has influenced the development of motorbikes. Once again it was the British who invented the first motocross competitions. In 1919 a "scrambler" type competition was organized at Camberley in Surrey; this was to all intents and purposes the first true motocross event. The program was divided into two different heats, one in the morning and one in the afternoon, the total time taken by contestants deciding the winner. The 60-km (37-mile) course included jumps and upward and downward slopes. It was won by the British rider Sparks, on a Harley-Davidson.

The first motocross track was also in Britain, where the Lancashire Grand National was held over a five-kilometer (3-mile) circuit with a total of 20 laps. But this was not motocross in the modern sense, even if the specialty was beginning to spread to other countries such as Holland, Belgium, Sweden and France, where one of the first international contests was held in Paris in 1939. The first official motocross event took place in 1947, when the F.I.M. recognized a Motocross des Nations (international motocross) competition, which was held in Holland. The year 1952 was another historic one for motocross racing, thanks to the introduction of the European Championships for 500 cc bikes only. The first 250 championship was held in 1957. Belgian riders dominated the first three editions of the European 500 Championship, followed in 1955 and 1956 by two Britons, although Sweden was already showing her potential. The European 500 Championship was elevated to "world status" in 1957 and the very heavy British four-stroke machines were joined by the German Maico, with a two-stroke engine, which was much more powerful, partly because its total weight was lower. Even the accessories industry was beginning to work for motocross: the Italian firm Ceriani was a notable example, their new, telehydraulic forks greatly improving suspension, which was by that time vitally important to the finished vehicle. In 1962 the European 250 event was also elevated to World Championship status and was won by a Swedish bike with a two-stroke engine: the Husqvarna.

In 1963 BSA tried playing another card against the technical development of two-strokes by bringing out a new machine with a progressive four-stroke engine and very compact crankcase design for the half-liter World Championship. After a year's refinement this bike, weighing just 116 kg (255 lb), won the colours in 1964 and 1965, while in the quarter-liter category Husqvarna was joined by CZ, who dominated the international scene from the mid sixties to 1970.

Of the four Japanese giants, Suzuki was the first to believe in motocross and for the 1970 season engaged champion Joel Robert, who immediately gave them their first world title. The following year Suzuki won the title in the 500 class too, starting a real hegemony. Yamaha also took part officially in the 250 World Motocross Championship in 1973, followed by Kawasaki who, however, concentrated on the 500 class.

Honda had of course to be there, to complete the Japanese line-up. After an unimpressive start in the mid seventies, they brought out a full range of models in the three different displacements.

After a few years in which competitions for 125s were not valid for world title events, the first World Championship race for this displacement was introduced in 1975. 1985 was the year of triumph for the Italian industry. As far as technical development is concerned, after a last, nostalgic appearance of a four-stroke engine on a BSA model, all bikes were developed as two-strokes. Fuel induction systems progressed from the classic type to disc and reed valves, and the Japanese have introduced valves on the exhaust system too in the last few years. But the most important improvement to motocross bikes has been in the suspension. The contribution made by motocross to the development of

modern methods of rear suspension is undeniable.

The use of light alloys such as magnesium has considerably reduced the weight of the bikes, so much so that modern regulations for the three displacements (125, 250 and 500 cc) have imposed a weight limit.

In Italy too motocross is now an established part of the motorcycling scene, thanks to the commitment of manufacturers like Gilera and Cagiva.

TRIALS

Balance and perfect synchronism with one's bike: the essence of trials riding. This sport, which originated in Britain back in 1911 when the first edition of the Scottish Six Days Trial was held, is undoubtedly one of the areas of motorcycling which has attracted the most public interest in recent years. Its success is mainly due to "indoor" shows which have introduced this sport, which is as silent as it is spectacular, to city squares, stadia and sports halls. The silence of a trials bike is due to its engine design, the engine necessarily being built to work at low power and rpm. Engines have been greatly improved, progressing from push rod-operated four-strokes to the less sophisticated two-strokes with both classic and rotary disc valve induction. However, in the last few years the technically indefatigable Japanese have very successfully relaunched machines with four-stroke engines.

The tyres of trials bikes are made for use at very low pressure and have small tread blocks, specially designed to adapt perfectly to all types of surface without harming the environment. The grip and compound mix of tyres is very important these days, because some stretches of stony or muddy ground need special types; but people do still compete in World Championships with mass-produced tyres.

A good frame can be an excellent weapon for the trials rider. Designs have progressed from the classic duplex frame to the split-spine frame with an open cradle and the guard plate of the engine crankcase bolted to the back and finally, closed duplex cradle frames which are better suited to sophisticated riding techniques using mono shock absorber rear suspension. New types of brake have also been developed in recent years, the classic central drum now being replaced by more modern disc brakes.

Apart from technology, an increasingly decisive influence on the result is undoubtedly the rider, as it is his considerable skill, experience and innate sense of balance which determine the outcome of a contest. Trial events are not speed competitions. In this sport what counts is not the intoxicating sense of speed, nor the sense of power which distinguishes other motor sports; not confronting obstacles in an aggressive way, as in motocross, nor trying to match the clock, as in enduro events. None of this applies in trials riding. The fundamental prerequisite to success in this sport is great courage, which the rider needs to tackle the various obstacles. Undoubtedly, if there were a direct confrontation between riders, the spectacle would be even more exciting. It is hard even for an

expert to explain in a word what a trial event is like without using clichés, as the rider really does have to perform miracles to avoid being penalized. A particular type of riding is involved. The course is carefully examined beforehand, in an effort to discover any possible pitfalls. The rider then sets out on his bike without changing gear, using his entire body to keep the vehicle in trim and on course, avoiding using the clutch and controlling his machine by skilful touches of the accelerator and brakes, virtually "on the spot," because he must not put a foot to the ground if he is not to be penalized. To determine the placings in a trial event there are "nonstop" zones, where the rider is penalized by five points if the bike stops, by one point if he puts a foot on the ground and by three points if he does so more than once. Obviously the winner is the one with the fewest penalties. In a World Championship, the course is usually about 30 km (18.6 miles) long with 15–20 nonstop zones, to be repeated three times. There is no limit to the bike's displacement, but 250 cc machines have proved most suitable, as they permit an ideal ratio between the weight and power of the rider and the power of the engine. The 250s are all single-cylinder machines, mostly with air cooling, although water-cooled models have also been used. The bikes for this sport certainly deserve a special mention. In the space of a few years, British and Spanish leadership has waned and Italian-built bikes are acquiring increasing importance.

An important point is that contrary to what happens with other off-road specialties, the trial bikes competing for the world title are virtually the same as those found in showrooms – apart from a few adjustments to suit the individual rider, such as the shape of the handlebars or positioning of the controls. They are normal bikes, therefore, modestly priced compared with the others. Not only is the purchase price reasonable; maintenance costs are relatively low too, as with the exception of the tyres, wear and tear on the different parts is virtually nil.

The most popular and prestigious sporting event in this field is the Six Days Trial, which is normally held in a different country each year and attended by riders from various countries. Some of the best have included British riders Sammy Miller, who dominated the scene in the sixties, and Mick Andrews, who was European Champion in 1971 and 1972.

ONE HUNDRED YEARS
OF DIFFERENT MARQUES

GREAT BRITAIN

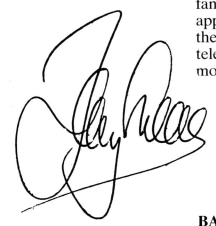

Britain has produced some great champions in her day. However, in recent years, motorcycling fans have tended instead to follow foreign aces. The British motorcycling industry, sadly, appears to be in something of a decline. Enthusiasm for the sport has been generated mainly by the racers themselves presenting a positive image of motorbike racing, especially through television appearances and other outlets. This spirit of enthusiasm will, no doubt, ensure many more successes for Britain in the future.

BARRY SHEENE

So great was the demand for civilian motorcycles when peace returned to the Western world in 1945 that there was a ready market for virtually anything with two wheels. Unfortunately, this sales boom encouraged a mood of complacency in British boardrooms and many factories continued to produce old-fashioned machines with only cosmetic changes or, at most, the adoption of telescopic front forks.

Meanwhile, the Japanese were doing intensive market research and soon started to export modern machines to Europe at competitive prices. As the quantity and variety of those machines increased, the British government's failure to protect its home industry through import controls compounded the industry's own complacency, with the inevitable result that it collapsed and was virtually dead by the mid 1970s.

While the death of any national industry is a commercial and economic tragedy, the demise of the British motorcycle industry was particularly sad because British designers, factories and riders had been in the forefront of development from the very dawn of motorcycling.

A comprehensive history of the British industry would fill a library, but a clear picture may be obtained by studying the achievements of the most famous manufacturers. Motorcycling is

predominantly a pastime of youth; hence the greatest degree of fame has always accrued to those manufacturers who have achieved most success in international sporting competitions such as Grand Prix racing, speed records and Six Days Trials.

AJS

In the early 1930s, Matchless bought the AJS company. Consequently, in the later years of production, many models in the two ranges were virtually identical except for the tank badges and other minor cosmetic differences. Before the amalgamation, however, the policies of the two companies were very different, for AJS sustained their interest in racing much longer.

Between 1914 and 1928 they won four Junior (i.e. 350 cc) TTs, set five Junior lap records, won five European Championships, won the 1921 Senior TT with a 350 cc machine (the only time ever) and set three Senior lap records. Their design team was very fertile, and after much experimenting they marketed a string of racing singles with chain-driven overhead camshafts

from 1927 onward – culminating in the world-famous 350 cc 7R (Boy Racer) from 1948 until the mid 1980s.

For the first few years the 7R was just another series-production racer. But at the end of 1954 Jack Williams was engaged as development engineer – and within six years, despite a tiny budget, he had so transformed the machine that MV Agusta asked for Alan Shepherd's engine to be measured after he had broken the Dundrod lap record and constantly disputed the lead with world champion John Surtees in the 1960 Ulster Grand Prix.

A three-valve version of the 7R was built in 1952 and an international team of riders rode it to five world records at Montlhéry in the autumn. Two years later Rod Coleman won the Junior TT on the three-valver – but it was shelved before Jack Williams arrived.

Both before and after the last war, AJS also built some special 500 cc racing machines which were not for sale. The first, a V-four, actually appeared at the 1935 London show with full touring equipment and the option of a super-charger in place of the dynamo! No orders were placed, so the factory converted two machines to racing trim, fitted compressors and raced them in 1936, 1938 and 1939. By that time they were

rear-sprung and water-cooled, and Walter Rusk set the first 100 mph (161 km/h) Grand Prix lap at Ulster before retiring and leaving Dorino Serafini to win on a Gilera four.

The postwar AJS works racer was the Porcupine twin. It was designed for super-charging, but that was banned before the machine was raced. Although Les Graham won the first 500 cc World Championship (1949) on a Porcupine, it was never developed to its full potential.

From the start in 1909 AJS always made their own engines. And as a background to their sporting activities they marketed a typical British range of side-valve and overhead-valve singles from 250 to 500 cc, big V-twins for sidecar duty and vertical twins.

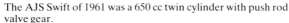

The AJS Swift of 1961 was a 650 cc twin cylinder with push rod valve gear.

The 1961 "Boy Racer" version of the AJS 7R 350 cc, one of the most popular and competitive mass-produced British racing bikes.

One of the very first versions of the Porcupine engine, with horizontal cylinders. On later models, the cylinders were fitted at an angle of 45 degrees.

Les Graham, on the Porcupine 500 cc twin cylinder, at the 1949 edition of the Senior TT. He won the 500 cc World Championship in the same year.

ARIEL

Of the wide variety of machines produced by Ariel during their 70 years of business, three very different types accounted for most of their renown. They were the over-head/valve single-cylinder Red Hunters of 250, 350 and 500 cc; the unique Square Four (500, 600 and 1000 cc) and the 250 cc Leader and Arrow parallel-twin two-strokes.

While the Red Hunters and the two-strokes (all designed by the talented Val Page) were aimed at the mass market, the role of the Square Four (designed by Edward Turner) was to bring prestige to the name Ariel – even at a financial loss on every machine sold. The original design (in 1928) incorporated not only four cylinders, separate front and rear crankshafts (geared together) and a chain-driven overhead camshaft, but also an integral three-speed gearbox and gear primary drive. This combination of novelties was considered to be commercially risky and so the first production machines, in 1931, had separate Burman gearboxes driven by chain.

Although the engine's smooth torque, quiet-ness and relative lack of vibration appealed to solo tourists, the demand for sidecar duty was so great that engine capacity was soon boosted to 600 cc by increasing the cylinder-bore size from 51 to 56 mm.

Next, in response to persistent demands for more flywheel inertia, even larger capacity, better oiling and lower cost, the crankshaft layout was revised and the stroke increased from 61 to 75 mm (to give 600 or 1000 cc according to bore diameter); push rods replaced the overhead camshaft and dry-sump oiling was adopted, with plain crankshaft bearings.

Only the 1000 cc version survived the 1939-1945 war, but with a telescopic front fork and link-type rear springing it was simply too heavy. So, for 1949, the cylinder block and head were cast in aluminum, reducing the weight by 25 kg (55 lb). Naturally, the engine then ran much cooler; this enabled the makers, four years later, to bring out the higher-performance Mark II with its distinctive four exhaust pipes. It was a thirsty machine, but it was certainly exclusive and offered docility or ferocious acceleration to suit the rider's whim.

The Red Hunters were popular with road riders and sportsmen alike. But the single that brought Ariel the most renown was the 500 cc HT5, on which the incomparable Sammy Miller dominated the trials scene from 1957 to 1963, winning a record 352 events and six British Championships.

As a civilized motorcycle-for-everyman, the Ariel Leader was a brilliant design: quiet, clean, comfortable, economical and stable. But the tooling costs for its pressed-steel monocoque chassis were high, and sales were low. Even when the weathershielding was omitted to make the sporting Arrow, sales were insufficient to offset the capital investment. Ariel learned – as others had earlier – that there is no commercial future in a car-on-two-wheels.

In 1939, Ariel built a bike for the Army using the 350 cc single cylinder engine of the Red Hunter.

BROUGH SUPERIOR

Affectionately known as the Rolls-Royce of motorcycles, the Brough Superior owed its aura of glamour as much to George Brough's showmanship as to his perfectionism. It is true that every Brough Superior had a lavish specification, a superlative finish and a correspondingly high price. But George Brough was essentially a self-publicist. His advertising exploited the fact that the legendary Lawrence of Arabia was one of his loyal customers. And at the annual London motorcycle show he made a habit of exhibiting some exotic new creation every year, several of which were strictly "one-off" products. Some others had a production run of only nine or ten machines.

In the 20 years of its existence the Brough Superior factory produced a total of no more than 3,000 machines, most of them big V-twins with JAP engines. And the first one set the extravagant style for the remainder. To distinguish it from other JAP-engine machines, the overhead valve gear and the lower ends of the cylinders were plated and the crankcase was sandblasted. Also, the bulbous, wedge-shaped black-and-silver tank was lined in gold leaf.

Except for the unconventional 1000 cc four-cylinder Dream exhibited in London in 1937, George Brough used proprietary engines from 500 to 1150 cc – MAG, Barr-and-Stroud and Matchless besides JAP. (Typically, the show model of the Dream was entirely gold-plated and called the Golden Dream.)

The famous SS80, with a 1000 cc side-valve JAP engine and a guarantee of 130 km/h (81 mph), was born in 1923. And to publicize it, George himself stripped and tuned his personal machine (called Old Bill), which won innumerable sprints and was the first side-valve machine to exceed 100 mph (161 km/h) at Brooklands.

Next, in 1924, came the overhead-valve version: the SS100 which, right up to the outbreak of war in 1939, broke many world records and Brooklands solo and sidecar speed records in the hands of such famous riders as Bert Le Vack, Freddie Dixon, Alan Bruce, E. C. E. Baragwanath (Barry), Eric Fernihough and Noel Pope. Several of these riders supercharged the engine.

Meanwhile, to sustain public interest, George Brough showed a succession of highly unorthodox roadsters. These included a 1000 cc side-valve transverse 60° V-four in 1927 and a car-type 900 cc side-valve straight four a year later. In 1931 viewers were stunned by a solo with an 800 cc four-cylinder Austin car engine and two close-coupled rear wheels with the drive shaft between them. And in 1938 there was an SS80 with a 50° Matchless engine installed transversely.

Designed with the help of Freddie Dixon and Ike Hatch (who was involved with the four-valve Excelsior Mechanical Marvel and the three-valve version of the AJS 7R), the flat-four Dream had perfect mechanical balance and excellent cooling. There were two crankshafts (geared together) – the lower one driving the transmission, the upper one the dynamo and ignition distributor. And there was a choice of three speeds with kickstarting or four speeds with hand starting.

However, in the "real world" it was the exploits of Fernihough, Baragwanath and Pope that captured the public imagination. For three years Fernihough fought a single-handed battle against Ernst Henne and the mighty BMW factory for the world speed record. Twice, at Gyon in Hungary, he captured the solo record and once the sidecar record. But in his 1938 bid, with extensive streamlining, he crashed fatally as a result of unsound aerodynamics.

The most advanced version of the Ariel 1,000 cc Square Four engine, with four separate exhaust pipes.

"Old Bill," or George Brough's personal racing bike in 1923: it won no fewer than 51 national acceleration contests and was the first motorcycle with a side valve engine to exceed 100 mph (161 km/h) on the track at Brooklands.

George Brough (with the goggles) at an exhibition in 1956, beside his 1,000 cc Dream four cylinder of 1939. It had cardan shaft transmission. The model shown was gold-plated throughout and was better known as the "Golden Dream."

This picture of the Dream four cylinder, taken from the back, shows the inlet ports, kick starter, gear lever and final drive power take-off.

Baragwanath confined himself to sidecars, breaking world standing-start records, winning sprints galore and reigning as king of Brooklands for many years. It was fitting that his supercharged machine – known to all as Barry's Big Blown Brough – should eventually go to the intrepid Noel Pope, who finally broke both the solo and sidecar Brooklands lap records in 1939. After the war he enclosed the machine completely in a streamline shell and made a bid for the world record at Utah. But his streamlining, too, was unsound and he crashed at 250 km/h (156 mph), fortunately without personal harm.

BSA

BSA, who for over sixty years was one of the most prestigious motorcycle companies on the British market, never regarded the big international competitions as the sole means of advertising and developing its products. The company mainly produced touring and "utilitarian" machines, from the big side-valve V-twins to the 500 cc overhead-valve Sloper, 250 cc side-valve Round-tank and little Bantam two-stroke (originally a German design) produced after the end of the war. Nevertheless there were plenty of sporting successes, particularly in races, the Six Days Trial, trials and motocross events (Jeff Smith won the 500 cc Motocross World Championship in both 1964 and 1965 and was eight times national champion).

Of the various models sold by the company, those that proved most competitive in the different areas were undoubtedly the 350 and 500 cc Gold Stars, two highly versatile machines designed by Val Page in 1937, constantly updated and improved versions of which were sold from 1938 to 1962.

BSA did not confine itself to the classic parallel-twin design used on bikes like the 500 cc A7 and 650 cc Golden Flash, but also produced the 750 cc Rocket Three, a slightly different version of the Triumph Trident.

Jeff Smith, 500 cc motocross world champion in 1964 and 1965, seen here on a BSA Gold Star in 1961.

The first model of a series which was to be world-famous: the BSA 500 cc Gold Star of 1938, derived from the Empire Star, on which Walter Handley achieved 107 mph (172 km/h) at Brooklands.

DOUGLAS

Douglas was another British name whose renown was based on an uncommon engine layout – the smooth-running, horizontally opposed (or boxer) twin. To suit chain drive the engine was mostly installed longitudinally, and mounted transversely only after the company's heyday was past. Two basic versions of the engine achieved distinction, the first having side valves, the second overhead valves.

The side-valve Douglases were mostly mild-mannered machines, culminating in the famous 350 cc EW introduced in 1926 with self-servo brakes and a top speed of 110 km/h (69 mph). But they first made their mark in 1911, when the original model – with an unusually high engine and direct belt drive – slashed the Land's End–John O'Groats (End-to-End) record to 39 hours 40 minutes, for a distance of about 1500 km (928 miles).

The racing version had a two-speed gearbox mounted under the rear cylinder, and in 1912 that was combined with a Scott-type double primary drive to give a total of four ratios. That was the layout used by Bill Bashall to win the Junior TT,

with his team mate Eddie Kickham finishing second and making fastest lap. A similar machine won the Spanish TT. In the following year, Billy Newsome was a close second in the Junior TT before Douglases filled the first three places in the Spanish TT. (Much later, the double primary drive was combined with a three-speed gearbox to provide a very early example of six speeds for racing!)

During the 1914-18 war the factory was fully occupied in supplying 25,000 350 cc side-valve WD machines to the forces. And such was their popularity with the military riders that the makers had a ready market in 1919 for a civilian version, together with a more powerful 600 cc machine that was in great demand for sidecar duty.

Soon afterward Douglas laid the foundations for a decade of sporting glory when they introduced three-speed, overhead-valve machines of 350 and 500 cc, with twin carburetors and disc-type front brakes, the larger model being the more successful. Surprisingly, it was three years before the engine and gearbox changed places – a logical step, since the engine (despite the adoption of aluminum cylinder heads) was considerably heavier than the gearbox, which by then had four speeds.

It took two or three years for the overhead-

The first Douglas, with a 350 cc engine fitted very high up, just below the fuel tank, and direct belt drive. In 1911, one of these bikes broke the Land's End to John O'Groats record.

The 600 cc Douglas opposed twin cylinder, in the 1925 version which earned a very good reputation in sand track and speedway racing.

The Victor is a development of the 250 C15 built by BSA in 1962 for trials competitions. This model is the Roadster Shooting Star 441.

Another Douglas which won the TT in 1923: Freddie Dixon's 600 cc machine, which was very low and fast.

◄ One of the last products by BSA, the A65 Star of 1962, with a 650 cc twin cylinder engine. A 500 cc version of this bike was also produced.

Tom Sheard after winning the Senior TT in 1923. It is interesting to note that someone had already invented the front disc brake over 60 years ago.

valve machines to overcome their initial weaknesses, and during that period their best performance was Cyril Pullin's achievement in exceeding 100 mph on a 500 cc machine for the first time in Britain, when he was electrically timed at 161 km/h for a half-mile (0.8 km).

But the Douglas development engineers were rewarded in 1923, when Tom Sheard won the Senior TT (after his team mate Jim Whalley had made fastest lap) and the legendary Freddie Dixon won the new Sidecar TT with a 600 cc version of the engine in a banking chassis. The following year Dixon made the fastest laps in both the Senior and Sidecar TTs and finished third in the Senior event. Then, in 1925, Len Parker won the Sidecar TT, with Dixon breaking the lap record.

Based on the outstandingly fast TT machines, the SW5 and SW6 catalogue racing models were already highly successful in sand racing when speedway racing came to Britain in 1928. With the brakes and left-side footrest removed they were soon supreme in the new sport, and Douglas achieved the pinnacle of their fame through the spectacular victories of Australian Vic Huxley and other superstars. In 1929 alone, the company sold 1300 DT5 and DT6 speedway racers.

When the Douglas family left in 1932, the company's policy changed completely. From 1935 onward there was a succession of transverse-engine models – first the side-valve 500 cc Endeavour with shaft drive, then a variety of overhead-valve 350s after the War. Alas, the glory days were gone and Douglas ceased production in the mid 1950s.

EXCELSIOR

Among the smaller manufacturers, Excelsior and New Imperial might have remained little known if it were not for the fascinating 250 cc single-cylinder engines they built to win the Lightweight TT in 1933 (Excelsior) and 1936 (New Imperial).

Inspired by the overwhelming successes of the

radial-valve Rudges in 1930 and 1931, Excelsior persuaded Ike Hatch (of Burney and Blackbourne) to design a radial-valve engine which they hoped would be even better than the Rudge – because they insisted that each inlet valve had an entirely independent downdraft port and Amal carburetor.

Across the front and rear of the crankcase mouth were separate camshafts, which opened the four valves through sloping push rods and rockers. That complex valve gear and the two carburetors caused the machine to be known as the Mechanical Marvel. Riding it in its very first race, Sid Gleave won the TT at record speed.

Subsequent changes included Bowden carburetors in 1934 and a single overhead camshaft, operating the valves through six Rudge-type rockers, in 1936. But the initial success was never repeated and Excelsior withdrew from racing in 1938, though continuing to sell Manxman series-production racers with conventional two-valve overhead-camshaft engines.

The Mechanical Marvel of 1934 used Bowden carburetors with butterfly valves. The port timing system had four valves, fitted radially.

In 1933 Sid Gleave won the Lightweight TT on the original version of the 250 cc Excelsior Mechanical Marvel, with four valves and Amal carburetors.

MATCHLESS

At the London show in the autumn of 1930, the 500 cc "Squariel" was not the only exciting overhead-camshaft four to make its debut. There was also the Matchless Silver Hawk, a 26° V-four that seemed even more desirable. It had not only an extra 100 cc but four speeds instead of three, battery ignition, rear springing and coupled brakes. And it was mechanically quieter, since it had no crankshaft coupling gears. At the time, it would have seemed inconceivable that the Silver Hawk would die within five years (with a total production of little more than 500) while the Square Four would evolve and survive for more than a quarter-century.

A year earlier Matchless had tested the monobloc cylinder construction, rear springing and coupled brakes in the 400 cc side-valve, three-speed Silver Arrow. That quiet, docile machine lasted only four years because of its mediocre performance. But the Silver Hawk was capable of surging acceleration and more than 130 km/h (81 mph), yet it would dawdle at a walking speed in top gear and could even be started by hand. Unfortunately, a tendency for the iron cylinder head to overheat was not rectified. More importantly – despite its many charms and technical ingenuity – it proved too expensive for the market, which has always preferred cheap performance to expensive refinement.

Founded by the Collier brothers in 1899, the Matchless factory enjoyed its racing heyday within the first decade. During that period Charles and Harry Collier together won three TT races (with two lap records) and established speed records for one hour, 24 hours and one mile, riding singles and V-twins with proprietary engines. Many years later their own 1000 cc Model H V-twin was famous for sidecar duty, while their 350 and 500 cc overhead-valve singles

This 400 cc Silver Arrow, ancestor of the Matchless Silver Hawk V-four, had a 26 degree Vee twin-cylinder side-valve engine. It also had rear suspension and interlinked brakes (integral braking).

One of the 50 500 cc scramblers (with no suspension or front brake) which were exported to California in 1957 to compete in one of the many track events which had become popular overseas: flat track racing. These bikes were nicknamed "sawn-off shotguns" because of their short exhaust pipes, which normally had no silencers. During a trial on a Matchless Sport Twin in 1958, Vic Willoughby touched 166 km/h (102 mph) on the MIRA circuit.

gained many successes in trials and scrambles.

Like AJS, Ariel, BSA, Norton and Royal Enfield, they followed the Triumph fashion of vertical-twin engines, the Matchless Sports Twin being particularly popular. But although it had a third main bearing in the middle of the crankshaft, it vibrated as much as rival twins with only two main bearings.

Surprisingly, the racing version of the twin (the G45) was not a success – and it was outclassed from 1959 onward by the single-cylinder Matchless G50, which was a 500 cc version of the 350 cc AJS 7R. Private owners much preferred the G50 to the Manx Norton because the engine was oiltight and trouble-free and had better acceleration. Indeed, Alan Shepherd, on a G50, finished second to Mike Hailwood (on the MV Agusta four) in the 500 cc World Championship in 1962 and 1963.

In the early sixties, Matchless models were the same as AJS ones, only the name differing. This is a 650 cc Majestic twin cylinder.

◄ A 350 cc single cylinder trials bike of 1959.

NEW IMPERIAL

New Imperial's straightforward push rod overhead-valve singles, with all-chain drive, already had a proud racing history, having won two Junior and three Lightweight TTs between 1921 and 1932. But in 1932 the factory had taken the bold decision to abandon the primary chain on all its catalogue models and adopt the continental practice of building the engine and gearbox as a single unit with primary drive by gears. After three years they decided they could sell more of those machines – the 150 cc Unit Minor, 250 cc Unit Super, 350 cc Unit Plus and 500-550 cc Unit Major – if the works racing machines also had unit construction and gear primary drive.

So one (and only one) machine was converted (with the engine running backward) and Bob Foster won New Imperial's last TT at record speed while on his honeymoon! It was a gallant personal and technical achievement.

On that basis the best-remembered name in British motorcycling is undoubtedly Norton, whose worldwide renown was based chiefly on the phenomenal successes of their works overhead-camshaft singles, especially in the prestigious Isle of Man TT races, throughout the 1930s and again for the first seven or eight years after the war.

NORTON

Norton's first TT victory was in 1907, when Rem Fowler won the twin-cylinder class on a machine with a Peugeot V-twin engine with automatic inlet valves. Nearly 20 years later a new 500 cc push rod overhead-valve engine scored two wins in the Senior TT – Alec Bennett in 1924, Stanley Woods in 1926 – and one in the Sidecar TT – George Tucker (1924). But it was the debut of the overhead-camshaft engine in 1927, when Bennett again won the Senior, that started Norton's long dominance of European road racing.

Designed by Walter Moore (who later went to NSU), modified by Arthur Carroll a few years later and painstakingly developed from then on by the legendary Joe Craig, the engine quickly acquired such a sterling reputation for reliability and speed that the Norton team became a magnet for the world's finest riders, including (before the war) not only Bennett and Woods but also Jimmy Guthrie, Tim Hunt, Jimmy Simpson, "Crasher" White, Walter Rusk, Freddie Frith and Harold Daniell.

In 1935, Stanley Woods' sensational win in the Senior TT on a rear-sprung 120° Moto Guzzi twin gave a warning that the single-cylinder unsprung racing machine was doomed – and the lesson was soon emphasized by Georg Meier's supercharged BMW twin and Dorino Serafini's supercharged Gilera four. At last, the end seemed to be in sight for Joe Craig's proud Nortons. But when

Rem Fowler pictured beside the Peugeot-engined twin cylinder machine on which he won the first edition of the Tourist Trophy, back in 1907.

In 1935 at Montlhéry, Jimmy Guthrie raised the hour speed record to 183.5 km/h (114 mph) on a 500 cc Norton single cylinder.

Like many other motorcycle companies, Norton signed a contract in 1939 to supply motorbikes to the Army. The model chosen was a redesigned version of the old side valve 16H. These rugged machines were widely used even in Africa, where they withstood the torrid climate well. The ones left over from the war helped supply the civilian market until Norton could resume normal production.

In 1938, as works rider for Norton, Harold Daniell had the first of his three victories in the Senior TT. Note the old style frame, of the single, open cradle type.

The Norton single cylinder engine of 1930-36, with overhead camshaft valve gear.

Norton Manx 500 cc racing bike, 1960 production model. Note the twin cam front drum brake.

international racing restarted after the war, three events combined to grant them a reprieve. First, supercharging was banned. Second, a new bunch of superstars flocked to the team, including Geoff Duke, Artie Bell, Reg Armstrong, Ray Amm, Ken Kavanagh and sidecar ace Eric Oliver. Third, Irishman Rex McCandless designed a much better frame – the so-called featherbed with pivoted rear suspension.

In total (starting in 1907) Norton riders won 33 TT races, filling the first three places 11 times. They won 11 European Championships before the war and eight world titles afterwards. And they broke the world one-hour record three times – Bill Lacey in 1931, Jimmy Guthrie in 1935 and Ray Amm in 1953. It all added up to a magnificent achievement.

Surprisingly – except for the ohc Manx racers and the International supersports models – the series-production single-cylinder roadsters never reflected the manufacturers' high reputation. They were commonplace in design and too expensive (in order to pay for the factory's racing activities!). In the early 1950s, however, Bert Hopwood designed the 500 cc Dominator vertical-twin engine. Once this was put in the featherbed frame it sparked off an extremely popular range of roadsters that soon grew to 600 cc, then 650 cc (the SS model) and 750 cc (the

Geoff Duke won the Junior TT in 1952, on a machine with a "postwar" closed, duplex cradle frame.

The Electra 400 of 1963 was derived from the Navigator of 1961. The engine was a vertical twin cylinder with electric start.

◀ Another twin cylinder engine, but 750 cc this time, for the Atlas of 1963.

The Norton Commando, derived from the Atlas (on the left is the roadster version of 1970) was clearly a sports machine. The engine was a 750 cc twin cylinder, later increased to 830 cc. The frame used the Isolastic system with rubber fittings to isolate it from the engine vibrations. The roadster and fastback versions were soon joined by a production racer. (PR, right).

Atlas). Finally, the biggest engine was canted forward and rubber-mounted in a new "backbone" frame to make the Commando, which was eventually bored out to 830 cc.

Though it was essentially a touring machine the Commando achieved a spectacular success in 1973, when development engineer Peter Williams tuned one of the 750 cc engines, stiffened the gearbox, made his own monocoque chassis-cum-fuel tank and scored a record-shattering, start-to-finish victory in the Formula 750 TT. It was a performance worthy of the manufacturers' great tradition.

At the time of writing, a handful of engineers are trying to perpetuate the name of Norton with an Interpol model powered by a twin-rotor Wankel engine. Several machines have been supplied to the British police but none to the civilian market.

ROYAL ENFIELD

Although they produced some tiny two-strokes and overhead-valve four-strokes from time to time, Royal Enfield were best known for reliable side-valve V-twins of 1000 and 1150 cc for sidecar duty – also for the 350 and 500 cc Bullet sports models and vertical twins of 500 cc (Twin and Meteor Minor), 700 cc (Meteor, Super Meteor and Constellation) and 736 cc (Interceptor). Well-known Royal Enfield design features included the rubber "cush-drive" in the rear hub (giving exceptionally sweet transmission), the integration of the oil sump with the crankcase and a floating shoe assembly in the front brake (giving a self-servo effect).

RUDGE WHITWORTH

Rudge Whitworth may not have been the first British manufacturer to specialize in four-valve cylinder heads (the Triumph Ricardo had appeared three years earlier, in 1921) but they certainly exploited the layout more successfully than any of their rivals, both for Grand Prix racing and for series production.

When Honda riders won 16 World Championships between 1961 and 1967, a myth was born that they had invented the four-valve arrangement with two pairs of parallel valves in a pent-roof head. In fact Rudge were breaking records and winning Grands Prix (including the Senior TT and European 500 cc Championship) with the same basic arrangement more than 30 years earlier.

In 1930 Rudge patented an improved design, in which the four valves were arranged radially. For several years that was sensationally successful in Junior and Lightweight TT races and other Grands Prix (including two European Champion-

After having competed for years on big Norton machines, Jimmy Simpson won his last TT, the Lightweight of 1934, on a Rudge 250 with radial valves.

In 1930 Rudge machines won two TT events with two different types of four valve engine. Here we see Walter Handley competing in the Senior event.

ships). And once more Honda "reinvented" the arrangement – 50 years later. But Rudge's most elegant four-valve arrangement – the famous semi-radial layout, with parallel inlet valves and radial exhausts – has yet to be "rediscovered" by the Japanese. It was introduced on the works 500 cc racing engine in 1931 and standardized on the supersports Ulster model from 1933 to 1939, when the war stopped production.

From the start of production in 1911 Rudge were in the forefront of technical progress. That year they introduced the Rudge Multi direct belt-drive transmission in which the pulleys on the crankshaft and rear wheel could be expanded and contracted in opposition by a lever to alter the overall gear ratio quite widely. A Rudge Multi, ridden by Cyril Pullin, won the 1914 Senior TT. In 1924 Rudge were the first to fit four-speed gearboxes. They were also the first to couple the front and rear brakes, and in 1931 the first to fit megaphones to their racing exhaust pipes. In the same year they experimented with a supercharged 250 cc V-twin with radial valves.

All Rudge's TT successes were especially convincing. Pullin's winning margin in 1914 was 6.30 minutes; the 1930 Senior race was run in the rain – yet Wal Handley established lap and race records, backed up by Graham Walker in second place. In the Junior race the same week, Tyrrell Smith, Ernie Nott and Walker filled the first three places with the new radial-valve engine. A year later Walker, Smith and Nott finished first, second and fourth on 250 cc radial-valve Rudges; and in 1934, a year after the factory had stopped racing, Jimmy Simpson, Nott and Walker rode the same machines privately to fill the first three places in the Lightweight event. And throughout the factory's racing activities, all successful innovations were incorporated in the following year's production machines.

Those models catered for the tourist, the amateur racer, the speedway rider and the Six Days cross-country trials rider. The Rudge Ulster remained the most popular model; although it was descended from the 1928 works racing machine, and was capable of 140 km/h (87 mph), it was also a "civilized" motorcycle with a hand-operated center stand, enclosed valve gear and an aluminum cylinder head.

SCOTT

In 1908 – when most British motorcycles were four-stroke singles with staccato power impulses and exhaust beats – the smooth torque and musical hum of a two-stroke twin would have been welcome, even without the genius of Alfred Scott's design. But Scott's new and highly unconventional 333 cc machine was not only quiet and unobtrusive: it also had a deceptively fine all-round performance, as competitors soon discovered at the prestigious Newnham hill-climb in the Midlands.

While other riders pushed their machines into life, Scott straddled his light, low-slung twin and paddled off effortlessly. Making little more noise than a purring cat, he then trounced his rivals with three devastating climbs – easily out-accelerating all the four-strokes and cornering more quickly too. That remarkable exhibition won him the twin-cylinder class, the variable-gear class and the open class, and he finally rode off with three gold medals. Such was the impact of that and subsequent performances that for the next three years the Auto-Cycle Union (the British sport's rule-makers) imposed a 25 percent handicap on the engine's capacity.

The secret of the machine's superiority lay in a technical specification that was in some ways as much as half a century ahead of its time. Scott chose the 180° parallel-twin layout, nowadays such a darling of the Japanese industry. He used all-chain transmission from the start of production in 1908. And his two-speed gear – with a rocking pedal to select either of two primary drives flanking the central flywheel – was positive and efficient.

The low open frame, of which the engine was an integral part, was a triangulated structure of straight tubes. And the telescopic front fork, though undamped, was strongly braced. The result was a low center of gravity and light, precise handling.

It is a remarkable tribute to Alfred Scott's foresight that the basic features of his design – engine, transmission and chassis – remained practically unchanged throughout more than two decades of high popularity during which his 500 and 600 cc Squirrel, Super Squirrel and Flying Squirrel roadsters – so distinctive in appearance – established a cult of almost religious fervour.

One of Alfred Scott's main preoccupations in the early years was the method of engine cooling. Dissatisfied with air cooling of both cylinders and heads, he tried water cooling – first of the heads only, then (more logically) of the cylinders only (to prevent distortion), before settling for total water cooling in 1914.

Another line of investigation was the use of a (cylindrical) rotary inlet valve to bypass the symmetrical port timing inseparable from piston control. Unlike modern rotary valves, however, Scott's valve also controlled the transfer ports. A year before the rotary-valve experiment, a Scott had made TT history by being the first two-stroke

Frank Philipp, one of the first aces to race for Scott, on a 1910 twin cylinder with two speed gears and air cooling; the bike had a few progressive features, such as an open frame and telescopic front fork.

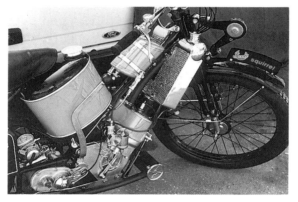

After the death of Alfred Scott in 1923, Scott bikes progressively lost the creative flair which had characterized all the new design. This model, from 1940, has a deformable parallelogramme front fork and foot-operated gears but has kept the open frame structure.

to complete the 255-km (159-mile) race.

When the chain-driven rotary valve was introduced in 1911, there was the added innovation that the engine was controlled not by a throttle in the carburetor but by advancing and retarding the timing of the valve. On the new and notorious 61-km (37-mile) Isle of Man Mountain course, Frank Philipp demonstrated the engine's potential by establishing the lap record at 80.63 km/h (50 mph). For the 1912 Senior TT the rotary valve was driven by gears instead of a chain, and the conventional throttle control was reinstated. Frank Appleby made the fastest lap and won by nearly seven minutes – and Philipp was a comfortable second until tyre trouble delayed him on the final lap.

With dual ignition and larger ports in 1913, Appleby led from the start but soon retired, leaving Tim Wood, a factory mechanic in his very first race, to uphold the factory's honour. Despite many stops to repair and replenish a leaking radiator, he raised the lap record to 83.86 km/h (52 mph) and won by five seconds – with a nail in the rear tyre! The following year Wood immediately hoisted the lap record to 86.08 km/h (54 mph), though mechanical trouble cost him the race.

Before racing resumed after the war, Alfred Scott left the company in 1919 to produce the unconventional Scott Sociable three-wheeler. And although the loss of his influence marked the beginning of a gradual decline in technical innovation (he died four years later), the popularity of the company's machines blossomed in the first postwar decade.

Their versatility and endurance was shown in 1920, when Scott machines won the team prize in the tough A-CU Six Days Trial. An aluminum cylinder block was introduced in 1921, and aluminum heads followed two years later. Harry Langman finished third in the 1922 Senior TT, second in 1924, and made the fastest lap in the new sidecar TT in 1923. Tommy Hatch was third in the 1928 Senior TT.

Except for the early rotary valve, Scott racers were substantially similar to the piston-ported

catalogue models. So the Squirrel sports model had a fanatical reception when it was marketed in 1922, as did the Super Squirrel in 1925 and the supertuned Flying Squirrel in 1926. Out-and-out racing versions included the Power-Plus TT Replica, the Sprint Special and the Speedway Special, which earned fame through the exploits of Eric and Oliver Langton and Frank Varey.

In the following years competition successes declined, while transmission, frame and fork design became orthodox. A spark of originality flared in 1934 with an experimental 1000 cc three-cylinder machine with fore-and-aft crankshaft. But the undying memory of the Scott Squirrels remains as a tribute to a British genius.

SUNBEAM

No British manufacturer established a higher reputation for the quality of it products than Sunbeam. Built by John Marston of Wolverhampton from 1913 to the early 1930s, Sunbeam machines were always sound and straightforward in design rather than exciting, but their workmanship was superlative and their black-and-gold finish immaculate.

At first they produced side-valve singles and V-twins, all with the luxury of oilbath cases enclosing both primary and secondary chains. Detail design was so thorough that they soon acquired a reputation for outstanding reliability. Indeed, Sunbeam's first two TT victories were achieved with side-valve engines. Those were the 1920 Senior race, won at record speed by Tommy de la Haye, with George Dance setting the lap record; and the 1922 Senior, in which Alec Bennett established both race and lap records.

It was company policy to race standard supersports models meticulously prepared in the factory rather than design special Grand Prix machines, and that policy was continued throughout the heyday of the push rod overhead-valve Sunbeams a few years later.

Unquestionably the most famous of those ohv singles was the 500 cc Model 90, on which the tiny but tough Charlie Dodson won the 1928 and 1929 Senior TTs; this was also marketed in touring guise as the Model 9. Dodson weighed only 54 kg (119 lb) (6 kg = 13 lb below the present minimum limit!) and had to have the riding position completely altered to suit his stature.

Sunbeam's first 500 cc overhead-valve engine, with a single exhaust pipe, was made in 1923 and George Dance quickly became king of the British sprint strips on a lightened machine capable of 145 km/h (89 mph). The following year both 350 and 500 cc versions were successful in several European Grands Prix, and Dance broke the one-hour and two-hour records in the 350 cc class.

The familiar twin-exhaust version of the engine appeared in 1925, with an overhead camshaft and hairpin valve springs (for the first time on a motorcycle). But the ohc engine lacked some of the pep of its predecessor, and push rods were

On a lightened version of the Sunbeam 500 with overhead valve gear (and a single exhaust pipe) George Dance was virtually unbeatable in acceleration contests for the entire 1923 season.

reinstated for 1926.

That layout then formed the basis for all subsequent sports and racing Sunbeams. Ridden by Dodson and Graham Walker (nearly twice Dodson's weight!), they enjoyed four years of considerable success. Besides Dodson's two TT victories, there were wins in the Ulster G.P. (twice), the 1929 French and Belgian G.P.s, and the 1927 European 500 cc G.P. on the Nürburgring, where D'Eternod, a Swiss sidecar driver, also took the 600 cc sidecar title.

After those four happy years Sunbeam fortunes waned, for sales of luxury machines plummeted in the industrial depression. The company was taken over first by ICI, then by AMC and finally by BSA. As a result the old Marston traditions were abandoned and design policy was radically changed. A range of high-camshaft, short push rod singles appeared just before the war; after the war came the S7 (touring) and S8 (sports) tandem vertical twins, with overhead camshafts and shaft final drive. They were all so different from the John Marston models as to be unrecognizable as Sunbeams.

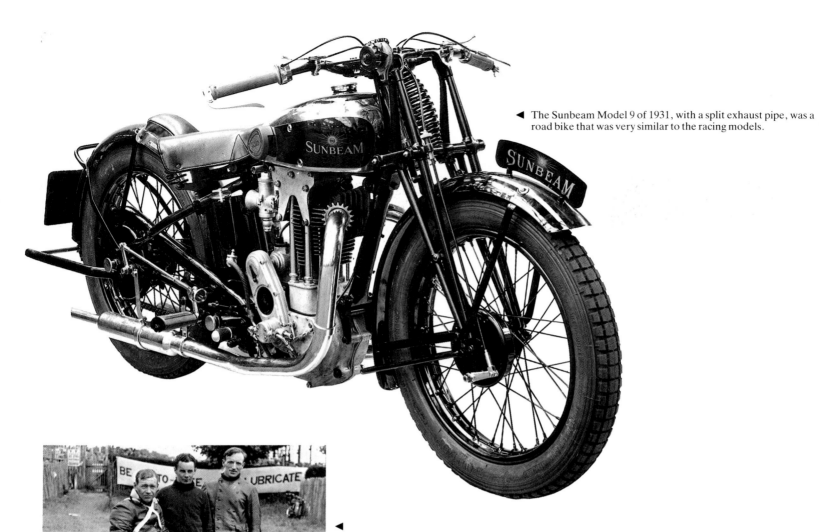

◀ The Sunbeam Model 9 of 1931, with a split exhaust pipe, was a road bike that was very similar to the racing models.

◀
Charlie Dodson (center), winner of the 1929 Senior TT, with his teammate Arthur Simcock (left) and Alec Bennett, with a specially prepared Model 90.

◀ The Sunbeam S7 500 was a successful touring model. The engine was a vertical twin cylinder with an overhead camshaft and cardan shaft transmission.

TRIUMPH

When Triumph launched the handsome 500 cc Speed Twin in 1938, they started a fashion that spread worldwide and is still alive. Designed by Edward Turner, the Speed Twin was often criticized for its engine vibration and skittish handling. But it was so successful commercially that most rival manufacturers quickly introduced similar vertical twins.

Yet the Speed Twin was by no means Triumph's first vertical twin. More than a quarter-century earlier they had made a 600 cc side-valve parallel twin with a 180° crankshaft. But the outbreak of war in 1914 killed the plans for its production. Twenty years later, Val Page designed a 650 cc overhead-valve vertical twin (Model 6/1) with 360° crank spacing and the unusual feature of double helical gears instead of a chain to drive the gearbox. That model immediately proved sufficiently robust and reliable for Harry Perrey to win a sidecar gold medal in the 1933 International Six Days Trial in Wales. But it was too expensive and bulky for commercial success and went out of production in 1936.

Before the birth of the Speed Twin, the factory built its reputation on single-cylinder machines. Riding one of the early side-valve models, Jack Marshall won the single-cylinder class of the 1908 TT. The 550 cc Model H was popular for many years before and after the 1914-18 war and was supplied in its thousands to the British army during that conflict.

The first overhead-valve Triumph was the four-valve Model R, designed by the famous engineer Harry Ricardo in 1921 as a supersports version of the model H. Ridden by Frank Halford, it quickly established world 500 cc records for one hour, one mile and 50 miles. The following year Walter Brandish, a newcomer to the TT, rode a Model R into second place in the Senior race behind Alec Bennett (Sunbeam). In 1923 four-valve Triumphs won Grands Prix in

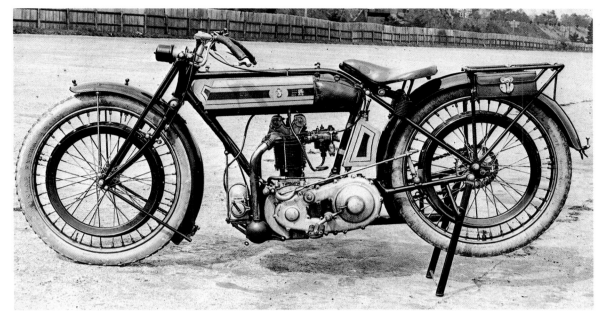

The prototype of the Triumph Ricardo on the Brooklands circuit. It was really a side valve Model H 550, the cylinder of which had been replaced by a 500 cc cast iron one with four valves in the cylinder head.

several countries, earned ISDT gold medals in Scandinavia and filled the first three places in the Liège–Paris–Liège marathon. But when Brandish, favourite to win the Senior TT, crashed during practice and broke a leg, the factory transferred its development efforts to a two-valve model on which Victor Horsman was breaking records galore at Brooklands. After he had raised the one-hour record in three successive years (1923, 1924 and 1925) the two-valve machine was put in series production as the Model T.

Another Val Page design in the mid 1930s was a range of sporting singles – the 250 cc Tiger 70, 350 cc Tiger 80 and 500 cc Tiger 90 – which were in great demand until Triumph decided to concentrate on the Speed Twin. A year later came a supersports twin – the Tiger 100 – which scored many sporting successes over a long period, both before the war at Brooklands and afterward in drag racing.

But Triumph's greatest popularity and sporting successes were achieved after the engine size was increased for 1950 and particularly after Doug

The 500 cc Speed Twin of 1938 on the track at Brooklands on the occasion of its official press release. This bike started the worldwide fashion for forward-facing vertical twin cylinders.

The first Triumph Ricardo engine. Note the parallel inlet valves and some of the five long studs fixing the cylinder head.

One of the TR5s belonging to the British team which won the International Six Days Trial in 1949. It used the same engine block as the Tiger 100.

Hele, one of Britain's finest development engineers, joined the factory from Norton in 1962. To introduce the 650 cc Thunderbird, the first three production machines were taken to Montlhéry, where they completed a 5½-hour high-speed marathon, finally lapping at more than 160 km/h (100 mph).

A few years later the supersports 650 cc Tiger 110 was marketed – and in 1958 Mike Hailwood and Dan Shorey rode one to victory in the Thruxton 500-mile (800-km) race. Later the same year, on the Bonneville salt lake in Utah, Bill Johnson raised the American Class C record (for 650 cc stock machines) to 237 km/h (148 mph), using a Tiger 110 with two carburetors – hence the new twin-carburetor Bonneville in the 1959 Triumph catalogue. In 1962 Johnson put a Bonneville engine in a streamline shell and broke the American speed record at 370 km/h (232 mph).

Doug Hele's work improved Triumph handling as much as engine performance, and in both 1967 and 1969 Bonnevilles won the 750 cc class of the Production Machine TT as well as the Brands Hatch and Thruxton 500-mile races. Doug Hele also prepared the 500 cc twins that filled the first two places in the 1967 Daytona 200, more than a lap ahead of the best 750 cc Harley-Davidson. Then – wanting a full-size 750 cc machine without the vibration of a big vertical twin – he added a third cylinder to the 500 cc twin to make the Trident, which won the first two Formula 750 TT races and every 750 Production Machine TT from 1970 to 1975.

Triumph machines were very versatile. As an example, the TR5 (a single-carburetor 500 cc twin) could be supplied for commuting, clubman racing, scrambling (motocross) or trials riding. At San Remo in 1948, the British teams rode TR5s in the International Six Days Trial and won both the Trophy and Vase competitions.

During the 1939-45 war the original factory in

Mike Hailwood, who together with Dan Shorey, won the 500 mile Thruxton race (1958) on a 650 cc Tiger 110.

Bill Johnson (second from left) with Joe Dudeck (second from right) in 1962, immediately after having established a new American speed record of 370 km/h (230 mph). Joe Dudeck designed the aerodynamic fairing enclosing the rider's seat and the 650 cc Bonneville engine fed by two carburetors.

The Triumph Thunderbird of 1963 proved a good production model for its displacement, i.e. 650 cc.

The Trident 750 of 1968 had a reliable and powerful engine with three cylinders side-by-side.

Coventry was destroyed by bombing and subsequent production moved to Meriden. Periodically that factory was plagued by industrial unrest, and as the industry contracted in the mid 1970s the shop-floor workers occupied the premises to prevent closure. With government assistance they eventually formed a cooperative. Alas, it proved better at producing huge debts than good motorcycles.

VELOCETTE

In the marketplace Velocette occupied a higher niche than Norton, appealing more strongly to connoisseurs of fine engineering. Yet their worldwide reputation, too, was based largely on achievements in international road racing. It is true that they won fewer TT races (eight), European Championships (three) and World Championships (two) than Norton. But that comparison reflected nothing more than the small size of the company (a family concern founded by the brothers Percy and Eugene Goodman) and the relative lack of strength-in-depth in their racing team.

Certainly there was no technical inferiority at Velocette. Indeed, they were a year ahead of Norton in winning a TT (the 1926 Junior) with a new design of overhead-camshaft engine (350 cc). But whereas Norton's 1927 engine could be regarded as little more than their successful push rod engine with a change of valve operation, Velocette had no such four-stroke experience to help them. Previously they were best known for a range of lively 250 cc two-strokes which eventually blossomed into the famous GTP – a handsome, reliable, economical touring machine capable of 100 km/h (70 mph). Yet their first overhead-camshaft machine (the work of Percy Goodman) was so sound in design that it won that 1926 TT race by the enormous margin of more than ten minutes.

Happily, Velocette were quick to give their ordinary customers the benefit of their racing experience by immediately marketing a sporting roadster (the KSS) with a guarantee of 130 km/h (81 mph). It was the first of a popular range of refined ohc roadsters with various levels of equipment.

When Harold Willis, himself a first-class TT rider, joined the company as development engineer in 1927 he soon enhanced Velocette's reputation for technical innovation. The following year they pioneered the ratchet-type foot gear change (now universal), experimented with pivoted rear springing, won their second Junior TT and many European Grands Prix, then established a string of world long-distance records from one hour to 12 hours. And once again the customer benefited, for in 1929 the company marketed the first genuine racing machine to go into series production: the Mark 1 KTT.

In 1931 and 1932 there was an abortive experiment with supercharging (always difficult with a single-cylinder engine). But throughout the

The Model KN, one of the first sports versions of the ohc Velocette 350 cc.

Bob Foster won the 1948 Belgian Grand Prix, on the Francorchamps circuit on a Velocette Mark 8 KTT. Two years later, he won the 350 cc class world title.

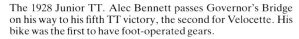

The 1928 Junior TT. Alec Bennett passes Governor's Bridge on his way to his fifth TT victory, the second for Velocette. His bike was the first to have foot-operated gears.

This is a Velocette Venom Thruxton of 1964. It had a 500 cc four stroke single cylinder engine (bore and stroke = 86 x 86 mm) with push rod valve gear, delivering 42 HP. It was the last sports bike by this famous British company.

decade the KTT continued to follow closely the development of the works machines, so that it was always in great demand by amateur racing men. The latest and greatest KTT was the Mark 8, marketed in 1939. It was an almost identical replica of the machine on which Stanley Woods won the Junior TT in 1938 and 1939, complete with massive cylinder and head finning and oil-damped air springing at the rear – a feature only recently resurrected by the Japanese.

But the most exciting example of Velocette's technical enterprise was the 500 cc supercharged vertical twin designed and built by Harold Willis in 1939 to challenge BMW and Gilera in 1940. It had two crankshafts geared together to rotate in opposite directions – one driving the super-charger, the other the transmission – with the cardan shaft enclosed in the left arm of the rear fork. Because of its deep exhaust note, Willis called it "The Roarer."

Tragically, Willis died of meningitis during the 1939 TT period, when Stanley Woods had ridden the machine for only two tentative but very promising practice laps. In any case, the war halted The Roarer's development and super-charging was banned when racing resumed in 1946.

Meanwhile the GTP two-stroke was dropped from the catalogue in the mid 1930s, following the introduction of the 250 cc MOV – a high cam-shaft four-stroke single with push rod valve gear, designed to offer refinement at a lower price than was possible with an overhead camshaft. The MOV was quickly followed by the 350 cc MAC and 500 cc MSS, both of similar layout. Inevitably, sports versions were marketed – the 350 cc Viper and 500 cc Venom – followed by the supersports 500 cc Thruxton, which was very popular for clubman racing.

Surprisingly, at the opposite end of the motorcycling spectrum, Velocette marketed the 150 cc LE utility model in 1948. With extensive enclosure, voluminous mudguards, legshields, footboards and luggage panniers, it was clean, comfortable and convenient to ride. Starting and gear change were by hand. The transverse boxer engine (soon increased to 200 cc) had side valves and water cooling, and was extraordinarily quiet and economical. However, civilian sales were never large and the LE was kept alive for many years by police contracts.

Alas, the postwar years soon proved that Velocette had no engineers capable of following in the footsteps of Harold Willis or the ageing Percy and Eugene Goodman – so design rapidly stagnated and the company died.

VINCENT

A British big-V-twin that needed no showman-ship, yet established an even sounder reputation and broke many more records, was the 1000 cc Vincent HRD (later simply Vincent). A late-comer to the industry, Phil Vincent bought the defunct HRD concern in 1928 to produce his patented spring frame, fitted with proprietary JAP and Python (Rudge) engines. Three years later he was joined by the famous Australian engineer Phil Irving. And the eventual worldwide renown of the small factory was entirely due to the blending of their very different temperaments – Vincent a dreamer, Irving practical and realistic.

Dual brakes were introduced in 1934. But that was also the year when the factory suffered overwhelming troubles with the JAP engines when they made their debut in the Senior TT. At the same time, the supply of Python engines came to an end. So Irving quickly designed an entirely new 500 cc single-cylinder engine that was an immediate success – and formed the basis for all Vincent machines from then on.

Available as the Meteor (standard), Comet (sports) and TT Replica (racing), the new model had been in production for only a year when Irving grafted two Meteor cylinders and heads onto a common crankcase, and so the 1000 cc Series A Rapide appeared in the 1937 Vincent-HRD catalogue. It was, as the advertisements claimed, the world's fastest standard motorcycle, capable of 180 km/h (120 mph) with full touring equipment.

Beloved by long-distance tourists and amateur sportsmen alike, it had one weakness: the engine's enormous torque was too much for the separate heavyweight Burman four-speed gear-box and clutch, which was the strongest available. Immediately after the war that problem was solved when the factory had the courage to launch the radical Series B Rapide, with self-servo clutch and integral engine and gearbox. There was no conventional frame – the power unit and 3.30-liter oil tank connected the steering head to the rear suspension.

The new model was a sensation and soon there was a sporting version, the Black Shadow (capable of nearly 200 km/h = 140 mph) and a racing version, the Black Lightning. Then came the Series C with a forged aluminum front fork and hydraulic damping front and rear.

Magnificently though the postwar twin fulfilled its purpose as an effortless tourer, its fame spread quickest through its overwhelming sporting successes in hill-climbs, sprints, clubman racing and national and world speed records. Those achievements were much too numerous to list here. In Britain George Brown alone broke more than 30 British speed records – and well over half of them were world records too. André Milhoux set records in Belgium, Rollie Free in the U.S.A., while South African and Australian records tumbled too. Finally, in 1955, Russell Wright and Bobbie Burns broke the world solo (298 km/h = 209 mph) and sidecar (262 km/h = 163 mph) records on a narrow road in New Zealand – and Burns went faster still at Utah later on.

In 1950 Vincent reintroduced 500 cc singles. And it was on the racing version, the Grey Flash, that John Surtees started the brilliant career that culminated in his seven World Championships for MV Agusta and one for Ferrari.

The final version of the big twin was the 1955 enclosed Series D Black Knight (Rapide equiv-alent) and Black Prince (Black Shadow equiv-alent). Since Irving had returned to Australia several years earlier, the ideas was Phil Vincent's alone. Unfortunately it was not a commercial success. The luxury market was in decline, and Vincent soon ceased production.

George Brown's bike Nero. This was a racing version of the Vincent twin cylinder, designed after the war. The front fork was from an AJS 7R, while the swinging rear fork was made by Velocette. Later, Brown built a supercharged engine. ▶

The 1,000 cc Vincent Black Shadow had a four stroke, twin cylinder engine with push rod valve gear, delivering 55 HP. Twin carburetors; special hydraulic front fork; cantilever rear suspension (1949). ▼

ITALY

We in Italy have a great motorcycling tradition: a veritable history of sporting and commercial achievements. We are great not just for the victories we have won, but for the brands that have competed on the racetrack and for our technological research. Two names sum it up: MV and Gilera. Unfortunately, we have suffered from a lack of protagonists in both sectors in recent years and are only now beginning to recover. When Italian riders were capable of winning again (I am referring to Lucchinelli and Uncini, in 1981 and 1982) the industry was not ready for them and we thus lost a good opportunity. But matters have improved a great deal now even if we are, alas, no longer at the forefront of racing events. The Italian motorcyclist is keenly aware of all the changes that are taking place in the sector and well able to compete and I do not doubt that within a few years, he will be able to find "at home" what he has been obliged to purchase abroad up till now.

GIACOMO AGOSTINI

The pioneer Italian brands

BIANCHI

In 1885 at the age of 18, after a three-year apprenticeship, Edoardo Bianchi opened a small machine shop in Milan for building velocipedes, electric bells and surgical instruments. Having abandoned the latter almost immediately, Bianchi concentrated on bicycles and as a result was one of the first Italians to become interested in motorcycles too. In 1897 he decided to test the prototype himself, with somewhat disastrous results. But Bianchi was a very determined man and, realizing that two-wheeled motorized vehicles had a future, he pursued his goals relentlessly, constantly testing and improving his designs. His efforts were well rewarded, Bianchi machines in fact being among the very few Italian brands that were truly abreast of the times. Indeed, the 500 cc C 75 single-cylinder and G 650 twin-cylinder proved highly successful as military vehicles in World War One. In the twenties and thirties Bianchi focused on 175, 250 and 500 cc four-stroke single-cylinder machines, which benefited from the brilliant experience of Nuvolari's

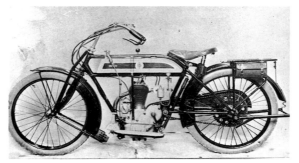
The 1919 Bianchi 500 had a vertical, single-cylinder engine, side-valve timing system and 3-speed gearbox.

The Aquilotto motor bicycle built in the fifties was of very simple construction and both purchase and running costs were very modest.

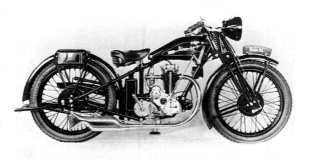
The 175 cc Freccia Celeste sports model of 1933 had an overhead camshaft and 3-speed gearbox with constant mesh gears.

The Orsetto scooter, driven by an 80 cc two-stroke single-cylinder engine, was not a commercial success despite its streamlined appearance (early sixties).

Freccia Celeste in sporting events. These machines were very reliable, and economical too. After World War Two, a series of models was marketed which was tailor-made for contemporary needs: the Bianchina 125 of 1946; the Aquilotto motor bicycle of 1952; the 175 cc Tonale of 1957 and the 80 cc Orsetto scooter of 1960. An unusual vehicle was the MT (Moto Tattica – Tactical Motorbike) 61, which went into production in 1963. Designed for the armed forces by the well-known engineer Lino Tonti, it was partly based on the company's highly successful racing models (this being the first Italian company to win a motorcross world championship event). But the MT 61 was also Bianchi's last technical and commercial undertaking: after the death of its founder, the company gradually succumbed to financial difficulties and closed down completely in 1967 (the bicycle side of the business was later revived by Piaggio). Bianchi's best racing results were achieved in the twenties, with the famous double-camshaft Freccia Celeste 350 (the first Italian bike with this type of engine, designed by Mario Baldi). Another big success was the 350-500 cc twin-cylinder of the sixties, designed by Lino Tonti.

The first version of the Bianchi twin-cylinder Grand Prix model (1960) had a displacement of 250 cc, double-camshaft valve gear and a power of 34 HP at 11,500 rpm.

BORGO

A well-known manufacturer of pistons, this company started out strictly as a motorcycle producer. It was in fact established in Turin in 1906 by the brothers Alberto, Carlo and Edoardo Michele Borgo, who were keen motorcyclists and thus began building their own machines, their most famous model being the 500 of 1914 with variable transmission. Borgo was quite successful commercially and in sporting events, but in 1911 the Turin company began making pistons for a third party and this activity gradually took over from motorcycle production, which in fact ceased in 1926.

DELLA FERRERA

Founded in Turin in 1909 by brothers Giovanni and Federico, the company immediately distinguished itself by the production of technically avant-garde, elaborately decorated and painstakingly finished vehicles. To begin with they built single-cylinder machines, then V-twins as well from 1913, the finest example of which was the 1925 model of no less than 1394 cc, which was particularly well suited to towing sidecars and fitted with half leaf spring rear suspension. Della Ferrera began a steady process of decline in the thirties, production being confined to unexceptional 175, 350 and 500 cc single-cylinder models. World War II hastened the demise of the Turin company, which ceased production in 1942, although the models already built were sold until 1948.

The 1914 Borgo 500 single-cylinder had an ignition magneto and opposed valves.

The 1925 Della Ferrera sidecar model had a 1394 cc twin-cylinder and a new Biflex front fork; it had leaf spring rear suspension.

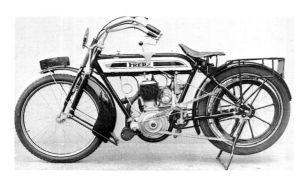

This 1914 Frera had a 500 cc four-stroke single-cylinder vertical engine.

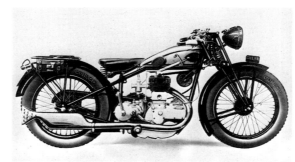

The new 1933 Gilera 500L had a foot-operated 4-speed gearbox of semi-unitary construction.

The Gilera Nettuno 250 (1946) had similar technical features to the Saturno 500. Bore and stroke 68 x 68 mm; 14 HP.

FRERA

Established at Tradate (Varese) in 1906, this was the first Italian motorcycle company to operate on a truly industrial basis, to the extent of becoming the biggest prewar Italian producer with an output of about 3000 units a year. Their success was partly due to the unusual design of their single- and twin-cylinder models. After the Great War, however, the company's creativity and productivity declined and it gradually became relegated to the sidelines. Frera survived World War Two as well, but ceased motorcycle production altogether in 1950.

GILERA

A highly skilled engineer and racer, Giuseppe Gilera founded his motorcycle company in Milan in 1909, after working for Bianchi and Bucher and Zeda. His first creation was a progressive 317 cc four-stroke single-cylinder, but he later built twin-cylinders as well. After World War One, having given up racing, he opened up a plant at Arcore. The Gilera 350 and 500 were soon among the most popular top-class single-cylinder four-strokes of the twenties and thirties, the finest example being the famous Saturno 500 of 1939, which stayed in production until 1959. Outstanding models after World War Two were the 150 of 1950, the 300 twin-cylinder of 1953 and the Giubileo 98 of 1959. In the five-year period from 1965 to 1970 Gilera was at the top of the industry with the four-stroke 125-175s, also available in off-road versions. But at the end of the sixties, the sudden closure of the U.S. market placed the company in serious difficulties. It had already lost the only heir to the company (Ferruccio Gilera had died suddenly in 1956). Therefore in 1969, Giuseppe Gilera sold the firm to Piaggio who, after a difficult transitional period, successfully relaunched it, partly through official involvement in enduro (1971–1974) and motocross (1979–1983) events. The Milan Shows of 1983 and 1985 confirmed the brilliant recovery of this splendid Lombard breed of motorcycle, an extensive range of new roadster and off-road models being available, which were greeted with considerable

The Saturno 500, introduced in 1939, was available until 1959. The single-cylinder engine had push rod valve gear. This is the final version.

The 1965 124 5V was the first Italian production model of this displacement to be given a 5-speed gearbox. The four-stroke single-cylinder engine had push rod valve gear.

The Gilera 250 NGR is a modern, very high-performance water-cooled two-stroke single-cylinder, with rotary disc inlet valve control.

Libero Liberati racing the Gilera 500 four-cylinder in 1957. ▶ This ace from Terni won the world title at the end of the season.

This is the 1957 version of the "300" twin-cylinder. Brought out in 1953, it was produced until the end of the sixties. Unit construction engine and gearbox. Chain primary drive.

This handsome 125 of 1968, built for reliability trials, had a four-stroke engine with push rod valve gear and a 5-speed gearbox.

enthusiasm by young riders (Arizona 125-200, NGR 250 RV, KK-KZ 125, Dakota 350). Apart from the more recent successes in enduro and motocross events, Gilera boasts a superb series of racing achievements spanning thirty years and more. Worth remembering are the International Six Days Trials of 1930 and 1931, the 500 class European Championship of 1939 and the brilliant sequence of eleven world titles won from 1950 to 1957.

Italian brands between the wars

BENELLI

In 1911 Signora Teresa Boni, the widow Benelli, set up a machine shop in Pesaro, to provide employment for her six sons. After World War I the engineer in the family hit upon the right area of specialization: motorbikes. The result was the first Benelli of 1919, a 75 cc two-stroke, although the first bike available commercially was the subsequent 100 cc version.

Nothing unusual so far. In 1927 the Benellis abandoned two-stroke machines in favour of four-strokes, producing a series of exclusive single and double camshaft models throughout the thirties in three displacements (175, 250 and 500 cc), which established the company at the top of the tree. The Pesaro firm was broken up in the Second World War, but made a strong and rapid recovery. Its greatest success in the fifties was the Leoncino 125, touring and sports models of which were available. Worth mentioning also is the Leonessa 250 four-stroke twin-cylinder of 1952. Giovanni, meanwhile, had split off from his brothers to found Motobi, also in Pesaro, which merged with Benelli in 1962 after a brilliant career distinguished by the "egg-shaped" 125, 175 and 250 single- and twin-cylinder models. The Benelli range continued to expand, from the motor bicycle (1958) to the twin-cylinder 650 Tornado (1967), all of a high standard, but the crisis of the sixties brought the company to its knees and the surviving partners had gradually lost their determination. In 1971 Benelli was thus taken over by the Italo-Argentine Alejandro De Tomaso, who relaunched it with several outstanding bikes like the 125-250 twin-cylinders (1972), the 350-500 four-cylinders (1973) and above all, the 750 six-cylinder (1974), later increased to 900 cc (1978). In the eighties, Benelli has been noted for its 50 and 125 scooters but has been much less in evidence, partly because much of its time has been devoted to assembling vehicles by Moto Guzzi, another member of the De Tomaso group. Among the major sporting successes of Benelli were victory in the British Lightweight Tourist Trophy of 1939 with Ted Mellors and the 250 class World Championships of 1950 (with Dario Ambrosini) and 1967 (with Australian rider Ken Carruthers).

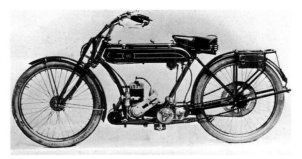

The 1921 Benelli 100 had a two-stroke vertical single-cylinder and a Bosch ignition magneto.

A double overhead camshaft engine was fitted to the 1939 Benelli 250 SS.

The 1932 Benelli 175 with overhead camshaft valve gear and a 4-speed gearbox.

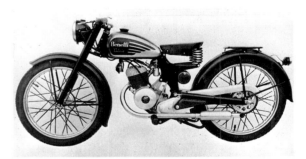

The 1949 Letizia 98. forerunner of the Leoncino 125, went on sale in 1953. It had a two-stroke single-cylinder engine.

After their merger with Motobi in 1962, Benelli also produced ▶ a 200 Sprite sports model with a horizontal-cylinder four-stroke engine.

One of the best-known racers of recent times to use Benelli machines is Renzo Pasolini, seen here on a four-cylinder from the second half of the sixties.
▼

The 1967 Tornado 650 had a four-stroke engine with two cylinders side by side, push rod valve gear and a 5-speed gear-box (bore and stroke 84 x 58 mm; 50 HP at 7200 rpm).

The Benelli two-stroke twin-cylinders, available in 125 and 250 cc displacements, were introduced in 1972. They had continuous duplex frames and 5-speed gearboxes.

The first mass-produced six-cylinder bike was the 750 cc Benelli "Sei," introduced in 1974. It had single-camshaft valve gear, a 5-speed gearbox and a power of 76 HP at 9000 rpm.

◄ From the 500 cc four-cylinder of the first half of the seventies, Benelli derived the 654 T of 1980, with a displacement of 650 cc, delivering 62 HP at 8650 rpm.

CM

From the initials for Mario Cavadegni, who founded the company in Bologna in 1930 with the technical assistance of Oreste Drusiani. Distinguished for its craftsmanlike methods of production, it first made 175, 250 and 500 four-stroke single-cylinder machines, then two-stroke ones as well after World War Two. A notable example was a 250 twin-cylinder launched in 1950, which was successful in both circuit and long-distance races. In 1956 CM built another very fine four-cylinder model, the Francolino 175, but this hand-crafted machine was too costly to build and the company was forced to close down in 1958.

GARELLI

Adalberto Garelli was a skilled engineer who in 1913, after working for Fiat and Bianchi, designed a 350 cc motorcycle engine with a split-single-cylinder engine, to overcome the problems inherent in two-stroke engines (loss of fresh gases through the exhaust) and four-stroke engines (valve breakage). Having made a bike to go with it, he proceeded to test it with excellent results, but it was only after World War I, in 1919, that he was able to begin mass production, having established a plant at Sesto San Giovanni (Milan). In a short time, Garelli became one of the top Italian producers of motorbikes and one of the biggest exporters. The company reached the peak of its achievement in 1925, then became interested in other types of production, finally devoting itself entirely to compressors for aircraft engines. However, it made a dramatic comeback after World War II with the legendary Mosquito, a miniature auxiliary motor for bicycles, more than a million of which were built from 1945 to 1952. Garelli subsequently devoted itself to the production of complete vehicles, from 50 to 125 cc, until it was taken over in 1961 by Agrati of Monticello Brianza (Como): a thriving bicycle manufacturer which had been producing motor bicycles and small scooters since 1958 with technical aid from Garelli.

After a long series of highly successful mopeds, from the single-speed automatic to the water-cooled "tubone" (which turned the Agrati-Garelli group into industrial giants in this sector), they resumed motorcycle production in the eighties, first with the 125 roadsters, then the Tiger 125 enduro model and finally the 320 trials bike. A modern version of the Mosquito has also been produced. Garelli's sporting successes are divided into two main periods. In the twenties there were the victories and championships of the 350, the first Italian bike to win a foreign Grand Prix, which established a long series of world records. In the eighties, Garelli has won four consecutive world titles with the 125 twin-cylinder and has been a strong competitor with an original bike in the 250 cc class.

The 1928 350 cc Garelli Alpina.

In 1964 Garelli began producing the Junior Special, a 50 cc motor bicycle; the "Export" version delivered 4.5 HP. It had a 4-speed gearbox.

The Garelli "NOI," introduced in 1982, is a modern example of a versatile, utilitarian moped. It has automatic transmission.

The 1983 Garelli 125 GTA 1983 has a two-stroke water-cooled single-cylinder engine. Power 22.5 HP at 8700 rpm; 6-speed gearbox.

GUAZZONI

Aldo Guazzoni began building motorbikes in Milan in the second half of the thirties, using British Calthorpe 350 and 500 engines. The company rapidly recovered from the turmoil of war, producing its own engines as well from 1950, which were highly original from a technical point of view. It was also the first Italian producer to offer a number of rotary disc (valve) two-stroke machines (1965) which did very well in speed and motocross events. The company ceased production in 1975.

Guazzoni, who specialized in low-powered bikes, produced this interesting 50 cc two-stroke rotary disc model in 1968; the "Export" version delivered 6 HP at 8200 rpm. Bore and stroke: 41 x 37.5 mm.

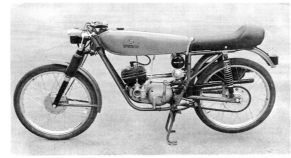

MAS

These initials stand for Motocicli Alberico Seiling, a dynamic company founded in Milan at the beginning of the twenties. With its rugged 175, 250, 350 and 500 cc single-cylinder machines, sports versions of which were also available, MAS played a leading role in the Italian industry of the thirties. It tried to preserve its position after the war, but having restricted its range to 125-175 machines, it encountered strong competition and in 1959 was forced to close.

MILLER-BALSAMO

Founded in Milan in 1921, this company used both its own and foreign engines until the end of the thirties. It produced a wide range of crafts-man-built machines, notable examples being the 350 and 500 cc sports bikes (with Rudge four-valve engines from Britain) and the fully faired 200, a magnificent example of functional avant-garde design (with a Miller two-stroke engine). After the war, Miller-Balsamo continued to produce the fully faired model and in 1954 started work on a handsome 175. In the ensuing years, the company became involved in other activities as well; these gradually took over and their last motorbike was produced in 1958.

MM

The partners who founded this company in Bologna in 1922 all had surnames beginning with the letter M (Massi, Mattei, Mazzetti, Morini), but settled on just two for the company name. In the twenties, MM mainly built bikes with two-stroke engines, primarily 125 and 175 cc, which did very well in races. But in the thirties they focused on machines with four-stroke engines of 175, 250, 350 and 500 cc displacement. These also proved successful in races, particularly the 175 and 350 cc versions – not only in speed contests, but in world championships too. After the war, MM's interest in four-stroke machines continued. The A/54 250 single-shaft of 1954 was the finest example but it was also the Bolognese company's swan song, as it closed down in 1957.

MORINI

In 1937 Alfonso Morini left MM, of which he had been a founder member fifteen years before, and began building lorries, which were much in demand at the time. However, Morini had been a brilliant racer with motorcycling in his blood; therefore once the war was over he restored his Bolognese company to efficiency, gave up producing lorries and devoted his attention to motorbikes. The first was a 125 two-stroke, which was immediately joined by a superb racing model, these two products putting Morini way ahead of the average Italian producer. In 1954, the company took another big step forward when it abandoned two-stroke machines in favour of four-strokes. In 1955 the famed Sette-bello appeared, which was to enjoy a brilliant career on roads and racing circuits; in 1963, it launched Giacomo Agostini on a brilliant career. Other important milestones for Morini were the Corsaro 125 of 1959 and the Corsarino 50 of 1963. The Corsaro was an agile lightweight sports bike which was also highly successful in the motocross versions, winning various national awards from 1967 to 1970 in the 100, 125 and 175 classes. In 1971 the third-generation Morini came out: this was the Bolognese company's best technical

The Morini 175 Settebello Corsa was one of the most popular bikes for "junior" motorcyclists for many years, notably used by Giacomo Agostini.

One of the final versions (1970–1971) of the 125 and 150 cc "Corsaro," with a 5-speed gearbox. The 125 cc version delivered 12.5 HP at 9600 rpm.

In 1963 the Corsarino 50 was introduced (this is the 1965 version), a four-stroke moped with push rod valve gear.

The road versions of the Corsaro were joined by the trail models in the second half of the sixties. The photo shows the 125 cc version of 1970, delivering 13.25 HP at 9800 rpm.

The 1972 Morini 3½, touring version. The twin-cylinder engine with push rod valve gear delivered 35 HP at 8200 rpm. It had a 6-speed gearbox and drum brakes.

The 500 cc road version of the Morini twin-cylinder was not as successful as the 350 cc model. The one shown came out in 1977.

Moto Morini's latest novelties are six-speed 350 and 500 cc Custom bikes, which go to join the established enduro and road models of the same displacements.

At the beginning of the sixties, Morini vehicles were raced by champions like Provini (seen here on a G.P. double-camshaft single-cylinder) and Agostini.

achievement, destined for a long life too, as it combined intelligent simplicity of design with advanced technical features. The third-generation Morini was a 350 cc twin-cylinder (also available in a sports version from 1974), increased to 500 cc (in 1977) and then reduced to 250 (in 1979). Derived from this motorbike were the Camel 500 (1981), the Kanguro 350 (1982) and finally, the very recent Excalibur 350-501 (1985). A large and thriving family of machines, therefore, to which the Turbo 500 (the first bike in the world to have this type of fuel supply) was to be added in 1979, when the project was abandoned as some special components were unobtainable in Italy. Morini's sporting successes were mainly due to the Settebello 175 (which forged a generation of riders and won numerous world titles); the Rebello 175 (which won the most punishing long-distance races, such as the Tour of Italy and the Milan–Taranto Rally of 1955) and the 250 Grand Prix (which narrowly missed winning the 1963 World Championship against the omnipotent Japanese, because the Bolognese firm had failed to compete in all the championship events.

MOTO GUZZI

Immediately after the Great War, two thousand lire was a pretty meager capital (barely enough to buy a used motorbike, in fact), yet it was enough to establish Moto Guzzi, which was soon to become one of the top names in the motorcycling world. The company was founded by Carlo Guzzi

and Giorgio Parodi. They had met in the Air Force during the war (Guzzi was an engineer, Parodi a pilot) and had agreed to build a new type of bike to a clever design by Guzzi. After the War was over they went into action, financed by Giorgio's father, the Genoese shipowner Vittorio Parodi. Carlo Guzzi in fact produced a 500 with a number of intelligent and practical features which made it extremely durable and reliable (almost a miracle in those days). This first 500, which was issued as the Normale in 1921, had a brilliant career lasting nearly half a century, the definitive version being the Falcone, which was produced until 1967.

But it was mainly after World War II that Moto Guzzi demonstrated its creative genius with an outstanding sequence of models, all with exclusive technical and aesthetic features true to the company's tradition: the highly popular Guzzino (1946–1965); the legendary Galletto (1950–1966); the faired Zigolo (1953–1966); the modernistic Lodola (1956–1966); the mythical Stornello (1960–1975). Finally, in 1965, began the saga of the V7, the big twin-cylinder machine that conquered foreign markets as well. And the story of the V7 is not yet over, as brilliant models have been developed from it, like the famous Le Mans supersports bike launched in 1975. After the intervention of the De Tomaso group in 1972 came another very important project in 1977 (by Lino Tonti again): that of the V35 and V50, from which other very famous models were derived, like the Custom bikes (1981) and the Lario 650 four-valve sports model (1983). Moto Guzzi was intensely active in races – particularly Grand Prix and world record events – up to the end of the

This is the 1929 Moto Guzzi Sport 14, which had an opposed valve 500 cc engine.

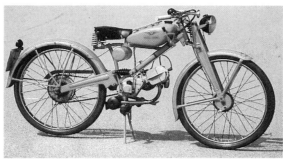

The Guzzino 65, with a two-stroke single-cylinder engine with a rotary valve port timing system, was introduced in 1946. The first versions had hand-operated gears.

The 1960 version of the Zigolo had a 110 cc horizontal-cylinder two-stroke engine delivering 4.8 HP at 5200 rpm and a 3-speed gearbox.

The Stornello Sport of 1962 could do 110 km/h (68 mph) thanks to its 8.5 HP engine. Bore and stroke: 52 x 58 mm; 4-speed gearbox; push rod valve gear.

In 1958 the Lodola 175 single-camshaft was replaced by the new 235 cc version with push rod valve gear, which delivered 11 HP at 6000 rpm.

The 1970 758 cc V7 "Special" (bore and stroke 83 x 70 mm; power 52 HP at 6500 rpm; shaft final drive).

One of the fastest sports bikes of the latter seventies was the Guzzi "Le Mans" 850 (this is the first version), delivering 81 HP at 7600 rpm.

The Guzzi V35 and V50 twin-cylinders appeared in 1978. The more powerful version delivered 45 HP at 7500 rpm. It had a 5-speed gearbox.

The sports version of he Guzzi V35 is called Imola. The 90° V-twin engine develops 36 HP at 8200 rpm.

◄ Bill Lomas on the fully faired Guzzi 350 double-camshaft single-cylinder (1957).

sixties. Among its greatest achievements were victory in the European Championship in 1924, the British Tourist Trophy of 1935 and 1937 (the first wins by a continental company), ten world titles in the period 1946–1957 and the Silver Vase (Vaso d'Argento) at the International Six Days Trial Motorcross of 1963. Moto Guzzi was also responsible for the most sensational Grand Prix model: the eight-cylinder 500 of 1953.

Lorenzetti racing the Guzzi 250 on the Monza circuit in 1953. It ► was a single-camshaft, single-cylinder with "duckbill" fairing.

SERTUM

Officine Meccaniche Fausto Alberti, founded in Milan in 1922, entered the motorcycle sector in 1931 under the trademark Sertum (the Latin word for crown). The company's technical and commercial commitment and expertise soon yielded brilliant results, and Sertum became one of the elite of motorcycle producers both nationally and worldwide. Sertum's success was due both to popular models (like the Batua 120 of 1933) and prestige ones (like the twin-cylinder with sprung frame of 1957). The Sertum range was then completed by excellent 175, 250 and 500 cc single-cylinder machines.

After the war Sertum suffered from a certain immobilism, which greatly restricted its sales volume. Despite its successes in motocross events (Sertum was virtually unbeatable in the period from 1946 to 1949), the market proved unreceptive to the medium- and high-powered models on which the Milanese company insisted on focusing its production. By the time Sertum began developing a modern 125 in 1950 it was too late to save the company, which in fact went bankrupt in 1952.

The Batua model by Sertum, introduced in 1933, had a pressed steel frame and a 120 cc two-stroke single-cylinder engine.

The engine of this 500 cc model from 1937 had twin cylinders fitted vertically side by side and a side-valve timing system.

Immediately after the war, Sertum introduced this 250 cc single-cylinder with push rod valve gear. Delivering 11.5 HP, it could do more than 110 km/h (68 mph).

AERMACCHI/HARLEY-DAVIDSON/ CAGIVA

At the end of World War II, Aermacchi obviously had to stop producing its famous fighter aircraft. But its Schiranna plant on the shores of Lake Varese was not idle, as it soon began producing the Macchi three-wheeler. Aermacchi then decided to enter the motorcycle sector and developed two unconventional models for the purpose: the U 125 large-wheeled scooter (1949) and the Chimera 175 faired motorbike (1956). The scooter sold well, while the bike was not a commercial success. Minus the fairing, however, the Chimera gave rise to a long series of models (including racing bikes) which were produced for twenty years in 175, 250 and 350 cc displacements. In 1960 Aermacchi began supplying Harley-Davidson with various 100, 125, 250 and 350 cc models suitable for the U.S. market. In 1973, having lost all interest in the declining motorcycle sector, Aermacchi sold the entire Schiranna plant to Harley-Davidson, who naturally continued producing models designed for the U.S. market but included some sporting versions, which were a major source of satisfaction to the Varese company (earning them four world titles in the 250 and 350 classes from 1974 to 1976). However, competition from the Japanese on the domestic market caused a financial crisis for the American giant which, despite the support of the AMF group in 1978, was forced to rationalize its production and decided to sell the Schiranna plant. A purchaser was soon forthcoming in the

The U125, which came out in 1949, was a type of scooter with big wheels, driven by a two-stroke single-cylinder engine (bore and stroke 52 x 58 mm; power 5 HP at 4300 rpm; 3-speed gearbox).

form of two brothers from Varese – Claudio and Gianfranco Castiglioni, who were motorbike and racing enthusiasts and owned Cagiva, a flourishing industry founded by their father (CAstiglioni GIovanni VARese), which manufactured trinkets. The Castiglioni brothers' enthusiasm soon breathed new life into the old company, which became the top Italian motorcycle producer, thanks above all to the two "125s" which were best-sellers in their category, the SST and the Ala Rossa, which also gave young riders a chance to compete in motocross events. In 1983 Cagiva signed an agreement granting exclusive technical and commercial rights to Ducati, and in 1984 it established an advanced research center at Rimini under the capable directorship of Massimo Tamburini. The fruits of this enterprise included the aerodynamic Ducati Paso 350-750, introduced at the Milan Show of 1985. Sporting successes by Cagiva also included the 125 world motocross title in 1985.

Excellent racing bikes were derived from the four-stroke road models with horizontal cylinders and push rod valve gear. This is an "Ala d'Oro" (Gold Wing) 350 from the sixties.

The Cagiva "Aletta Rossa" 125 has a water-cooled two-stroke engine with reed-type inlet valves (1986).

◄ The Chimera 175, with full "bodywork" to conceal the mechanical parts, came out in 1956. Four-stroke single-cylinder engine, bore and stroke 60 x 61 mm. Push rod valve gear.

The Aermacchi "Ala Verde," which came out in 1960, had a 250 cc engine. This is the 1965–1966 model, with a 4-speed gearbox (bore and stroke 66 x 71 mm; 16 HP at 6500 rpm).

The 1974 Harley-Davidson SS 350, last in line of the four-stroke single-cylinder machines with push rod valve gear, had a duplex cradle frame and delivered 27 HP at 7000 rpm.

The Cagiva Elephant is driven by a Ducati four-stroke twin-cylinder engine with desmodromic valve gear. It is produced in 350 and 650 cc versions.

APRILIA

Founded at Noale (province of Venice) in 1938 by Alberto Beggio, who named it after a Lancia car that was much in vogue at the time, this company devoted itself entirely to bicycle production for almost thirty years. However, Alberto Beggio's son Ivano was a great motocross enthusiast and finally, in 1965, succeeded in persuading his father to let him build a 50 cc off-road bike. The result was an interesting "special," which launched Aprilia as a motorcycle manufacturer. After the 50 the company built a 125, then a 250 – all off-road bikes with strong technical and aesthetic qualities. They were immediately tested in competitions, performing well even at an international level, particularly in motocross events. From 1975 to 1983 Aprilia used Italian Hiro engines, then switched to Austrian Rotax in

order to extend its range to cover road, enduro, rally, motocross and trials models, with two- and four-stroke engines, in displacements from 50 to 600 cc. Since 1985, Aprilia has also produced racing models, experience in this field being regarded as vital to the development of production models with advanced technical and aesthetic features.

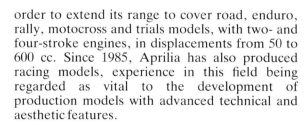

The 1986 Aprilia F1 50 is one of the most sophisticated examples of a modern sports moped. It has a two-stroke engine and aluminum alloy wheels.

The 1979 Aprilia RC 250 had a two-stroke single-cylinder engine delivering 38 HP at 7800 rpm. It had a 6-speed gearbox.

The Aspes Yuma was one of the most popular 125 sports bikes in Italy in the second half of the seventies. The two-stroke single-cylinder engine of the later versions had a power of 19 HP at 9800 rpm.

This Beta 240 is typical of trials bikes of the early eighties. It is driven by a two-stroke single-cylinder engine delivering 18 HP at 8000 rpm.

The Bimota SB2, with a Suzuki 750 four-cylinder engine, was one of the fastest roadsters at the beginning of the eighties.

The Ceccato 75 four-stroke single-cylinder, introduced in 1953, had single-camshaft valve gear and delivered 6 HP at 10,400 rpm.

ASPES

This company started out as a bicycle manufacturer at Gallarate in 1955, the unusual name being derived from the surname (Aspesi) of the wife of one of the founder members. In 1968 it produced its first motorcycle – a 50 cc off-road bike which distinguished itself from the wide range of vehicles in this sector by its advanced technical and aesthetic features. In 1971 the company began building its own 125 cc engines, winning the national motocross championship in this category in 1976. Financial difficulties forced the company to close down in 1982.

BETA

This Florentine firm originated in 1904, the name being derived from the initials of its founder members, Bianchi (Enzo) and Tosi (Arrigo). For decades they just made bicycles, their first mopeds and motorbikes being produced in 1948. Franco Morini engines were used to begin with, then from 1957 they produced their own two- and four-stroke engines. In 1960 the plant at Osmannoro was opened, followed by the one at Rignano sull'Arno in 1973. Since the seventies Beta has specialized in off-road bikes, first enduro ones only, then motocross (winners of many events including two national championships in 1976) and finally trials models.

BIMOTA

Bimota, from the initials of its founder members (Bianchi, Morri and Tamburini), was established in Rimini in 1968 as a manufacturer of central heating plants. Since 1972 the company has been entirely devoted to motorcycle production, making special frames and also a few racing models (in 1975 a Bimota with a Yamaha engine, piloted by Cecotto, won the 350 world title). After that, Bimota concentrated on supersports roadsters with progressive features, a high standard of finish and Japanese four-cylinder engines, which have been very successful both in Italy and abroad. The company introduced the futuristic Tesi in the same year. In 1985 the first all-Italian Bimota appeared, the DB1, with a Ducati 750 twin-cylinder engine.

CECCATO

This firm at Alte Ceccato (near Vicenza) in Veneto has always specialized in automobile

equipment but entered the motorcycle sector in 1949, when it produced the Romeo auxiliary motor for bicycles. It then rapidly advanced toward more ambitious projects like the 75, 125 and 175 two- and four-stroke light motorbikes, producing a fine 200 twin-cylinder model as well in 1953. From 1954, it was noted for its fast 75-100 single camshaft models (designed by engineer Taglioni before he joined Ducati), which established various world records. Ceccato stopped producing motorcycles in 1963.

DUCATI

Founded in Bologna in 1926 by the brothers Adriano and Marcello Ducati as SSR (Società Scientifica Radio), Ducati changed direction completely at the end of the war. In fact, in 1946 it began building an excellent four-stroke auxiliary

This is a 1958 Ducati single-cylinder Grand Prix model, with desmodromic valve gear.

The 1961 Ducati Diana had a 250 cc single-cylinder engine with overhead camshaft valve gear operated by a vertical shaft and two bevel gear pairs. Power 19.5 HP at 8000 rpm (version for U.S. market). Bore and stroke 74 x 57.8 mm.

The Ducati 750 Super Sports twin-cylinder of 1973 (bore and stroke 80 x 74.4 mm; 72 HP at 9500 rpm; 5-speed gearbox).

The Ducati Scramblers were produced from 1968 to 1974. The two initial, 250 and 350 cc versions were joined in 1969 by the 450 cc model. They had a single-cylinder engine with single-camshaft valve gear and a 5-speed gearbox.

This is the first version of the 1970 "Desmo" 350. The single-cylinder engine with desmodromic valve gear had a bore of 76 mm and stroke of 75 mm. 250 cc and 450 cc versions with the same characteristics were also produced.

The second generation of Ducati 90° V-twins started with the 1977 "Pantah" 500 model. This also had desmodromic valve gear, but the camshafts (one per cylinder head) were operated by toothed belts.

FANTIC MOTOR

This company was established in 1968 at Barzago (province of Como), with the aim of producing "fantastic bikes." And it succeeded, its output covering nearly all of the huge number of different types of motorcycle. It started with minis and midis, which were a great success in the United States too, then progressed to the 50 (1970) and 125 (1973) off-road bikes, always producing avant-garde vehicles which did brilliantly in sporting events, above all in the endurance sector (they won the 125 world title in 1981). The company successfully invaded the "American-style" Chopper field with 50 and 125 cc models (1972), of original design but with good handling qualities. It then became involved in the emergent trials sector, with a range of models and displacements: 125 (1977); 200 (1978); 240 (1980);

The 1978 Fantic "Caballero 50." This is the RC version, delivering 8.5 HP at 12,000 rpm.

The 1983 Fantic Strada 125 has a water-cooled two-stroke single-cylinder engine delivering 18.6 HP at 7500 rpm.

This is the 1983 Fantic Raider 125, an enduro bike with a two-stroke single-cylinder engine delivering 16 HP at 7000 rpm.

motor for bicycles called Cucciolo (Cub), which was extremely popular, over half a million being built up to 1950. After the unhappy interlude of the futuristic Cruiser 175 Ghia enclosed scooter (1952), with the arrival of engineer Fabio Taglioni in 1954, Ducati entered a period of technical exclusivity which reaped considerable rewards and in which it was the envy of the whole world. From 1956, after the famous 100 and 125s which won long-distance events, engineer Taglioni introduced desmodromic valve gear, which enabled four-stroke engines to achieve even the highest rotational speeds with complete safety. This was a unique device in the motorcycling field; Taglioni first tested it successfully on racing bikes, then transferred it to production models. Three families of bikes figure prominently in Ducati's history, all with a sporting bias: the 125, 175, 250,

350 and 450 single-cylinders, some with desmodromic valve gear (1956–1978); the Scrambler single-cylinders, also from 125 to 450 cc, which pioneered the on/off-road formula so fashionable today (1968–1975) and the big L-twins. The latter – which first appeared as 750s in 1968, their displacement gradually being increased to 1000 cc – are still in production today and gave rise in 1977 to the brilliant series of Pantah 500, 600, 650 and 750 machines. Ducati twin-cylinders are distinctive for their structural originality, slim front profile and very high performance. Ducati had two particularly successful periods in sporting events: 1954–1956, when the 100-125s triumphed in Italian long-distance races, and 1956–1959 – three years of success in world speed contests with the desmodromic 125s. And we must not forget the victory in the Imola 200-mile event of 1973.

300 (1983) and 301 Mono (1985), the latter winning the World Championship. Finally, it produced the brilliant 125 roadsters (1981), the original Sprinter moped (1982) and the imposing series of 50, 125 and 250 enduro models.

FB MINARELLI AND FRANCO MORINI

The two biggest Italian (motorcycle) engine manufacturers have common origins dating from 1951. In that year, in fact, in Bologna, Vittorio Minarelli and Franco Morini founded FBM (Fabbrica Bolognese Motocicli), whose first product was the unusual Gabbiano 125 lightweight motorbike with an open frame. In 1956 the two partners split up, Vittorio Minarelli establishing FB Minarelli (restyled Motori Minarelli in 1968) and Franco Morini founding the company of the same name. Both specialized in engines, mainly 50 cc, in all possible variants from quiet, single-speed automatics to supercharged six-speed models like the Minarelli P6 and Franco Morini Turbo Star. Recently a few models have been given water cooling, while Minarelli has begun producing the Yamaha 125 engine under license. Minarelli has also done brilliantly in sporting events, winning the 50, 75 and 175 class World Championships from 1966 to 1975 and the three 125 class world titles in 1979, 1980 and 1981.

Provini racing at Monza in 1957 on a Mondial 125 cc double-camshaft with dustbin fairing. Seven-speed gearbox; ▶ duplex cradle frame; speed about 200 km/h (125 mph).

Tarquinio Provini on the double-camshaft Mondial 175 during the 1956 Tour of Italy.

The Mondial single-cylinder with single-camshaft valve gear was one of the most brilliant 125s of its period. This is the 1950 version.

The engine of the 1971 Mondial "Record" 50 was a two-stroke single-cylinder which delivered 5 HP at 7800 rpm in the "export" version.

FB MONDIAL

Established as FB or Fratelli Boselli in 1936 (Boselli Brothers – the brothers being Carlo, Ettore, Giuseppe and Luigi), this company manufactured lorries to begin with. However, Giuseppe was a good racer, and after the war he persuaded his brothers to build motorbikes as well, having added the word Mondial to their trademark. Their first bikes were an overwhelming success, winning ten world titles in the 125 and 250 classes from 1949 to 1957. They produced excellent road models: 125 (1950); 200 (1952) and GS 175 (1955); followed by the 125-175 Serie Oro (Gold Series) from 1960, all of which had four-stroke engines. From the mid sixties, despite producing a greater variety of models, their machines became less exclusive, engines of other brands being used as well, and Mondial gradually faded into anonymity, disappearing from the scene in 1978.

ISO

Founded in 1948 by Enzo Rivolta, Isothermos of Bresso (Milan) began its career as a motorcycle producer with the Furetto 65, a small scooter which was not a success. However, the company learned from this experience and in 1950 brought out the Isoscooter 125, whose technical and aesthetic qualities earned it a place among the industrial giants in this sector. The Isomoto 125 (still of 1950) was also a success, being virtually the same as the Isoscooter minus bodywork.

The "Isomoto," introduced in 1950, had a split-single two-stroke engine. The wheels were of very small diameter (12 inches). Power 6.7 HP.

ITALJET

Founded in 1958 by Leopoldo Tartarini (winner of the motorcycling Tour of Italy in 1953 and 1954), this company was originally called Italemmezeta because it used 125 and 175 engines by the East German company MZ (the initials read *emme zeta* in Italian). Having terminated the contract with MZ because of difficult relations, the Bolognese company

The 1965 Italjet Mustang with a 50 cc engine.

assumed its present name in 1961, producing further outstanding models (including non-sports bikes), all with strong aesthetic qualities and the best engines available on the international market, like the British Triumph 500 and 650 cc (1965), the Japanese Yamaha 125 cc (1974) and the Italian Piaggio 50 cc (1980). An indication of Italjet's flair for styling is the fact that the Pack 50, a folding "mini" with a Ciao (Piaggio) engine, received much-coveted recognition from the New

The Laverda 200, which came out in 1962, was a twin-cylinder with push rod valve gear. Bore and stroke 52 x 47 mm; power 11 HP at 6500 rpm.

The 1970 Laverda SF 750. It had chain-operated single-camshaft valve gear. The twin-cylinder engine (bore and stroke 80 x 74 mm) delivered 57 HP at 6500 rpm. Five-speed gearbox.

This is the twin-cylinder version with double overhead camshaft valve gear and four valves per cylinder, brought out in 1976 and produced in 350 and 500 cc versions. Six-speed gearbox.

York Museum of Modern Art. In the eighties, Italjet has begun producing its own 250 and 350 cc engines, both two- and four-stroke, for strictly off-road trial and enduro bikes. Italjet is the only Italian company to produce a leisure "three-wheeler," the Ranger 125.

LAVERDA

This company at Breganze near Vicenza in the Veneto originated in 1873, but the motorcycle factory was opened by Francesco Laverda in 1949. All the Laverda bikes were original both technically and aesthetically, starting with the first 75 and 100 cc models, which were also famous for their success in long-distance races. However, Laverda's greatest triumph were the 750 twin-cylinders (1967–1976), which fought brilliantly in motorcycling marathons and advertised the company overseas as well. Another motorcycle with star quality was the 1000 cc triple cylinder (1969–1982). The 350-500 twin-cylinders (1975-1977) were not a great success, but the company soon recovered with the 125, initially with a Zündapp engine (1977), then with an original engine (1981). An outstanding machine was the sensational 1000 prototype six-cylinder (1978). After going through a difficult period from 1983 to 1984, Laverda has fully recovered, as demonstrated by the 1985 Milan Show, at which the Lesmo 350 triple cylinder was much admired.

MALAGUTI

This company was founded in Bologna in 1932 as a bicycle factory by former racing cyclist Antonino Malaguti. In 1950 it moved to San Lazzaro di Savena on the outskirts of Bologna and began producing motorbikes as well. It was one of the first Italian companies to launch a 50 cc off-road bike, the Cavalcone Cross (1971), and has developed a wide range of "50s" with very different characteristics to suit all tastes, as well as specializing in models for children. It recently entered the true motorcycling sector (in 1985) with the Runner 125 Enduro.

MALANCA

This company was founded in 1947 at Pontecchio Marconi (Bologna) by Mario Malanca, as a bicycle factory. Since 1956 it has also built mopeds, first with engines by other companies, then (in 1960) with original engines. In 1973 Malanca started work on a 125 twin-cylinder which, suitably updated, is still in production. An on/off-road version is also available. From 1972 to 1975 Malanca did well in speed contests in Italy and abroad, in the 50 and 125 classes.

The 1982 Laverda RGS 1000 with a three-cylinder-in-line engine delivering over 80 HP at 7300 rpm (bore and stroke 75 x 74 mm). Double overhead camshaft valve gear.

MI-VAL

Metalmeccanica Italiana Valtrompia (MI-VAL for short) is a thriving company near Brescia which started producing motorcycles in 1950. To begin with it just built 125 and 175 cc two-stroke machines, then four-stroke models as well, of 125, 175 and 200 cc displacement, from 1954. For a few years after that it built the Mivalino three-wheeler under license from Messerschmitt. It was soon on a par with other Italian manufacturers in the mid-range and was also very active in sporting events, particularly off-road motocross and enduro competitions using machines of 125 and 250 cc displacement. It made an unsuccessful attempt at producing mopeds in the sixties and then seemed to lose interest in motorbikes too, its absence from the Milan Show of 1969 putting an end to its motorcycling career.

The Malaguti "Cavalcone" 50 had a two-stroke single-cylinder engine with a bore and stroke of 39 x 42 mm.

The Malanca 150 two-stroke twin-cylinder. The engine, with a 5-speed gearbox, was also produced in a 125 cc version.

The Motom 48 had a 48 cc four-stroke engine with push rod valve gear. This is the 1958 version, delivering 2.2 HP at 6500 rpm.

MOTOM

Established in Milan in 1947 by the brothers Ernesto and Giuseppe Frua (then magnates of the textile industry), this company was responsible for producing the first true motor bicycle – a small, economical motor vehicle which was rationally designed as a whole, rather than being a mere assemblage of different parts (as was the custom then). This explains the success of the Motom 48: over a half a million were built in fifteen years with only minor changes and it is still in use today, thanks to its incomparable sturdiness and durability. In 1950 Motom further demonstrated its flair for original design when it introduced the Delfino 150, a comfortable vehicle with medium-diameter wheels. In 1953 another outstanding machine appeared: the fully faired T 100. Its praises were sung at the Milan Art Triennial but it was less successful than its predecessors from a technical point of view. After that Motom's inspiration seemed to dry up, its products failed to keep pace with the times, and despite the introduction of a few new mopeds like the Nova (1965) and Daina (1968), the Milanese company was forced to close down in 1971.

MV AGUSTA

In the middle of the war, in 1943, Costruzioni Aeronautiche Giovanni Agusta, which had been founded at Cascina Costa di Gallarate in 1923 by the Sicilian pioneer of the same name, researched and developed a two-stroke 98 light motorbike to be produced as soon as peace returned. Domenico Agusta, who had inherited his father's company in 1927 at the age of twenty, was a keen motorcyclist and as soon as the war was over, he gave an enthusiastic go-ahead to the project. He also changed the company name to MV Agusta (MV is short for Meccanica Varghera, Varghera being the place where the motorcycle production plant was situated). Up to 1955 MV concentrated on popular models, famous examples being the Pullman bike and Ovunque scooter, both of which had 125 cc two-stroke engines. The Pullman was the model produced in the greatest numbers. In subsequent years MV undertook more ambitious projects, such as the single-camshaft 175s (including the famed Disco Volante = Flying Saucer); it was also the first motorcycle producer to pioneer direct injection and hydraulic transmission. The company further upgraded the quality of its machines in 1965, at the beginning of its third decade, when the extraordinary four-cylinder 600 (the first modern maxi) and later to become the 750 sport in 1969 and 800 Super America in 1975, appeared at the Milan Show. Having abandoned popular models, MV also produced an outstanding 250 twin-cylinder (1966), later increased to 350 (1969), a sports version of which was subsequently available (1974). The fourth chapter in MV's history should have unfolded in the mid seventies: apart from anything else, a new four-cylinder engine had already been designed, in various versions from 750 to 1200 cc. But unfavourable market conditions and the company's increasing commitment to helicopter production (Agusta had re-entered the aeronautical sector in 1952) had created some degree of hostility at a managerial level to motorbikes, which were regarded as making unprofitable use of the company's resources. Furthermore, the death of Domenico Agusta in 1971 had deprived the motorcycle lobby of its strongest champion, and in 1976 the fateful decision was thus made to give up motorbikes, including racing models, which in thirty years had provided MV and Italy with an outstanding number of successes yet to be surpassed, even by the Japanese: 75 world titles; 275 victories in international Grands Prix and over 3,000 victories in all types of speed contest.

This first MV was designed in 1942 but went into production only in 1947. The engine was a 98 cc two-stroke single-cylinder.

The 1966 MV 600 had a four-cylinder engine with double overhead camshaft valve gear, a power of 52 HP at 8000 rpm and shaft final drive.

In 1974 MV brought out this completely new version of its 350 twin-cylinder. With a bore and stroke of 63 x 56 mm and push rod valve gear, the engine delivered 32 HP at 7650 rpm.

The 1975 MV America Sport 750 had a four-cylinder double-camshaft engine with 80 HP at 7900 rpm.
▼

The 1953 MV Pullman 125. The engine was a two-stroke single-cylinder (bore and stroke 53 x 56 mm), delivering 6 HP. It had a 3-speed gearbox.

PARILLA

Immediately after the war, Giovanni Parrilla (with two r's) was in charge of a workshop in Milan which specialized in injection pumps for diesel engines. But his great hobby was motorbikes. Therefore, at the first opportunity, he gave up building pumps and designed a fabulous 250 single camshaft model with Alfredo Bianchi. In 1946 he started a small production run of these bikes, under the trademark Parilla (he dropped one of the r's, convinced that the name sounded better without it). These bikes did well in competitions and earned the company recognition, but little money. Giovanni Parrilla then brought out a series of popular 98, 125 and 250 cc two-stroke machines that were a commercial success, plus the Levriere scooter. However, in 1953 he raised the tone again with the high-cam Fox 175 and the Setter 250 and Veltro 350 twin-cylinders. The 175, various versions of which were built for nearly a decade, had a brilliant career. The Slughi of 1958 – a handsome machine with a unitized body designed by Cesare Bossaglia – was highly progressive, but the time was not yet ripe for it and in fact the industry was in a state of crisis. Parrilla was forced to close down in 1967, despite having successfully invaded the "go-kart" sector.

From 1966 to 1972 Agostini won twelve world titles in the 350 and 500 classes, on MV Agusta triple-cylinders. ▼

The 1956 Parilla 175 SS was driven by a single-cylinder engine with "high cam" valve gear. Bore and stroke 59.8 x 62 mm; power 12.8 HP at 7800 rpm.

The 1958 99 cc Parilla "Slughi" had a unitized body of pressed steel, in two halves. The horizontal single-cylinder engine was available in two- or four-stroke versions (the latter delivering 6 HP at 7200 rpm).

RUMI

Donnino Rumi, who owned a factory producing textile machinery in Bergamo, decided immediately after the war to build motorcycles as well. He naturally wanted something special and developed a progressive two-stroke 125 twin-cylinder, which did well for nearly twenty years. Rumi also built two types of scooter, the Scoiattolo (1952) and the Formichino (1954), the latter having a unitized body cast in light alloy. In the second half of the fifties more conventional models were built as well, but these were not particularly successful and the textile machinery side of the business put the company in serious financial difficulties. Rumi tried to make a comeback in the sixties with another bike which was out of the ordinary, a four-stroke V-twin available in various displacements, but it was no more than a swan song and the company was forced to close down shortly afterward.

SWM

Founded in 1971 by an off-road champion (Fausto Vergani) and a manufacturer of central heating systems (Piero Sironi) who was a keen off-road motorcyclist, SWM (for Speedy Working Motors or Sironi Vergani Moto) soon took over leadership of the off-road motorcycle sector in Italy. Up to 1975 SWM motocross and enduro

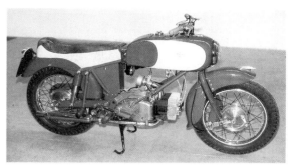

The Rumi 200 of the mid fifties had the same technical features as the better-known 125. The two-stroke twin-cylinder engine (bore and stroke 52 x 49 mm) delivered 10.6 HP at 6000 rpm. Four-speed gearbox; speed 110 km/h (68 mph).

The Rumi 125 trail bike of 1955.

bikes used German Sachs engines, adapted by SWM in the light of their brilliant racing experience (in 1975 they won the Vaso d'Argento – Silver Vase – at the International Six Days trial. Then Sachs began producing a new, seven-speed engine which, despite the corrective efforts of SWM, was not up to scratch. The Italian company (based at Rivolta d'Adda in the province of Milan) then fitted its bikes with Austrian Rotax engines and extended its interest to cover the trials sector where it did very well, its finest achievement being victory in the 1981 World Championship. However, declining fortune in the enduro and motocross sector caused a financial crisis for the Lombard company, which reacted too sluggishly, with a few unsuccessful road models. Collapse was inevitable and SWM closed down in 1984, but reappeared the next year on a much smaller scale as SVM (Società Veicoli Milanese).

The 1979 SWM Trial 320 was driven by a 276 cc two-stroke single-cylinder engine delivering 18 HP at 6400 rpm. It had a 6-speed gearbox.

SCOOTERS

The scooter phenomenon grew at a tremendous rate in Italy after World War II and then spread throughout the world. It had in fact already manifested itself at the end of World War I in various European countries, above all Britain, and in the United States. Ancestors of the modern scooter included the American Autoped, German DKW Lomos, French Monet-Goyon Velauto, Czech CAS and British Whippet, Unibus and Skootamota. But all of them were short-lived. By contrast, the Italian scooters produced after World War II (Lambretta and Vespa, basically) were a huge success, and are still popular today despite formidable opposition from the Japanese since the beginning of the eighties. How does one explain this very different reception? For one thing, the scooters of the twenties were by-products of the motorcycle industry, dependent upon its limited technology and artisan methods of production. They were thus impractical and too costly for the mass market. Little more than motorized versions of the child's scooter, they did not appeal to sportsmen and women (who preferred motorbikes) and were too expensive for others (who travelled on foot or made do with bicycles). The Italian Lambretta and Vespa scooters built after World War II were brilliantly designed (quite independent of motor-cycles) and had very high industrial potential (something unheard of up till then in the two-wheeled motorized vehicle sector); they were therefore truly practical, economical, safe to use and accessible to all.

The history of the Italian scooter was thus written almost entirely by Lambretta and Vespa: machines built by Innocenti in Milan (founded in 1932) and Piaggio at Pontedera (dating from 1884). These companies were veritable industrial giants who had, even in wartime, been planning how to transform the industry once the fighting was over. Although not established as historical fact, it could well be that the idea for scooters came to Innocenti and Piaggio not by reference to the early machines of the twenties but by observing the minibikes created during the war to give greater mobility to certain army divisions. Two of these in particular may have inspired the modern scooter: the Italian Volugrafo, built in Turin, and the British Welbike, which originally fitted into a drum designed to be dropped by parachute and was manufactured for some time after the war under the name Corgi. The Vespa, designed by brilliant aeronautical pioneer Corradino d'Ascanio, was the first to appear, in the spring of 1946. The Lambretta came out a year later. In 1946 Piaggio built just 2500 Vespas, but after that production spiralled. If you include the figures for Lambretta, 300,000 scooters were built in Italy in 1954 and just two years later, Piaggio celebrated the millionth Vespa leaving the assembly line. Innocenti stopped producing scooters in 1971 (this was continued under license abroad): in 24 years, it had built four million. Piaggio, which is still actively involved in production, boasts a record of nearly nine million Vespas built, including those manufactured under license. Memorable machines in the Piaggio range, after the first 98 cc vehicle, include the 125 of 1948, the 150 GS sports model of 1954, the 50 of 1962 with a rotary valve port timing system and 2% lubrication, the 125 (a more powerful version of the 50) of 1965 and the Primavera 125 of 1967 with its descendants ET3 (1976) and PK (1979). After the overwhelming success of the Ciao moped (1967) with its descendants Bravo, Boxer and Si, came the Vespa Nuova Linea PX of 1977 in 125, 150 and 200 cc displacements, which has been continually updated and even given an electric starter and separate lubrication. Other important projects have been the PK 125 automatic with progressive hydraulic transmission (1983) and the corresponding 50 version, then the brilliant 125 T5 supersports model (1985) and finally – a source of great interest at the 1985 Milan Show – the Vespa two-stroke direct-injection engine, developed and tested over a period of ten years. Outstanding vehicles produced by Innocenti – after the first A 125 of 1947 and B 125 of 1948 – included the C 125 of 1951, the LD 125-150 of 1954 (the first fully enclosed Lambretta) and the sporty TV 175 of 1957, with a completely new engine, frame and bodywork, which signalled a new technical era for the Milanese scooter. From this TV 175, the Li 125-150 (1959) and powerful 200 X Special with disc brake (the first to be fitted to a scooter) were developed. Worth mentioning too are the Lambretta Cento (introduced at the Amsterdam Show of 1964), which was the first Innocenti scooter to have a unitized body, and the original Lui 50-75 (1968) with bodywork designed by Bertone, which was not well received, perhaps because it was too futuristic in style.

The 125 cc Italian Volugrafo of 1941.

The British 1941 Welbike, an air-droppable folding scooter.

The 1946 Vespa 98.

The 1951 Lambretta C125.

The two big rivals of the fifties and sixties: Vespa and Lambretta. The models shown here are of 125 cc displacement.

The 1967 Piaggio Ciao 50.

The 1968 Innocenti Lui 75 SL.

The 1977 Vespa PX 125/150.

The 1975 Lambretta Lince 200. It was built under license in Spain.

The 1986 Suzuki Hi (49 cc).

GERMANY

The German motorcyclist is keenly interested in all areas of sport and very much a sportsman himself. He covers tens of thousands of kilometers a year, in all weathers, because he enjoys using the bike as an alternative to the car. As you may know, there are no speed limits in Germany, therefore I believe that it is the job of racing professionals like myself to educate people to use motorcycles wisely. Modern bikes are of a high technical standard and their efficiency is such that the performance they offer is far in excess of requirements. At the same time they are safer than they used to be: more stable, and with better brakes. Riding a motorbike is a real pleasure these days – you need only get on a Honda to realize that. For that matter, one of the largest European manufacturers, BMW, builds vehicles every bit as good as the best foreign competition: German motorcyclists are fastidious and demanding, and provide a good yardstick for the European industry.

ANTON MANG

A good way to begin a history of the motorcycle in Germany is by drawing attention to a fact that may be surprising: there have been no fewer than five hundred and forty manufacturers since 1885, when Gottlieb Daimler first tested his Reitwagen (ride-wagon/vehicle to be ridden like a horse). The different names include Adler, BMW, DKW, Hercules, Hildebrand & Wolfmüller, Horex, Imperia, Kreidler, Maico, Megola, NSU, Sachs, Triumph (TWN), Tornax, Victoria, Zündapp and various others. Also included are a few curious names like Abendsonne (setting sun), Eisenhammer (iron hammer) and Roter Teufel (red devil).

In 1869, when the French engineers Michaux and Perreaux travelled from Paris to St. Germain on their bicycle fitted with a steam engine, nobody in Germany thought that motor carriages or bicycles had a future. And Gottlieb Daimler, having made a few short trips on his Reitwagen, turned his attention to four-wheeled vehicles. The Reitwagen had a 264 cc petrol-fuelled internal combustion engine (bore 58 mm, stroke 100 mm) and developed 0.5 HP, and with its two wheels and wooden frame reached a speed of about 12 km/h (7½ mph).

It was only in 1894 that engineers Hildebrand & Wolfmüller of Munich began producing the Hildebrand & Wolfmüller bike with a displacement of 1488 cc. They called it Motorrad (motorcycle). This creation of theirs had a water-cooled four-stroke twin-cylinder engine, developing 2.5 HP at 240 rpm, and a top speed of about 40 km/h (25 mph). The connecting rods linked up directly with the rear wheel, which acted as a flywheel. It has been said that two thousand were built, but this figure is clearly inaccurate and probably no more than eight hundred were produced. Hildebrand & Wolfmüller was the first motorcycle company and the first to achieve mass-production. The bike was sold only up to 1897, as new French models developed in the meantime had created a demand for more up-to-date, functional machines, with the result that Hildebrand & Wolfmüller's sales volume fell and the factory had to close. Things were fairly quiet on the German motorcycling scene up to the beginning of the century. It is true that Star of Dresden produced a few machines patented by the Werner Brothers in Paris, but motorization did not really catch on until after 1900. Fafnir of Aachen (Aix-la-Chapelle) started mass-production, also of Werner-patented vehicles, while in Munich Joos built motorbikes and twin-cylinder engines. In 1901 there were thirteen different brands: Adler (Frankfurt am Main), with De Dion engines; Cyklon (Berlin), with Werner and Zedel engines; Dürkopp (Bielefeld), with an original engine; Excelsior (Brandenburg), with Minerva and Zedel engines; Germania S & N (Dresden), with Laurin & Klement engines; Magnet (Berlin), with original single-cylinder and V-twin engines; NSU (Neckarsulm), with Zedel engines; Opel (Rüsselsheim), with an original engine; Presto (Chemnitz), with Minerva and Zedel engines; Progress (Berlin), with a Zedel engine; Torpedo (Geestemünde), with a Zedel engine; Welt-Rad (Schönebeck) with an original engine, and Westfalia (Ölde) with De Dion, Fafnir and Zedel engines. Of these two brands, NSU and Opel, were to become famous.

In 1902 Corona brought out Fafnir engines at Brandenberg, where Brennabor also began operation. Komet appeared on the scene in Dresden, with the French Ixion two-stroke engine, and Wanderer at Schönau Chemnitz, was also to become famous as a producer of automobiles and motorbikes fitted with their own brand of engines.

In 1903 TWN (Triumph Werke Nürnberg) of Nuremberg began production, their bikes being fitted with Fafnir engines. Hercules was also based in Nuremberg, as was Victoria, which started up in 1904. Germany was increasingly alive to the new motorcycling adventure.

The 1971 Maico GS 400 was a powerful trail bike with a two-stroke single-cylinder engine delivering 40 HP at 6500 rpm. Bore and stroke 77 x 83 mm.

The 1974 Kreidler RM 50 had a two-stroke single-cylinder engine (bore and stroke 40 x 39.7 mm) delivering 6.25 HP at 8500 rpm. The cylinder barrel had a nickel-silicon carbide (Nikasil) lining. Pressed steel frame; 5-speed gearbox; speed 85 km/h (53 mph).

The 1969 Maico GS 125 motocross racer had a two-stroke single-cylinder engine with a rotary disc inlet valve.

In 1914, at the outbreak of World War I, twenty-three more companies were operating in the motorcycle sector, but many of them were to close down shortly afterwards. It was at this period that the first motorcycles were imported from Britain, France and Belgium: the FN, for example, was very popular with German motorcyclists.

Motorcycles became more common immediately after the war, and in the roaring twenties the use of motorbikes and motorbike racing became widespread in Germany. There were over five hundred companies building them between 1919 and 1930, of which only half were left after 1926. The largest number (about 10%) were based in Berlin, with many others at Munich, around Nuremberg, at Hamburg, in the Ruhr, at Bielefeld, Dresden, Leipzig, in Saxony, at Magdeburg and at Stuttgart.

Any survey of German motorcycle production, however brief, cannot fail to mention the number of technical innovations that were introduced. For example, in 1935 the K 500 version of the Imperia, produced at Bad Godesberg, had a 500 cc supercharged two-stroke twin-cylinder boxer engine with shaft drive and automatic transmission, hydraulic brakes and other very modern technical features. There were motorcycles with electric motors (Bullo of Bremen, of 1924–1926), with diesel engines (Befag and Deloma of 1921–1924), and even a Wankel engine (Hercules). Frames of special design were often used and other completely new features added, like the cantilever suspension adopted by NSU from 1911.

From 1956 onwards, a few companies produced small sports bikes of up to 50 cc. These included Hercules-Sachs, Zündapp and Kreidler of Stuttgart. The last engines of this type delivered over 6 HP and were extremely reliable. Outstanding speed records were set by Rudolf Kunz in 1965, at Salt Flats (in the U.S.A.), with his 50 cc "record cigar" model, which achieved 210.6 km/h (130.86 mph) and on one stretch of the course even reached 225 km/h (138.80 mph). The chief designer of this model had been Johann Hilber. In 1980 the limit in displacement for speed records was increased from 50 to 80 cc, putting an end to the famous little engines with a piston the size of a liqueur glass.

Other important names were Tornax, Triumph (TWN), Victoria, Maico and Standard, all of which produced models that were world-famous. In 1929 a woman called Hanni Köhler travelled from Cairo to Cape Town on a 750 cc Victoria sidecar model, of the Bergmeister type. Other riders embarked on similar journeys across unexplored regions of the world, the names Ardie and Hercules figuring prominently in these adventures. Maico started production in 1926, and after World War II did brilliantly in motocross and off-road events. At the beginning of the fifties the company produced the highly successful Taifun model (400 cc, two-stroke twin-cylinder), but then ran into difficulties.

Little has remained of the industry and technological achievements of these companies, their designers and famous racing motorcyclists. Only the memory lives on.

ADLER

Adler started producing motorbikes in 1901, with De Dion engines. Up to 1907 the company also built its own V-twin engines, but automobile production had developed to such an extent in that period that motorcycles were discontinued. A new line of Adler bikes did not appear until after World War II, in 1949. The company, which had appointed the engineer Friedrich as head of technical research, produced some magnificent two-stroke models in a space of nine years,

This Adler MB 250 S was produced in 1956. The two-stroke twin-cylinder engine delivered 18 HP. It had a 4-speed gearbox and 16-inch tyres.

starting with the M 100 (98 cc, two-stroke single-cylinder), followed by the 198 cc M 200, the first of a long series of two-stroke, twin-cylinder engines. They were beautifully built, a delight to two-stroke engine buffs and a good model for the Japanese two-stroke twin-cylinder motorcycles of the early sixties. Right from the start Adler took part in sporting events: first with series models, then with purpose-built speed and motocross versions. The 250 cc RS model, initially with an air, and then with a water cooling system, made a name for itself. This company, which was based at Frankfurt am Main, won numerous sporting contests and its racers Günter Beer, Hallmeyer, Lohmann, Luttenberger and Walter Vogel became household names.

The last models produced were the Favorite (16 HP) and the Sprinter (18 HP), both of 250 cc; but undoubtedly the most famous – to the point of being regarded as a symbol of the German motorcycle of the fifties – was the earlier MB 250 S model (of 1956–1957), which delivered 18 HP and was fitted with rear suspension with a vertical sliding wheel. Improvement of the rear suspension by the addition of a trailing arm was not sufficient to boost sales volumes to an acceptable level, and in 1958 Adler was sold to the Grundig radio company.

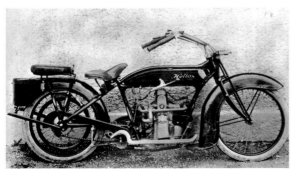

The 1922 Helios, with a BMW boxer engine fitted longitudinally. It had a displacement of 486 cc and delivered 6.5 HP at 2800 rpm.

The first BMW production model with an hydraulic, telescopic front fork was the 1935 R 12. 750 cc engine; 18 HP at 3400 rpm; side-valve timing system.

The 1940 BMW R 75 was a military motorcycle with sidecar which had transmission with locking differential, 8 forward and 2 reverse speeds. 750 cc boxer engine; 26 HP; speed 95 km/h (59 mph).

The new BMW range, with completely redesigned boxer engines in 500, 600 and 750 cc displacements, was brought out in 1969. They had 4-speed gearboxes and duplex cradle frames.

BMW

Bayerische Motoren Werke AG was established in 1917, to build aircraft engines for use in the war. From 1920 it built engines for Flink and Helios motorcycles (of Munich) and in 1922 the engineer Max Friz produced the first complete BMW bike, the R 32, with a twin-cylinder boxer engine and side valves. In 1923 this model was placed on the market (486 cc, 8.5 HP at 3300 rpm, speed approximately 95 km/h (60 mph)). This was the start of BMW's motorcycling history. It covers four periods: the first from 1923 to 1929; the second from 1930 to 1945; the third from 1948 to 1969 and the fourth up to the present day. In the twenties, production was geared to sporting events. In that period engineers Rudolf Schleicher and Rudi Reich and the head of the test team, Joseph Hopf, developed the R 37, R 42, R 39, R

The R 51 of 1938 had plunger rear suspension in addition to the telehydraulic fork. 494 cc boxer engine; 24 HP at 5600 rpm; push rod valve gear.

The BMW R 69S was one of the fastest bikes of the sixties. The 600 cc twin-cylinder engine (bore and stroke 72 x 73 mm) delivered 42 HP at 7000 rpm. Continuous duplex cradle frame; Earles type front suspension; top speed 170 km/h (105 mph).

The R 90S, of 1973, had a 900 cc engine (67 HP; speed 200 km/h = 125 mph). It was the first BMW machine with a handlebar fairing and a twin disc front brake.

47, R 52, R 57, R 62 and R 63 – all with opposed twin-cylinder engines of 500 to 750 cc and shaft drive (except for the R 39, which had a 250 cc, single-cylinder engine). The first competitions were mainly entered by privateers on the R 32, but from 1924 the company participated officially, using normal R 37s piloted by riders like Rudolf Schleicher, Rudi Reich and Franz Bieber. They had their first successes, and from then on BMW enhanced its reputation as a producer of fast, reliable and carefully finished models. In fact, bikes were put into production once they had proved themselves on the racetrack.

In 1924 Franz Bieber won the first championship for the German company with his victory in the ADAC road event at Schleiz. This was to be followed by many other sporting successes achieved by riders like Paul Köppen, Toni Bauhofer, Sepp Stelzer, Ernst Henne, Karl Gall and others. By then BMW was famous, even if it had not yet managed to beat the very fast British

In January 1983, Hubert Auriol won the Paris–Dakar Rally on the BMW 1000 (76 HP; 165 km/h = 103 mph).

◄ Wilhelm Noll and Fritz Cron won the world sidecar championship in 1954. BMW were undisputed leaders in this event for many years, winning numerous world titles.

The BMW R80, introduced in 1984, has the classic "boxer" twin-cylinder engine in the 800 cc version, delivering 50 HP at 7000 rpm.

The very recent K75 has a water-cooled triple-cylinder engine with double-camshaft valve gear. The cylinders are horizontal. Bore and stroke 67 x 70 mm. Power 75 HP at 8500 rpm.

competitors, and the company was consolidating its fortune in commercial terms as well.

The second stage of BMW's history began in 1930 and was characterized by the use of technical innovations even on ordinary mass-produced models and the introduction of supercharged engines. The models produced in this period included R 11, R 16, R 2, R 3, R 4, R 12 and R 17 with pressed steel frames and, from model R 12 onward, with telescopic front forks. Racing models were, however, given tubular frames. BMW was now at the forefront of events, even in international competitions: in 1938 Georg Meier won the European Championship and the following year the Senior TT on the Isle of Man. But World War II put a stop to this ascent.

The first postwar BMW was put on the market in 1948. This was the 250 cc model R 24, with a very simple single-cylinder engine and shaft drive. It was a new beginning, the company's position being reinforced by the 500 cc model R 51/2

(derived from the prewar R 5 and R 51) and 600 cc R 67 and R 68. The most famous riders were Georg Meier and Walter Zeller. In 1955 entirely new models appeared, with Earles-type front forks and trailing-arm rear suspension: these were the 250 cc R 26, 500 cc R 50 and 600 cc R 60 and R 69.

By that time BMW was exporting its bikes to the United States and worldwide, and this enabled it to survive the contraction in the motorcycle market until the next boom, which occurred at the end of the sixties and marked the beginning of the fourth stage in the company's history.

Meanwhile, the Japanese had revolutionized the world motorcycle market and BMW also had to come up with something new. In 1969 it launched models R 50/5, R 60/5 and R 75/5, a new line of motorcycles but still with opposed twin-cylinder engines and shaft drive. It was its first success after the difficult years of the fifties. In

1984 and 1985 a completely new series came out, with flat three- and four-cylinder engines and double overhead camshafts. These were models K 100 and K 75. The models with twin-cylinder boxer engines are, incidentally, still being produced. From 1954 to 1974, BMW won no fewer than nineteen world championships in the 500 cc sidecar category.

One must not forget, either, that Ernst Henne had won the world speed championship on a motorway near Frankfurt in 1937, at 279.5 km/h (173.67 mph) on a 500 cc BMW bike (of approx. 95 HP).

Today, BMW is the only German motorcycle company to have weathered the financial storms of the last sixty years – and, moreover, with high-powered bikes. Its production plant is now in West Berlin (at Spandau), while the design, testing and administrative departments are still in Munich.

In the thirties, split-cylinder, water-cooled supercharged two-stroke DKW machines were enormously successful. This is the 250 cc twin-cylinder model, produced from 1935 to 1937.

This DKW UL 250 supercharged racing model was produced from 1938 for privateers and had a 250 cc two-stroke engine.

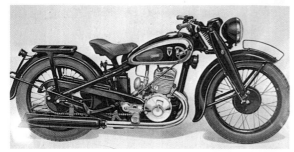

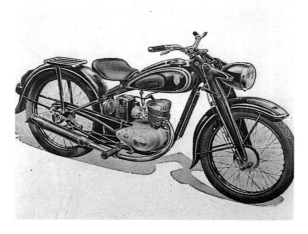

The 1939 DKW SB 500 had a 15 HP two-stroke twin-cylinder engine and a 3-speed gearbox. This model had an electric starter motor.

The DKW RT 125, produced from 1939 to 1957, was the most copied motorbike in the world. The engine was a 125 cc two-stroke single-cylinder. In 1949, the power was 4.8 HP.

DKW

Another famous company was DKW. Founded by J.S. Rasmussen at Zschopau in 1919, the company immediately became world-famous for its two-stroke engines, which were much used in sporting events. Its biggest success was victory in the Lightweight TT, held on the Isle of Man in 1938. The rider on that occasion was Ewald Klüge, who piloted a 250 cc supercharged single-cylinder water-cooled rotary-valve model, delivering about 30 HP. Designers like Hugo Ruppe, August Prüssing, Arnold Zöller and Hermann Weber undoubtedly played an important part in the company's success before World War II. At the end of the twenties DKW was the biggest motorcycle producer in the world, production of

The 1956 MZ GS 175 was a trail bike with a rugged two-stroke single-cylinder engine. Earles type front fork.

This is the MZ 125 racing bike of 1958, minus fairing. The two-stroke single-cylinder air-cooled engine had a rotary disc inlet valve.

The biggest DKW built after World War Two, the 1955 RT 350, had a two-stroke twin-cylinder engine (18 HP, 350 cc). It is still very popular today.

two-stroke engines reaching the one million mark shortly before 1939. Many other companies used DKW engines and DKW's fame was not just due to its sporting successes. All displacements were produced, from 98 to 498 cc, with single- or twin-cylinder engines and air or water cooling systems. Particularly famous models were the 145 and 173 cc Reichsfahrtmodell of 1921; the 206 cc model from 1925 onward; the 498 cc water-cooled twin-cylinder of 1929; models SB and NZ (200 and 500 cc) and the little 98 cc RT of the late thirties. The company started up again after World War II, having moved to Ingolstadt in West Germany. The factory in East Germany continued production, first with the trademark IFA, then MZ. The most famous models were the RT 125 of 1949 (the most copied motorcycle in the world) with a 5 HP engine, and the RT 350 of 1955, with a 350 cc, 18 HP air-cooled two-stroke twin-cylinder engine, telescopic front fork and trailing-arm rear fork.

The company also built some spectacular racing bikes after the war – notably the three-cylinder model with which riders like H. P. Müller, Siegfried Wünsche, Ewald Klüge, August Hobl, Cecil Sandford and others were so successful in numerous trials and championships.

The DKW, by analogy with the Volkswagen, was a Volksmotorrad (a people's bike), mainly appreciated for its economy and reliability. Only a few racing models were produced. DKW suffered during the recession in the motorcycle industry and in 1966 merged with Zweirad Union of Nuremberg. At the end of the seventies it became part of the Fichtel & Sachs group of Schweinfurt, using two-stroke engines of 50 to 175 cc displacement produced by that company. The brand is still famous in Germany, thanks both to sporting activities – world championships and to trophies like the Six Days Trial – and to the reliability of its ordinary models built for the general public.

The 1970 Hercules GS 100 was also produced in a 125 cc version. The engine, made by Sachs, was a two-stroke single-cylinder with a 6-speed gearbox. This trail bike had an Earles type front fork. The power of the lower-capacity version was 13 HP at 7500 rpm.

The 1971 Hercules GS 50 trail bike. The Sachs two-stroke engine (bore 33 mm, stroke 44 mm) delivered 6.75 HP at 8000 rpm. It had a 6-speed gearbox.

HOREX

Horex, based at Oberursel near Frankfurt, began producing complete motorcycles in 1924 and subsequently devised a few models that were to become famous. After a number of four-stroke single-cylinder engines, with side or overhead valves, a 796 cc four-stroke twin-cylinder with an overhead camshaft, designed by the engineer Hermann Reeb, came on the market in 1933. This engine was also used by Tornax, Victoria and other companies. In 1950 the 350 cc Regina model came out: a single-cylinder with push rod valve gear, which was to arouse considerable public interest in later versions as well. In 1955 the 392 cc Imperator ohc twin-cylinder was a big success, followed shortly afterward by the 349 cc Resident single-cylinder with push rod valve gear. Various versions of these models were built in an effort to save the company, but to no avail: the Horex works were bought up by Daimler-Benz in the mid fifties and used to make parts for buses and lorries. Horex had been very active in sporting events in the thirties and fifties, using famous riders like H. P. Müller, Roland Schnell, Fritz Kläger, Georg Braun and others. The company has always figured prominently in motorcycle racing and some small firms are now using the name again.

The 1974 Hercules M 125 was an "all-terrain" bike derived from a military model. The engine was a Sachs two-stroke single-cylinder with a 5-speed gearbox. Power 12.5 HP at 7000 rpm.

The 1974 Hercules W 2000 was the first mass-produced motorcycle in the world to be driven by a Wankel engine. Delivering 25 HP at 6500 rpm, it had a 6-speed gearbox and was air-cooled.

HERCULES

Hercules started producing motorcycles with Fafnir engines in 1904. By the twenties the firm was very well known and used many types of engine by companies such as JAP, Bark, Columbus (owned by Horex), Küchen and others. The models produced by Hercules had two- and four-stroke engines with side valves, overhead valves or overhead camshafts, and displacements of 73 to 498 cc. Sporting achievements were largely responsible for the economic success of this company, which became part of the Fichtel & Sachs group toward the end of the sixties. Their most famous model was produced at the beginning of the seventies: this was the W 2000 with a Wankel engine, manufactured until 1978–1979. Today, Hercules is the second motorcycle company in Germany after BMW, despite its small output.

NSU

One of the oldest German motorcycle firms was NSU, which started up in 1900. Its last model (the 174 cc ohc Maxi delivering 12 HP) was sold in 1964, but 168,985 NSU bikes were still registered in West Germany in 1965. The NSUs of 1953–1954 and 1955 gained no fewer than five world championships (three of which were won by Werner Haas, one by Rupert Hollaus and one by H. P. Müller). Erwin Schmider of Wolfach in the Black Forest, the motorcyclist who took part in the greatest number of trials both nationally and internationally, won many of his gold medals and other awards on an NSU Max. The Max was the model with which NSU wrote an important chapter in the history of motorcycle technology. It had an overhead camshaft operated by link rods (like the engines on some Bentley sports cars) and was designed by Albert Roder. The first model went on the market in 1952, the last being sold in 1963. Another famous engineer and designer of NSU motorcycles and engines was Walter-William Moore who, after working for the British company Norton, moved to Germany and NSU in 1929. He stayed with the company until 1938 and perfected their famous 498 and 348 cc single-cylinder ohc engines, with which riders like Tom Bullus, Bernd Rosemeyer, Heiner Fleischmann, Oskar Steinbach, Wilhelm Herz, Ted Mellors, Fergus Anderson, Hans Schuman and others contested so many national and international events up to 1939. From 1931, NSU had been gaining increasing weight on the international

The 1916 NSU, with a 1000 cc twin-cylinder engine.

market too. The pioneering era for motorcycles in the twenties, with the old four-stroke single-cylinder and V-twin engines, was now over: a new era was beginning, featuring models of completely new design with drop fuel tanks. NSU, who had managed to stay afloat during the worldwide economic crisis at the end of the twenties, was more active at this period in the sporting field, which increased its economic burden. The OSL models, in displacements from 198 to 562 cc, were all single-cylinders with overhead camshafts. They sold so well that in 1938 63,000 motorcycles (and 136,000 bicycles) were produced by a workforce of 3,600. But NSU's finest hour was yet to come. The company started up again after World War II. The Fox model of 1949, with a four-stroke engine and overhead

valves, was a revolutionary type of small motorcycle. The OSL 251 and the two Konsul single-cylinder models of 350 and 500 cc followed the old OSL tradition. Then in 1952 – as already mentioned – the Max appeared, the most famous and spectacular NSU machine.

The company had also resumed its sporting activities, first with the old single-cylinder models of Walter-William Moore, then with the 350 and 500 cc supercharged twin-cylinder racing bikes. They were piloted by Wilhelm Herz, Heiner Fleischmann and, in the case of the 500 cc model with sidecar, Hermann Böhm and Karl Fuchs. But when the F.I.M. banned superchargers in 1951, new research was needed. A team composed of Albert Roder, Walter Froede, Ewald Praxl and the chief foreman, Richard Horch, started work on a 500 cc dohc four-cylinder racing bike, which was unsuccessful. They then decided to design 125 and 250 cc racing models with double overhead camshafts. Werner Haas and the Austrian rider Rupert Hollaus won the World Championships in 1953 and 1954 on machines of this type. Reginald Armstrong, Hans Baltisberger, Roberto Colombo, Otto Daiker, Romolo Ferri, Bill Lomas, H. P. Müller and others also achieved excellent results with them.

Meanwhile the 250 cc Sportmax racing model, inspired by the normal Max and Supermax models, was being designed. One of the most famous riders who obtained numerous placings with this bike was John Surtees, but in 1955 the world champion was H. P. Müller. Sammy Miller, who was later to become one of the best racing motorcyclists in the world, also rode the Sportmax. The Geländemax won trophies and

This 1910 NSU touring model had a 6 HP four-stroke twin-cylinder engine with valve gear using overhead inlet valves and side exhaust valves. The displacement was 600 cc. A system similar to the modern cantilever type was used for the rear suspension.

This 22 HP NSU 500 SS with a 500 cc single-cylinder engine and overhead camshaft valve gear was produced from 1931 to 1934. It was the most famous single-cylinder NSU machine before World War II.

The NSU Quick was produced from 1935 to 1953. It had a 98 cc two-stroke single-cylinder engine delivering 3 HP. It was a lightweight machine, a very popular first bike for young people.

The NSU 201 OSL, with a 7 HP 200 cc four-stroke single-cylinder engine with push rod valve gear, was produced from 1937.

The NSU Fox was produced from 1949 to 1955. It had a 98 cc four-stroke single-cylinder engine delivering 6 HP and an overhead valve timing system.

The 1955 NSU 250 Sportmax, shown here in the version with full aluminum fairing, was derived from the "Max" production model. It won the world title with Müller. The engine was a four-stroke single-cylinder.

The NSU Supermax, produced from 1956, was a great success and was available until 1963. The 250 cc engine, with "Ultramax" single-camshaft valve gear, delivered 18 HP.

championships in trials, participating in various editions of the Six Days Trial and similar events. In 1951 a very important person joined NSU: Gustav Adolf Baumm. Together with Froede, he created models that were to break numerous world speed records. These included the "NSU record kneelers" with 50, 98 and 125 cc engines. In 1954 Baumm himself broke eleven records, but he was killed in an accident at Nürburgring in 1955. In 1956 H. P. Müller continued the battle for the world speed records at Salt Flats in the U.S.A., establishing no fewer than thirty-eight world records in the categories up to 50 cc, 75 cc, 100 cc,

125 cc, 175 cc, 250 cc, and 350 cc (he broke the record for the 125 and 350 cc categories with a 125 cc engine). The maximum speed he attained was 242 km/h (150 mph) over a kilometer with a flying start. On that memorable occasion Wilhelm Herz had also fitted a supercharged engine to a classic racing model, with specially designed integral fairing. He won sixteen world championships in the categories up to 350 cc, 500 cc, 750 cc, and 1000 cc (in the 500 and 1000 cc classes, with a 500 cc engine). The maximum speed he attained was 339 km/h (210 mph) over a mile with a flying start.

The German motorcycle market was in a very

bad way in those years. World War II had been followed by a period of rapid economic growth (the Wirtschaftswunder – the economic miracle), with the result that more and more people were interested in four-wheeled vehicles. Thus while spectacular world records were being established on the one hand, on the other the prospects for the motorcycle market were being virtually reduced to nil. NSU began turning its attention to small motorcars like the famous NSU-Prinz, and motorcycles gradually faded from the scene. NSU is now part of Auto Union.

ZÜNDAPP

In 1921 the Zündapp factory in Nuremberg started producing motorcycles, gradually becoming famous for its advanced technology and sporting achievements. This company was active for over sixty years – up to 1983 – earning an excellent reputation in the motorcycle sector. Its first bike was a simple 211 cc two-stroke single-cylinder, but its best machines were produced in 1941 (the 750 cc KS 750 with a four-stroke opposed twin-cylinder engine with overhead valves, a driving wheel on the sidecar and special gear change with reverse, designed for the Wehrmacht) and 1951 (the 600 cc K 601, still with a twin-cylinder (boxer) engine with overhead valves, shaft drive, telescopic front fork, plunger rear suspension and chain gearing). The K 601 was dubbed Green Elephant, because of its colour and engine power. The most popular model was the 198 cc DB 200, various versions of which were produced. In 1958 Zündapp sold their plant at Nuremberg to Bosch and continued to produce small motorcycles, mopeds and bicycles with roller-driven auxiliary motors at their Munich plant.

In sporting terms Zündapp was active mainly in reliability trials, winning the Six Days Trial and other important contests on several occasions. But this type of competition did not have the impact of speed racing, with the result that their industry was not boosted by sporting activities. Zündapp began participating in road events only in the eighties, by which time it was too late: the Japanese could build excellent bikes at lower cost. The company therefore ended up selling all its machinery to China.

The 1925 Zündapp EM 249 was driven by a single-cylinder engine with a separate gearbox.

The 1929 Z 300, with a single-cylinder engine.

The 1938 Zündapp DS 350 had a four-stroke single-cylinder engine with push rod valve gear, delivering 18 HP.

The Zündapp KS 601 twin-cylinder boxer is the postwar version of the prewar KS 600. Push rod valve gear and shaft final drive. Continuous duplex cradle frame.

The 1941 Zündapp KS 750, with a horizontal twin engine.

The 1957 Zündapp 250S had a two-stroke single-cylinder engine, a pressed steel frame and Earles front suspension.

The 1972 GS 125 trail bike had a two-stroke single-cylinder engine delivering 19 HP at 7900 rpm (bore and stroke 54 x 54 mm). Five-speed gearbox.

This KS 50, with a (thermosiphon) water-cooled single- ▶ cylinder engine, is typical of the latest models by Zündapp.

UNITED STATES

In some respects motorcycling is much more popular in Europe than in America, especially from a competitive point of view. There are fewer contests here and fewer people go to them, apart from annual events like the Laguna Seca race. Nevertheless interest is growing, maybe partly due to the success of American riders in recent world championships. And this is attracting the general public, the ones who use bikes.

The United States are a big market, undoubtedly the most important for the Japanese industry. But different models are preferred here, except in a few rare cases: big, comfortable bikes (because of the 55 mile an hour speed limit) or machines midway between bikes and dragsters. The image of the motorcyclist, which was rather negative in the past, has improved today, partly as a result of the increased popularity of we racers, who are often asked to talk about the subject on television.

Kenny Roberts

KENNY ROBERTS

Harley-Davidson twin-cylinders were very popular in the twenties: this is a 1000 cc model from 1924, with opposed valves.

HARLEY-DAVIDSON

Harley-Davidson originated at Milwaukee in Wisconsin in 1901 when three young men in their twenties, the brothers Arthur and Walter Davidson and their friend William S. Harley, decided to build a motorcycle in their spare time. This first model, completed in 1903, had a single-cylinder engine with direct belt drive, fitted to a bicycle frame, in front of the pedals. The bike worked well enough, but its makers were conscious of their lack of experience and Harley enrolled at the Faculty of Engineering of the University of Wisconsin, passing on his knowledge to his partners as he acquired it.

The improved Harley-Davidson began to be known and appreciated. Output rose from 50 machines in 1906 to 154 in 1907 and 450 in 1908. In 1909 the first Harley-Davidson motorcycle with a V-twin engine was produced and the company has remained faithful to this design to the present day, albeit with countless improvements. The displacements used varied from 750 to 1200 cc. By about 1920 the brand was also popular in Europe, where it did very well in races. In those years the company also brought out a "little" 345 cc

single-cylinder, mainly built for the European market. However, production remained centered on powerful V-twin models which were updated after World War II by the addition of telescopic forks, rear suspension, hydraulic tappets and electric starters.

Harley-Davidson is now virtually the only United States producer and builds models – still V-twins – from 1000 to 1350 cc in Grand Touring, sports and Chopper versions.

Before World War II, Harley-Davidson models had displacements varying from 750 to 1200 cc. The photograph shows the 1935 750 twin-cylinder.

In the fifties and sixties, Harley-Davidson bikes were the most powerful in the world. This is the 1200 cc Duo Glide of 1960, with hydraulic tappets.

This handsome 900 cc twin-cylinder of 1965 was unmistakably a sports machine. Note the single exhaust pipes, both on the same side.

The 1350 cc Harley-Davidson Sturgis, with toothed belt final drive, was brought out in 1980. It had aluminum alloy spoked wheels and a twin disc front brake.

INDIAN

The founder of Indian was a man by the name of Oscar Hedstrom, a racing cyclist who was dissatisfied with the performance of the first motorcycles imported to the United States to "pull" cyclists during track races. After exhibiting his first bike in 1900 Hedstrom received many orders and therefore decided to devote himself to motorcycle production, working first with Charles Henshaw, then with George Hendee. The bike was sold to the public in 1901, under the name

One of the most famous models produced by Indian was the Scout of the mid-twenties. It had a twin-cylinder engine with side valves.

Indian; it had a bicycle-type frame, the engine being fitted in place of the saddle support tube, and chain drive. Three were produced in 1901, rising to 143 in 1902 and 546 in 1904, when a twistgrip throttle control was fitted, with rigid-rod transmission.

The first V-twin was produced in 1905. The company continued to expand and soon became the biggest in the world. In 1914 it employed over 3,000 people and produced 35,000 machines; it was known in Europe and technically avant-garde to the extent of marketing a twin-cylinder model with integral leaf-spring suspension and an electric starter.

Indian was still a leading company in the twenties, overall production amounting to 250,000 units. Its most popular model was the Scout, with a V-twin engine. Its greatest achievement was at the beginning of the thirties when it built the 1200 cc Four, with four cylinders in line: an elegant and powerful model, which was available for about ten years. However, the company was hard hit by the Depression in those years and after a brief recovery during World War II, when it supplied vehicles to the Army, its predicament worsened and it closed down in the fifties.

AMERICAN FOUR-CYLINDERS

In the first decades of this century the U.S. motorcycle industry boasted a considerable number of longitudinal four-cylinder models alongside the typical V-twins, which were famous even abroad. The earliest was the Pierce Arrow of 1909 with a displacement of 750 cc, two-speed transmission with shaft drive and a beautiful frame made up of thick tubes, which doubled as fuel and oil tanks. This highly sophisticated machine was also very expensive; the company soon found itself in financial difficulties, and was forced to close down.

Next on the scene was the Henderson, designed by William Henderson in 1911, with a displacement of about 780 cc (later increased to 1076 cc), opposed valves, chain drive and a tubular frame; it could do 100 km/h (62 mph) and was soon popular (in Italy it was sold by Lanfranchi). The Henderson four-cylinder was the first bike to use force-feed lubrication for the main and big-end bearings. In 1917 Henderson was taken over by Excelsior, a company founded by a German immigrant called Ignaz Schwinn. The resultant Henderson-Excelsior underwent various modifications and was soon the fastest bike on the market: the 1922 model K De Luxe, with a 1300 cc engine, could easily do 160 km/h (100 mph) with the rider in the upright position and was favoured by the American police, because no car could outstrip it. In 1924 a specially prepared model was capable of exceeding 200 km/h (125 mph). Despite its good qualities, Excelsior did not survive the slump of 1929 and disappeared from the market a couple of years later. However, William Henderson had left Excelsior in 1919 and set up in business on his own again. He designed another four-cylinder, the Ace, which obviously had a lot in common with the Henderson-Excelsior. Built at Philadelphia it was, however, exceptional from an aesthetic point of view too, in terms of its shape, tasteful colour scheme and nickel plating. Of approximately 1200 cc displacement, it had opposed valves, a three-speed gearbox and chain drive. The 1924 model developed over 40 HP and had drum brakes on both wheels; in that same year it established a world speed record of over 215 km/h (134 mph). But this bike was also very expensive, and despite excellent sales both at home and abroad the company was plagued by financial troubles until it was taken over in 1927 by Indian, who derived their famous model Four from the Ace.

Militaire designed a bike of the same name in 1913–1914 with a 1100 cc engine later increased to 1600 cc, a three-speed gearbox and highly original features such as lateral stabilizing wheels and, for a time, a steering wheel. This company also had a difficult time financially; in 1917 it changed its name to Militor, but despite filling sizeable orders for military vehicles it disappeared in 1922.

The last "big" American four-cylinder was built by Cleveland in 1925 with the aid of a former employee of Henderson, the engineer De Long. The first Cleveland had a displacement of about 750 cc, opposed valves, a three-speed gearbox, a tubular frame and a dual front fork. The displacement was soon increased to 1000 cc. The Tornado model of 1929, with drum brakes on both wheels and a new, very low and streamlined frame, could do 100 mph (160 km/h). It was a luxury machine and Cleveland also fell victim to the Depression, closing down in 1930. Thus the only four-cylinder left in production was the Indian Four.

Detail of the four-cylinder-in-line engine of the 1914 Henderson.

The 1936 Indian 1000, with four cylinders in line.

NER-A-CAR

Motorbikes at one time were an economic means of transport for the less wealthy. Therefore every effort was made to improve their practicality and ease of operation. One of the most unusual interpretations of the utilitarian motorbike was the Ner-a-Car, designed by J. Neracker at Syracuse (New York) in 1921. It had a long, low profile, with an open cradle and metal body covering the mechanical parts, except for the cylinder head and block. The two-stroke engine was of about 250 cc; the transmission included a progressive friction gear, comprising a disc pressed against the engine flywheel. It had indirect steering, with helical spring suspension. The machine was ridden from a very comfortable position, with ample leg-room. However, the bike was so much out of the ordinary that it was not a great success, even the British version with a 350 cc four-stroke engine failing to convince prospective buyers and in 1926, Ner-a-Car disappeared. Nevertheless its originality has ensured it an important place in the history of the motorcycle.

FRANCE

Many of the most important pioneers of motor sports were born in or worked in France, which has always been tremendously keen on motorcycling. Oddly enough, however, after a spectacular start the French motorcycle industry failed to sustain a high level of enthusiasm and productivity. French racers have also had long periods of "absenteeism" from the world championships and returned to positions of absolute preeminence in speed contests only in the early seventies. One area in which they have, however, always been very strong and, for a long time now, undisputed world leaders is in track endurance contests. Then again, that unique sporting event known as the Bol d'Or originated in France.

CHRISTIAN SARRON

Although France was one of the very first countries to build motorized two-wheeled vehicles, and although the very word "motorcycle" was invented in Paris at the end of the last century by the Werner brothers, the French industry cannot be said to have contributed subsequently to any very great extent to the technical progress and evolution of the motorcycle, except with the outstanding Peugeot model of 1913, with double-camshaft valve gear and four valves per cylinder.

French companies built a number of very good bikes in the twenties and thirties, but none of them was truly technically avant-garde. The French motorcycle industry recovered rapidly after World War II and in fact flourished for some years, mainly producing utilitarian models, scooters and above all, mopeds. But before long, a crisis of the kind that affected Italy and Germany at about the same time placed most of the French companies in serious difficulties, causing many to shut down. The moped industry survived, indomitable, and is still very much alive and well today, even if it no longer enjoys the type of international prestige it once did.

Very few motorcycles are produced in France today and nearly all the great names belong to the past. Famous examples were Alcyon, which was the first company in the world to use valve gear

The 1919 Monet-Goyon Vélauto had a vertical single-cylinder engine with a big external flywheel. The petrol tank was fitted above the rear wheel and the seat was made of wicker.

with four valves per cylinder; Monet-Goyon, who started production in 1917 and stopped in 1957; and Koehler Escoffier. The latter was taken over by Monet-Goyon in 1929.

Other, much more important companies were Dresch – which operated for about fifteen years, finally closing down in 1939 – and Dax, which was only active in the thirties.

In a class of its own was Terrot, which was founded in 1901 and operated until the end of the sixties. After World War II Terrot found itself in difficulties and was acquired by the Peugeot group. At the top of its range was a handsome 500

cc four-stroke single-cylinder with push rod valve gear; it also produced a few very interesting scooters with two-stroke engines.

Jonghi was well known for many years for its sturdy, high-performance vehicles. In 1931 this company produced its first, 350 cc single-cylinder bikes, from which excellent sporting models were derived. Their range was subsequently extended to include 175 and 250 cc models as well as less powerful bikes (which were fitted with two-stroke

Vélosolex is perhaps the world's most famous producer of mopeds. This is the 1970 Flash 50, with shaft final drive. This company merged with Motobécane in 1975.

engines of another make). Jonghi continued operation after the war, producing both two- and four-stroke-engined vehicles, and did well in endurance contests (Bol d'Or) and long-distance world speed championships before closing down in 1956. Magnat Debon started producing motorcycles in 1906 and was one of the leading French companies for many years, before being absorbed by Terrot in the thirties. It shut down at the end of the fifties. René Gillet began building motorbikes in 1898 and stayed in operation until 1957.

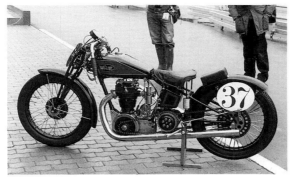

The 500 cc Gnome & Rhône racing bike came out in 1927. The four-stroke single-cylinder engine had push rod valve gear and an external flywheel.

This Gnome & Rhône AX2 was a special military bike with a pressed steel frame. It had a four-stroke twin-cylinder boxer engine with side valves.

GNOME & RHÔNE

This company started out building aircraft engines, for which it became justly world-famous. In the twenties and thirties its engines were manufactured under license. Motorcycle production began in 1919 and soon became a very important part of the company's activity. Its single-cylinder models, which were very popular in the twenties, were joined by powerful twin-cylinder models with shaft drive. After World War II the company mainly produced low-powered bikes with two-stroke engines. It ceased operations in 1959.

MOTOBÉCANE

This French company is best known nowadays for its mopeds and lightweight motorbikes. Established in 1922, Motobécane produced a very wide range of two-stroke models in displacements up to 300 cc and four-stroke models in higher displacements for a number of years. In addition to the excellent single-cylinder versions, bikes with four cylinders in line and a unit construction

gearbox in displacements from 500 to 750 cc appeared in the thirties.

After World War II the company continued to produce excellent models of medium displacement too, with four-stroke engines, but then – following the crisis at the end of the fifties – it concentrated on mopeds and lightweight bikes with two-stroke engines. It merged with Vélosolex in 1975.

The 125 cc two-stroke twin-cylinder produced by Motobécane was very popular for many years, not just in France but in various other European countries. This is the 1970 version.

PEUGEOT

The most famous French motorcycle company is undoubtedly Peugeot, which originated in 1899 and rapidly became world-famous for its avant-garde products (it even supplied engines to other manufacturers like Norton). In 1913 it made a racing bike which was a source of inspiration to engineers worldwide for many years to come: a beautiful 500 cc twin-cylinder, with four valves per cylinder and a double overhead camshaft, operated by a gear train.

Peugeot withdrew from racing at the end of the twenties. At that time its range of production models was very extensive and included light-weight bikes driven by two-stroke engines and more powerful ones with four-stroke single or V-twin engines. This was one of the first companies in the world to fit unit construction gearboxes to all its models.

After World War II Peugeot concentrated on bikes of 250 cc and under (all with two-stroke engines) and mopeds. In recent years it has confined its production to mopeds and scooters.

The 1971 Peugeot V 104 50 moped, with a two-stroke single-cylinder engine and telescopic front and rear suspension.

◄ This 1904 Peugeot had a four-stroke single-cylinder engine with side valves and an interesting Truffaut front suspension system.

171

JAPAN

My country entered the world of two-wheeled vehicles by observing, with humility, what was made in Europe and has now reached the point where it is a treasure house of state-of-the-art motorcycle technology. Commercial development of the sector has gone hand in hand with sporting achievements. At one time there were few Japanese racers and they were not very well known, but things have changed a great deal in the last few years: the sport now has a huge following and provides the chief incentive for the industry. The vast majority of those who use bikes for pleasure dream of becoming top racers one day and use their vehicles accordingly, which – given the fact that these modern "toys" are capable of speeds well in excess of 200 km/h (125 mph) – can be dangerous. We racers therefore have the serious responsibility of making people understand that roads are not racetracks. Then there is another class of motorcyclist in Japan, to which I belong, which regards motorcycles and motorcycling as a form of art. Modern art. We are people who love bikes and preserve them, like a piece of history that must not be lost.

TAKAZUMI KATAYAMA

Honda's first products were auxiliary motors for bicycles. This is the 1948 Cub 50.

The Japanese motorcycle industry, which has dominated markets the world over for years now, started up after 1945. To begin with it developed on the internal market only with models which were undoubtedly behind those of their European contemporaries from a technical point of view, then expanded in more and more explosive fashion on the various world markets with increasingly sophisticated and efficient models. The Japanese industry produced its first, really valid, up-to-date models after thorough examination and assessment of the best products of the European industry. However, it soon began to blaze a trail of its own, moving to a position right at the forefront of technology with highly original products. In the fifties numerous small and medium-sized motorcycle companies were active in Japan, but these gradually disappeared, leaving the way free for the big four (Honda, Yamaha, Kawasaki and Suzuki). Lesser companies included Tohatsu, Bridgestone, Lilac and Marusha.

HONDA

In 1948 Soichiro Honda, an enterprising individual born in 1906 in the little Japanese village of Komyo, founded what was to become the biggest motorcycle factory in the world at Hamamatsu. At first it recycled materials left over from the war to make small auxiliary motors for bicycles, but after a year it began producing an engine entirely of its own construction. In subsequent years Honda opened other plants at Tokyo, Kamijvujo, Saitama and Nuchura in addition to the works at Hamamatsu, while at the same time the Honda Motor Co. Ltd. gradually increased its capital.

Honda confined its range of products to vehicles of small displacement, but produced in very large numbers. A turning point for the Japanese company came in 1959 with the creation of the American Honda Motor Co., aimed at both the United States and Europe. All Honda's products followed a pattern that was to characterize the company in the future: the introduction of a new model or the start of a new commercial policy coincided with or was preceded by participation in sporting events. In fact, in 1959 Honda entered no fewer than 125 four-stroke twin-cylinder bikes in the legendary Tourist Trophy contest, of which four were successful. That was the start of a magnificent series of victories in international racing which culminated in Honda winning 41 world speed titles in 1985 (nineteen rider and twenty-two brand). But Honda's successes are not confined to speed contests: the Japanese company has in fact

172

Over 15 million Honda Cub 50s were built. The one in the picture is from 1958.

This is the 1953 Honda Dream 125.

participated in and won events in nearly all the sporting disciplines. It has had five victories in motocross 500 world championships, won three world championships in trials, and six endurance titles (with no fewer than ten victories in the Bol d'Or), not to mention its successes in the African races, including the Paris–Dakar rally. In 1960 it built a 250 in both road and racing versions, and in the sixties the Japanese company opened numerous branches in Europe. The year 1968 saw two important events: the company withdrew (temporarily) from racing and the number of bikes produced since the establishment of Honda reached the ten million mark. But 1969 was the decisive year for the Japanese company and world motorcycling in general. That year saw the birth of the CB 750, which attracted millions of motorcycle enthusiasts back to the sport. With the crisis in the fifties the motorcycle had been relegated to the role of an economic means of transport, rather than a product for an elite following. At the end of the seventies the CB 750, together with a few British and Italian bikes, established a new fashion and a new form of motorcycling. This four-stroke four-cylinder machine was the first in a series that lasted until the eighties, when it was replaced by the "V" range. The four-cylinder format was available with different engines, in 350, 400, 500, 550, 650, 900 and 1000 cc versions. An interesting model in

Mike Hailwood was the top Honda racing motorcyclist in the sixties, competing with the six-cylinder in the 250 and 350 classes (see photo) and with the four-cylinder in the 500 class.

The Honda CB 750 came out in 1969. It had single-camshaft valve gear, a 5-speed gearbox and an electric starter. The front disc brake was hydraulically actuated. Bore and stroke 61 x 63 mm; power 67 HP at 8000 rpm.

The CB 400F was derived from the CB 350F, which it replaced in 1974. A sixth speed was added to the transmission. Bore and stroke 51 x 50 mm; power 37 HP at 8500 rpm.

The 1978 CX 500 (later increased to 650 cc) was very different from Honda's usual models: the engine was a water-cooled V-twin with push rod valve gear, delivering 50 HP at 9000 rpm.

The 1979 CB 900F with a four-cylinder-in-line engine and double-camshaft valve gear with four valves per cylinder. Power 95 HP at 900 rpm.

The Honda CB 125K twin-cylinder of the early seventies was a great success. It also had single-camshaft valve gear and an electric starter. Bore and stroke 44 x 41 mm; power 15 HP at 10,500 rpm.

The CBX 1000, with a six-cylinder-in-line transverse engine and 24 valves, caused a sensation when it came out in 1978. It delivered no less than 105 HP at 9000 rpm.

This is the CB 350F, which came out in 1972, with four cylinders in line, an overhead camshaft, electric starter and front disc brake. Bore and stroke 47 x 50 mm; power 34 HP at 9500 rpm.

The CB 750K had a double-camshaft, 16-valve engine with four cylinders in line, exactly like that of the CB 900F.

This comfortable grand touring bike is the latest version of the Gold Wing, with four opposed cylinders and single-camshaft valve gear operated by toothed belts.

The XL 500S was the model which marked Honda's entry into the high-powered enduro bike sector.

The CX 650 Turbo was not a great commercial success. It had a supercharged twin-cylinder engine and electronic fuel injection.

In 1985 Freddie Spencer won the world title in both the 250 and 500 classes, on the very fast Honda racing machines.

The CB 1100 R was produced in limited numbers for high-speed enthusiasts.

the 1000 class was the GL Gold Wing, a four-cylinder boxer type with cardan shaft final drive which appeared toward the end of the seventies and is still an excellent grand touring bike for marathon riders the world over. But Honda's production also includes two- and four-stroke single-cylinder (the latter including the XLs, which contributed to its success in enduro and African races), twin- and multi-cylinder models, not forgetting mopeds and scooters.

The CBX 750F (91 HP) is the newest type of machine with four cylinders in line.

At the beginning of the eighties. Honda introduced some new water-cooled, 90° V-type four-cylinder engines, with double-camshaft valve gear and 4 valves per cylinder, like the one fitted to this VF 750F, which delivers 90 HP at 10,000 rpm.

Enduro bikes are also available in smaller displacements, along with road models. This type has a single-cylinder engine in displacements from 125 to 200 cc, and single-camshaft valve gear.

This NS 400R, with a two-stroke three-cylinder water-cooled engine with reed inlet valves, is clearly inspired by Grand Prix models. It delivers 72 HP at 9000 rpm.

KAWASAKI

Like another company that figured prominently in the history of motorcycling – Piaggio-Vespa – Kawasaki's first bike was produced by the aeronautical industry, but not as directly as the most famous scooter in the world.

Kawasaki was in fact founded in 1878 by Shozo Kawasaki as a shipbuilding concern, and expanded in 1937 to cover the aeronautical field as well. This side of the industry developed a motorcycle engine which appeared in 1949 and was called KE. It was a 148 cc single-cylinder model which was used by many other companies, as was the KH (two-stroke, 250 cc), made in 1952. A year later Kawasaki came to an agreement with Meihatsu to manufacture complete motorbikes. In the meantime the KB-1 was built: a 60 cc two-stroke engine which served as an auxiliary motor for bicycles.

In 1954 the first two bikes which can be regarded as the forerunners of true Kawasaki machines appeared. These were a 125 Meihatsu with a Kawasaki 125 KB-5 engine and a scooter fitted with the 60 cc KB-2.

Not until the sixties was a bike produced under the name Kawasaki. This was the B8, with a 125 cc two-stroke single-cylinder engine and four-speed gearbox.

The continual development of Kawasaki Industries led to the creation of the Kawasaki Motorcycle Co. Ltd. in the mid sixties, with a branch in America. Although Kawasaki was already appreciated as a manufacturer of low-powered and off-road bikes, the real breakthrough came in 1968 when it introduced the H1 500 cc Mach III, a very powerful (60 HP) air-cooled two-stroke, triple cylinder bike.

This was followed by a racing version, which was an ideal – if costly – solution for "privateers" who up till then had had to be content with using British single-cylinder models for racing championships. The success of the Mach III in the road and racing versions persuaded Kawasaki to sell a complete range of three-cylinder models in 250 cc (known as S1), 350 cc (S2) and 750cc (H2) displacements. A racing version was derived from the latter which was highly successful in the United States too, where the "dark green" team (Kawasaki's official colour in racing events) completely dominated the scene.

The motorcycle section of the Japanese holding company realized the need to produce four-stroke engines too and in 1972 Kawasaki introduced the 900 Z1, a machine that was to make history. It was a 900 cc four-stroke model with four cylinders in line, five-speed transmission and an output of over 80 HP. It too was the first of a series, being followed by the 750, 1000, and 650 and finally the standard-bearer, the KZ 1300 A.

In its different versions, the four-stroke engine is still Kawasaki's strong point; the range being completed by highly progressive twin-cylinder roadsters and single-cylinder enduro models.

In racing terms Kawasaki boasts numerous successes in both the endurance field – in which the "dark greens" have won five world titles (two rider, three works) – and speed contests, where they have won the world championships eighteen times (nine rider, nine works).

At the beginning of the seventies, the two-stroke three-cylinder H1 500 "Mach III" was one of the fastest bikes around. Bore and stroke 60 x 58.5 mm; power 60 HP at 7500 rpm.

This is the 750 cc version of the two-stroke three-cylinder, which came out in 1972 and delivered 74 HP at 6800 rpm.

The brilliant "Avenger" two-stroke twin-cylinders, produced toward the end of the sixties in 250 and 350 cc displacements, were very successful.

The real breakthrough for Kawasaki came with the 900 Z1, the first high-powered four-stroke machine produced by this company. Four-cylinder engine; power over 80 HP.

The single-camshaft twin-cylinder Z 400 (1975) was quite popular because of its good handling and low running costs. The engine delivered 36 HP at 8500 rpm.

The first medium-capacity Kawasaki four-cylinder was the 1977 Z 650. As in the Z 900, double-camshaft valve gear was used. Bore and stroke 62 x 54 mm; power 64 HP at 8500 rpm.

Kawasaki also mass-produced a four-cylinder model with fuel injection in the early eighties. This was the GPz 1100, with a 108 HP engine.

The 1979 Z 1300 had an impressive engine with six cylinders in line, water cooling, double-camshaft valve gear and shaft final drive. Power 120 HP at 8000 rpm.

The GPz 550 four-cylinder, derived from an earlier 500 cc model, was a big success. The engine delivered 64 HP at 9000 rpm.

Like all the other Japanese companies, Kawasaki made a supercharged bike: the ZX 750 Turbo which was not, however, a great success.

This is the recent (1985) GPz 600 R, with a four-cylinder water-cooled engine. The stated power is 75 HP. Square section tubes; weight 195 kg (430 lb).

Although not used for racing like its Yamaha and Honda counterparts, Kawasaki also has a 600 cc four-stroke enduro model. This is the KLR 600, the latest version of which has an electric starter motor.

Kawasaki's major sporting successes have been in the 250 and 350 classes, in which they won eight world titles from 1978 to 1982 with riders Ballington and Mang (in the photo). The bikes were two-stroke twin-cylinder models with rotary disc valve induction control. The cylinders were arranged in tandem.

Another, highly successful Kawasaki bike was the GPz 900 R with a water-cooled engine with four cylinders in line and four valves per cylinder, developing 115 HP at 9500 rpm.

The most recent maxi-version Kawasaki is the 1000 RX, which is completely new despite being a natural development of the 900. The stated power is 125 HP.

Another important addition to Kawasaki's range was the 1000 GTR, the first true grand touring model by this Japanese company: 115 HP; 245 kg (540 lb); 29 liter (6.38 imperial gallon) petrol tank.

SUZUKI

The story of Suzuki begins at Hamamatsu, a town some two hundred kilometers (125 miles) from Tokyo, where Michio Suzuki, who came from a family of cotton growers, took the first step toward the creation of the giant of the motor industry which bears his name by establishing a firm to build textile machinery. But progress did not stop there. Having launched his business technically and commercially, Mr. Suzuki turned his attention to the automobile sector. Concentrating on the fact that around the 1930s Japan was importing about twenty thousand vehicles a year, Suzuki purchased an Austin Seven, which he studied in order to design his first automobile. Unfortunately, the new vehicle was blocked by the restrictions which the Japanese government had imposed on nonessential industry. The car in question was driven by a 750 cc four-cylinder water-cooled engine delivering 13 HP at 3500 rpm.

Suzuki's arrival on the two-wheeled vehicle scene dates from the early fifties, when the company brought out a motor bicycle with a 36 cc two-stroke engine. The engine was called Power Free. A year later (March 1953) came an enlarged version of the Power Free, the 60 cc Diamond Free. The first "true" motorbike was the Colleda, a 90 cc four-stroke single-cylinder which appeared at the end of 1953. This first version was followed by many others, also with 125 cc engines (these being called Colleda CO) and in 1955 a completely revised model called COX appeared, accompanied by a version with a two-stroke engine (Colleda ST), also of 125 cc.

Meanwhile, in June 1954, the company had assumed the name Suzuki Motor Co. Ltd. and two years later the Colleda TT appeared, a 250 cc two-stroke twin-cylinder. Until the sixties Suzuki's production was entirely based on less powerful models (maximum displacement 250 cc), but in 1961 the Japanese company opened an office in Britain, with the result that their sphere of interest was increasingly extended toward models designed for Europe and the United States. The real springboard to success was the model T20 Super Six introduced in 1963, a two-stroke twin-cylinder which caused a sensation in Europe and the United States, earning Suzuki a solid reputation. After that came a big leap in power with the introduction of the T500 Cobra, a two-stroke twin-cylinder which finally launched the Japanese company into the motorcycling world thanks also to its involvement in speed contests, using a bike closely derived from the mass production model.

Another milestone in Suzuki's history was the GT 380, a two-stroke triple cylinder with a RAM Air system for cooling the cylinder heads. In its rise to fame Suzuki introduced the GT 750, another three-cylinder but with a water cooling system, which only went out of production shortly before the eighties.

Suzuki suffered a setback with its RE 5 with Wankel engine, which – like the NSU and Mazda cars that used the same type of power unit – did not have the success hoped for.

Another turning point in the Japanese company's history came in 1976 when it introduced the first four-stroke maxis: the four-cylinder GS 750 and twin-cylinder GS 400. From that moment a new era began for Suzuki, which is still continuing, and all credit is due to the company for having achieved such brilliant technological diversity.

This technological capacity of theirs has been fully demonstrated in both speed and motocross events. Since Suzuki entered its first race way back in 1953, the company has won no fewer than twenty-one world motocross titles (in the three classes), one world title for endurance and twenty-eight for speed.

Suzuki won four rider world titles in the 500 class, two of which (in 1976 and 1977) were with Barry Sheene. The bike had four cylinders arranged in a square and rotary disc inlet valves.

The 500 cc Suzuki twin-cylinder appeared toward the end of the sixties. The two-stroke engine (bore and stroke 70 x 64 mm) delivered 47 HP at 7000 rpm.

The Suzuki two-stroke air-cooled three-cylinders were produced in 380 and 550 cc displacements. The latter delivered 50 HP at 6500 rpm (early seventies).

For some years the most powerful bike produced by Suzuki was the GT 750 water-cooled three-cylinder, introduced in 1971. Stated power 65 HP at 6500 rpm.

Interesting from a technical point of view, but unsuccessful commercially: the RE 5 with a water-cooled Wankel engine. Power 62 HP at 6500 rpm (mid-seventies).

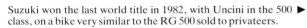

Suzuki won the last world title in 1982, with Uncini in the 500 ▶ class, on a bike very similar to the RG 500 sold to privateers.

Suzuki entered the four-stroke maxi sector in 1976 with the GS 750 four-cylinder with double-camshaft valve gear. Power 70 HP at 8500 rpm.

◀ The 1980 DR 400 S was the first high-powered four-stroke "enduro" bike produced by Suzuki.

The Katana, produced in 550, 750 and 1100 cc displacements, was highly progressive from an aesthetic point of view. The engine was a four-cylinder with double-camshaft valve gear.

The RG 500 Gamma is a faithful replica of the very successful racing model: a two-stroke four-cylinder with 6-speed gears, delivering 95 HP. The cylinders are arranged in a square and induction is controlled by rotary disc valves.

The RV 90 is a cross between a fun bike and moped. It has a small two-stroke single-cylinder engine with a 6-speed gearbox.

The only supercharged Suzuki was the XN 85, with a turbo-supercharger, delivering 85 HP at 8500 rpm.

Suzuki does not produce only road bikes but also motocross and on/off-road machines. One of the most interesting enduro models is the DR 600, a four-stroke single-cylinder originally of 400 cc.

One of the most beautiful and powerful bikes of the eighties, the GSX 750 R, also directly derived from a top enduro competition model. It is a 749 cc four-stroke four-cylinder. Maximum stated power 100 HP at 11,000 rpm.

YAMAHA

A few romantics of the motorcycling world maintain that the noise a motorbike makes is sheer music. Yamaha has every right to do so, given that it was founded in 1955 by Nippon Gakki, one of the biggest manufacturers of musical instruments in Japan.

The first Yamaha bike, dating from 1955, was the 125 YA-1, a 123 cc two-stroke single-cylinder. The YA-2 derived from it won the prestigious "Good Design Award," handsome recognition of the quality of the then new industry.

In 1957 Yamaha brought out a 250, the YD-1, the first of a long series of vehicles, modern versions of which are still being produced today. In 1960 a motor bicycle appeared together with the 50 cc MF-1, which was followed two years later by the 50 and 55 cc MF-2.

Yamaha made its debut in world speed championships at the same period and is still active in this sector. Its two-stroke models encountered stiff opposition from the very powerful Italian (Benelli and MV Agusta) and Japanese (Honda) four-stroke machines, especially in the 250 and 350 classes. Yamaha has won no fewer than forty-five world titles in the 125, 250, 350 and 500 categories, with twenty-two victories in the rider results and twenty-three in the brand ones.

In 1970 Yamaha produced its first four-stroke model, a 650 XS-1 which was disappointing from a technical point of view. Fortunately for the company, its two-stroke twin-cylinders continued to reap commercial and sporting rewards. Still in 1970, Yamaha won the 250 class World Championship with the TD-2. Its second four-stroke model, the TX 750 of 1972, was not successful either, but the late lamented Jarno Saarinen repaired Yamaha's dented image in the sporting world when he piloted the new four-cylinder 500 model to victory in its first race. Kenny Roberts and Giacomo Agostini also subsequently raced this model. In any case, the problems with the company's four-stroke machines did not affect its business overseas, where imports of low-powered Yamahas continued unabated.

In the mid seventies a bike was introduced which was to constitute a milestone in the history of motorcycling: the XT 500. With this four-stroke single-cylinder model – which virtually initiated the fashion for enduro bikes – Yamaha took part in numerous African races, thus acquiring the experience needed to produce a long-distance racing model, the Ténéré, from the name of the Algerian desert which has always been the toughest part of the legendary Paris–Dakar rally.

Contemporary with the XT 500 Yamaha continued its efforts to enter the four-stroke roadster market, with models like the XS 750, XS 1100, XJ 650 (from which a supercharged version was derived) and maxi twin-cylinders of classic design for the American market, like the XV

The first Yamaha four-stroke machine was the 650 twin-cylinder with single-camshaft valve gear. Bore and stroke 75 x 74 mm; power 53 HP at 7000 rpm.

The 250 and 350 cc two-stroke twin-cylinders were manufactured for many years in numerous versions. Bore and stroke 54 x 54 mm for the 250 and 64 x 54 mm for the 350.

The 1976 RD 400 twin-cylinder. The engine delivered 38 HP at 7000 rpm. Weight 155 kg (342 lb).

The big enduro models with four-stroke single-cylinder engines were launched by Yamaha with the 1977 model XT 500. Bore and stroke 87 x 84 mm; power 30 HP at 6250 rpm.

Yamaha finally entered the big four-stroke multicylinder sector in 1977, with this double-camshaft 750 with three cylinders in line. Bore and stroke 68 x 68 mm.

This XS 650 SE is a Custom bike with a twin-cylinder engine and single-camshaft valve gear.

In the sixties, Yamaha was actively involved in the world speed championships, winning the title in the 125 (1967 and 1968) and 250 (1964, 1965 and 1968) classes, with racers Ivy and Read.

At the end of the seventies Yamaha introduced this hefty 1100 cc four-cylinder with double-camshaft valve gear and a power of about 95 HP. Shaft final drive. Speed 215 km/h (134 mph).

The various technical schemes undertaken by Yamaha include this high-powered V-twin. This is the 1980 XV 750 SE model, delivering 61 HP at 7000 rpm.

Yamaha was also caught up in the "turbo" craze and in 1981 introduced the XJ 650 turbo, derived from their four-stroke, four-cylinder model.

This is the FJ 1100 with a double-camshaft four-cylinder engine and frame of unusual design. The power is 125 HP at 9000 rpm.

The RD 500 LC, introduced in 1984, was inspired by racing models. The two-stroke engine has four cylinders in a V and is water-cooled. Power 84 HP at 9500 rpm.

This is the XT 550 Enduro, which replaced the excellent XT 500 with equal success. Four-stroke single-cylinder engine delivering 38 HP at 5500 rpm.

series (750 and 1000). Another significant bike in the eighties has been the RD 500 LC, a two-stroke four-cylinder, which is a clear "replica" of the bike used by Kenny Roberts in the world speed championships.

Yamaha finally established itself in the four-stroke sector with the FJ 1100, an advanced, high-powered four-cylinder which was well received by maxibike fans.

However, this company – which has incidentally extended its production to include marine engines, fishing boats and motor sleds – has produced its most successful model yet in the FZ 750, a four-stroke four-cylinder with five valves per cylinder: a beautiful piece of engineering, available to the bike-loving public, who have given it the title of "Bike of the Year, 1985" in Italy.

From this first bike, many others have been derived which will carry Yamaha's production forward into the future.

Yamaha's greatest victories in the 500 class were achieved by the formidable American rider Kenny Roberts, who dominated the world championships for several years, winning the title in 1978, 1979 and 1980.

The very recent Yamaha DT 125 LC has a two-stroke single-cylinder engine with reed inlet valves delivering over 22 HP at 8000 rpm.

At the beginning of the eighties Yamaha updated their 250 and 350 cc two-stroke twin-cylinders, giving them new water-cooled engines. The inlet valves are reed type. The latest versions have shutter exhaust valves. The RD 350, introduced in 1984 (see photo), delivers 59 HP at 9000 rpm.

▼

The FZ 750 four-cylinder, introduced at the end of 1984, immediately attracted the notice of motorcycle enthusiasts and engineers by its progressive features and performance. The 20-valve engine is water-cooled and delivers 100 HP at 10,500 rpm.

Carlos Lavado has been the company's top racing motorcyclist in the 250 class in recent years, piloting the very fast two-stroke twin-cylinders with reed inlet valves.

This bike did and still does represent the "African myth" for many people. It is the XT 600 "Ténéré" with a giant petrol tank for long-distance races. The four-valve single-cylinder engine delivers 44 HP at 6500 rpm (bore and stroke 95 x 84 mm). Dry-sump lubrication.

SPAIN

Although Spain appeared on the international motorcycling scene relatively late, she did so with products which – obviously after an initial development period – proved themselves thoroughly up to date, managing to win a number of world speed and later, trials championships. Spain has never had any big motorcycle companies or produced high-powered bikes, but her racing divisions have often developed highly progressive vehicles capable of beating the best foreign competition. Spaniards seem to have an innate love of motorcycling and some very great champions have been Spanish – men who have done a lot for international motorcycling. As far as mass production is concerned the Spanish companies have been manufacturing very good bikes for a long time now, in the off-road sector as well. People are enormously interested in the subject and Spain will continue to provide the world with very great riders in the future.

ANGEL NIETO

DERBI

This company from Barcelona was established in 1951, mainly producing small vehicles such as mopeds and scooters, its largest models being lightweight road bikes of 125–1275 cc, all with two-stroke engines. Derbi's mass production programme has been brilliantly supported by participation in world speed contests, in which it has distinguished itself as the most "decorated" Spanish make (winning nine titles in the 50 and 125 classes). Thanks to its production of low-powered utilitarian models (for which it had installed modern equipment) it survived the difficult post-Franco era well and is now the only "healthy" independent Spanish industry.

BULTACO

Francisco Bultò, known as Paco, left Montesa (of which he was technical director) in 1958 to found Bultaco in Barcelona. This new brand soon became a leader of the Spanish industry. All its

models were two-stroke, and its trials and motocross bikes in displacements from 100 to 350 cc were outstanding. Particular credit is due to the company for having been the first to manufacture very lightweight trials bikes (from 1964) which won two world titles after the world championships for this category were introduced in 1975. It also did well in speed events, winning eight world titles in the 50 and 125 classes.

The financial crisis and industrial disputes of the post-Franco period toward the end of the seventies placed Bultaco in grave difficulties, and despite repeated attempts at recovery the company was forced to stop production in 1982.

MONTESA

This is the oldest Spanish company, founded at Barcelona in 1945. Its first products were 125 cc two-stroke lightweight road bikes, and it was the first Spanish company to compete in the world speed championships for this displacement. It subsequently followed the national trend, producing 125 to 350 cc motocross and trials models, all with two-stroke engines. It distinguished itself in trials, winning four world championships

between 1975 and 1980.

Thanks to an agreement with the Japanese company Honda (which needed a local partner to break into the Spanish market), Montesa survived the stalemate of the late seventies and early eighties and has managed to keep up production, which is almost entirely focused on their successful two-stroke single-cylinder trials bikes, in 125, 250 and 350 cc displacements.

OSSA

Given the heavy demand for motor vehicles after World War II, in Spain as elsewhere, Ossa of Barcelona decided in 1951 to build motorbikes alongside its traditional lines of film equipment. It also specialized in two-stroke motocross and trials models, in displacements from 125 to 300 cc. However, the company did not neglect the racing sector, developing a progressive 250 with an aluminum frame. Ossa was another victim of the post-Franco period and although it managed to hold out for longer than Bultaco, it was forced to close down in 1985.

The Bultaco Metralla was popular in the sixties. This two-stroke single-cylinder sports bike had a displacement of 250 cc.

Bultaco played a leading role in trials events. This is a 1975 Sherpa, of over 300 cc displacement.

▼

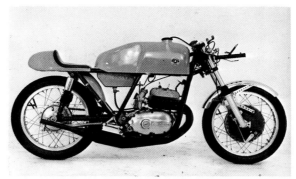

This 1966 350 SS was closely derived from production models. The engine was a two-stroke single-cylinder. Continuous duplex cradle frame.

Bultaco's best racing results were achieved by Ramon Torras ▶ in 1964–1965 (250 class).

The excellent Cota della Montesa was one of the best trials bikes of its period. This is the 1971 247 version.

Ossa was better known for its outstanding enduro and trials bikes than its road models. This is the 1968 Enduro 250.

The Ossa 250 Grand Prix model nearly won the world title in 1969. The unitized body was of sheet aluminum.

This is the 1978 Montesa Cota, with a two-stroke single-cylinder engine.

The Mick Andrews Replica of the second half of the sixties was very popular with trials riders.

This is the 1980 Ossa Trial 250. It also has an air-cooled two-stroke single-cylinder engine.

Montesa has been highly successful in the enduro field. This is the H6, with a 360 cc two-stroke single-cylinder engine.

SOVIET UNION

People tend to be a little scathing about Soviet motorcycling, especially as regards production.

In fact, while Soviet racers do manage to attract attention even in world events – although only in their favourite areas of specialization (speedway and cross-country) – their mass-produced vehicles are distinctly behind the times.

This backwardness is basically due to the fact that the various government "plans" for motorbikes insist on very simple, robust types, not just for the obvious reasons of economy and durability but also because the Soviet Union does not have a proper network of garages; therefore the easier a bike is to maintain, the better it is for all concerned. Then one must not forget the social and climatic conditions of the country and finally, the total lack of competition. In fact, the Soviet market permits the importation only of a very few Czechoslovakian or East German models which have to fit the same requirements and are not exactly modern either. However, if it is lacking on a technical level (and an aesthetic one), Soviet production makes up for this in terms of numbers to the extent that the Soviet Union is the second biggest producer in the world, after Japan. In fact, in 1985 about two million motorbikes were produced and almost as many motor bicycles (two-wheeled vehicles in circulation number well over twenty million) and the annual increase has always been big, especially after 1956. In that year, in fact, the 20th Communist Party Congress made an historic decision on motorization by establishing that "in the interests of the people and the nation, new, individual means of transport need to be built, and their production increased."

The first Russian motorbike was built in Moscow in 1908. It was called Doux and was driven by a 275 cc Swiss Moto Rêve four-stroke twin-cylinder engine. But the social conditions, climate and state of the roads did not encourage production, which on the eve of World War I in 1913 did not exceed a hundred units a year.

After the war and the Revolution, nearly ten years passed before anything more was heard of the motorbike. In 1925 came the prototype of the Soyuz (which in Russian means union), a four-stroke single-cylinder model, while in 1928 it was the turn of the Ish 1 or, to be more precise, a monumental 750 kg (1653 lb) sidecar model driven by a 1200 cc four-stroke twin-cylinder with shaft final drive.

However, these prototypes were not mass-produced because they were rightly considered to be too complex. Much simpler bikes were needed.

The first such vehicle was the L 300, the first Soviet bike to be mass-produced (1933–40) by

The Doux 275, the first motorbike built in Russia (in 1908). It was in fact little more than an assembly, the engine being a Swiss Moto Rêve while various other parts also came from abroad. Produced in Moscow, the Doux weighed 70 kg (154 lb) and had a top speed of 50 km/h (31 mph).

The engine of the Doux, the Swiss Moto Rêve, was a four-stroke twin-cylinder with side automatic inlet valves and overhead exhaust valves operated by push rods and rocker arms. The ignition magneto and pulleys for the direct drive belt are clearly visible (there were no friction gears). With a total displacement of 275 cc, it developed 2.5 HP.

both the Red October Works at Leningrad and the Ish works at Ishevsk. The L 300 was an exact copy of the 1929 German DKW E 300, just as the subsequent 1M 350 four-stroke, AM 600 four-stroke, Strela (arrow) two-stroke of 98 and then 125 cc and 750 cc M 72 four-stroke twin-cylinder with cardan shaft final drive were copies of other well-known American, British and

European bikes.

The only original Soviet design in the period between the two wars was the L 600 two-stroke twin-cylinder sidecar model with water cooling and cardanic transmission with reverse gear. Also built by the Red October Works at Leningrad (1935–40), it was used in particular by the Fire Brigade, because the engine had a water pump attachment. It weighed 650 kg (1433 lb).

However, production figures were still very low, partly because very few bikes were destined for private hands. The others were for the Army, the Post Office and youth organizations. In 1940, on the eve of World War II, production stood at just 6,800 units.

After the massive destruction of war, the process of rebuilding and reconversion to civilian production affected motorbikes too. A very important step was the establishment at Serpuchov of a central organization for the study, research and testing of motorbikes, which was also intended to reorganize and strengthen the motorcycle industry. Numerous indigenous designs were developed by this institute, including racing bikes. Unfortunately, many of them (including one for a rotary engine) had to be stopped at the experimental stage because, as already mentioned, the Soviet market cannot cope with sophisticated models. However, the institute continues to provide a valuable stimulus for the national industry.

The policy of copying models by other countries was pursued after the war too, although accompanied by a few original models. The following belong to the first category: the Ish 350 (taken from the DKW NZ); the Dnepr 650 (BMW); the Kovrovetz 175 (Jawa-CZ) and the Viatka (Piaggio Vespa). Original designs include Riga and Verkhovina, the V 150 M scooter, the Planeta and the Jupiter, both of which are two-stroke 350s by Ish, the first a single-, the second a twin-cylinder.

There are at present eight Soviet factories producing motorbikes, situated in the most heavily industrialized areas which specialize in metallurgy. To rationalize production, each factory makes just one specific model or at any rate, very similar versions. Nearly all these models are named after the town where they are built, or a river or mountain range nearby. The oldest factory still in operation is Ish, founded in 1928. All the others have been built since the war. It is hard to establish their order of importance in terms of output or turnover, given the traditional reserve of the Soviet authorities. However, the list should include KMZ of Kiev in the Ukraine (Dnepr sidecar), IMZ of Irbit (Ural sidecar), Ish of

The Ish 350 came out in 1949 and, suitably updated, is still in production (the 1967 version is shown here). It is a four-speed two-stroke single-cylinder, which in the model currently in production delivers 21 HP at 5800 rpm, with a speed of 120 km/h (75 mph); weight 160 kg (353 lb).

The Ish 350 "Jupiter 3" with a twin-cylinder engine, 1958 version.

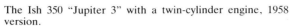

The Viatka, a copy of the Italian Vespa, built from 1956 to 1966. Two-stroke engine, displacement 150 cc, power 4.5 HP at 5000 rpm, 3-speed gears operated by left-hand twistgrip control, weight 120 kg (264 lb) and top speed 80 km/h (50 mph).

The V 150 M scooter (1979) delivers 6 HP at 5800 rpm.

The 175 cc Voshkod 3, a two-stroke four-speed single-cylinder of Czech inspiration. The version shown is from 1978. This bike is still produced in much the same form as the one shown and has a power of 10.5 HP at 5800 rpm, weight of 125 kg (275 lb) and maximum speed of 110 km/h (68 mph).

The Soviet motorbike which is best known in the West is the 650 cc Dnepr MT 10-36 sidecar model, shown here in the 1980 version with shaft drive to the sidecar wheel as well, to assist driving on rough ground. The engine, of clearly Teutonic inspiration, has opposed cylinders, overhead valves, develops 36 HP at 5200 rpm, has a 4-speed gearbox and a top speed of 105 km/h (65 mph) with a total weight of 320 kg (705 lb).

Ishevsk (Jupiter and Planeta 350), MMVZ of Minsk (M 125), Kovrovetz of Kovrov (Voshkod 175), Verkhovina of L'vov (mopeds), Riga of Riga (mopeds) and Tula of Tula (scooters). KMZ of Kiev produces 150,000 sidecar models a year and employs 9,000 workers, its twenty assembly lines covering an area of 120,000 sq. m (1,291,680 sq. ft; the entire factory covers 200,000 sq. m = 2,152,800 sq. ft). Ish has built the largest number of bikes (over five million).

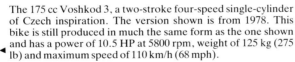

The Verkhovina Sport two-stroke in the 1978 version.

OTHER COUNTRIES

Apart from those described separately, which have proved the most important, various other countries have contributed to a greater or lesser extent to the development of motorcycling by producing models which were often highly progressive from a technical point of view or by being the birthplace of designers and racers who were to become world-famous. A few countries may even be regarded as "praiseworthy" for the incentive they gave to the motorcycling cause by the production of innovatory or at any rate extremely interesting machines. Some companies which grew to a considerable size and exported to other countries were founded and developed in small countries.

AUSTRIA

Austria is a country of mountains and forests, a perfect environment for the motorcyclist. Motorization of this country in fact began as long ago as 1899, when the new motor bicycles began to be produced. Sixty-five manufacturers have been active between then and now. Of the companies estabished in 1903 – Austria of Vienna, Cless & Plessing of Graz (both of which closed down in 1907) and Puch, also of Graz – only the latter has survived and is today the biggest motorcycle producer in Austria. In 1904 OB was founded; it built motorcycles with engines of its own make and shaft drive to the rear wheel; production ceased in 1907. In 1905 Niesner (which used Fafnir and Minerva engines), Block & Holländer (which fitted its own single-cyclinder and V-twin engines and was active until 1911) and Styria with Fafnir engines, which operated until 1908, were founded.

The next wave of motorcycle production began after World War I with more than forty companies, twenty-four of which did not make it to 1930. After World War II, only eleven companies were producing motorcycles and scooters; there are now three: Puch, KTM and Rotax.

PUCH

Puch started out producing four-stroke engines, but from the end of the twenties two-stroke, split-single-cylinder engines predominated.

Famous models were the 496 cc twin-cylinder of 1932; the 248 cc S 4 of 1933; the 792 cc four-stroke four-cylinder with side valves of 1936 and, in the period from 1952 to 1956, the 248 cc SG and SGS models. Nowadays the company produces models of between 125 and 600 cc, with Rotax engines.

The split-cylinder two-stroke engines gave

The little Puch SL 125, produced for a number of years from 1951, had a split-single-cylinder two-stroke engine, delivering 6 HP; it distinguished itself among low-powered bikes in reliability trials and was also one of the touring bikes best suited to mountain roads.

particularly good results at low rpm and thanks to these engines Puch was incredibly successful in the Six Days Trial and other important sporting events. After World War II, Puch introduced a heavy-duty pressed steel frame which was strong enough for the sidecar model as well (the famous Felber sidecars, also produced in Austria, were used). Puch is one of the few European motorcycle companies which has managed to resist invasion by the Japanese.

A typical representative of Puch road models from the sixties and seventies is this 1970 M 125 with a two-stroke single-cylinder engine.

Puch has been manufacturing excellent off-road bikes for a long time. This is the GS 175 trail bike of 1973 with a two-stroke single-cylinder engine.

ROTAX

Rotax was established at Wels during World War II as a second Fichtel & Sachs factory for the production of small two-stroke single-cylinder engines. It subsequently built scooters for Lohner of Vienna. Soon after that it became part of the Canadian Valcourt group of Quebec, building engines for motor sleds. Today, it mainly produces motorcycles and powerful 600 cc four-stroke single-cylinder ohc engines. The famous two-stroke racing engines with rotary-disc inlet valves designed by Heinz Lippitsch, and all the engines of Can-Am motorcycles, are also produced by Rotax.

KTM-80.

KTM

KTM started up in 1953. To begin with it used 93 and 123 cc Rotax engines, then engines of its own make or produced by Fichtel & Sachs (West Germany) and Puch. The company soon became famous in off-road (trail and motocross) events and achieved a good volume of exports to the United States (sometimes using the Penton trademark). Nowadays it sells mopeds and 80 cc models as well as enduro bikes from 125 to 600 cc, some of which have Rotax engines.

The 1972 KTM GS 175 had an original engine (like all its successors). In this case, it was a two-stroke single-cylinder.

SWITZERLAND

CONDOR

In 1901 Condor appeared on the market, its motorcycles being fitted at first with MAG engines, then later with Villiers two-stroke engines. Condor became famous above all for its 680 cc twin-cylinder boxer model with shaft final drive, which went into production after 1945. This model – as well as a subsequent 250 cc single-cylinder machine with push rod valve gear and shaft final drive – was produced for the Swiss Army. Condor also developed another four-stroke single-cylinder model for the Army, with an Italian Ducati engine and overhead camshaft. Condor is the only Swiss motorcycle company still in existence, although its production is now confined to bicycles and mopeds.

The Motosacoche racing bike was produced from 1920 to 1926. It had a 1000 cc four-stroke single-cylinder (MAG) engine delivering about 20 HP. The maximum speed was 135 km/h (84 mph). It had a Sturmey Archer 3-speed gearbox.

EGLI

In 1975 Fritz Egli became famous as a builder of motorcycle frames to which British, Italian and Japanese engines were fitted. He also builds special racing machines and works with a team of famous riders.

MOTOSACOCHE

Switzerland has had twenty motorcycle manufacturing companies, starting in 1899, the year in which Motosacoche was founded. Henri and Armand Dufaux started out producing small engines for bicycles, but devoted themselves almost immediately to the production of motorcycles and engines of 250 cc to 1000 cc, under the MAG trademark. MAG engines were soon used by motorcycle manufacturers throughout Europe, including Britain; the company, whose head office was in Geneva, became the biggest engine producer in Europe. Most of its motorcycles and engines were for export. They were excellent products, and people still talk about them today. Notable examples were the 496 cc model with an overhead valve V-twin engine, of 1926; the 1000 cc ohv V-twin of the same year; the 498 cc ohv single-cylinder of 1929 and the 850 cc twin-cylinder side-valve model of 1932.

The two world wars did not disrupt Switzerland as they did other countries, and production continued unabated. The name MAG was famous throughout the industry and its quality was compared to that of Swiss watches. MAG also had factories in other countries. Engineers Dougal Marchant and Bert Le Vack were in charge of the company until 1930. A four-stroke single-cylinder engine was designed after 1945 and in 1953 a 250 cc four-stroke overhead camshaft twin-cylinder appeared, designed by the German Richard Küchen. This engine was not successful and in 1957 Motosacoche MAG stopped producing motorcycles.

This 1955 Condor 598 cc was a special military motorbike. The engine was a four-stroke twin-cylinder boxer with a side-valve timing system. It had shaft final drive.

UNIVERSAL

One Swiss company which played an important part in motorcycle production was Universal. It started up in 1928, fitting 170 cc Belgian PA engines to Helvetia motorbikes. It subsequently used Jap, Anzani, Jlo and other engines until 1936, when it started producing 680 and 1000 cc V-twins for the Swiss Army. After World War II Universal used 600 cc twin-cylinder boxer engines with side or overhead valves and shaft drive, like BMW. Before it closed down in 1964, the company's production programme also included four-stroke single-cylinder engines with push rod valve gear.

ZEHNDER

Zehnder also appeared on the scene in the twenties (1923), immediately becoming famous. It used its own, very interesting 110 and 250 cc two-stroke engines for its motorcycles. In 1928 Zehnder was taken over by the German company Standard and it closed down in 1939.

CZECHOSLOVAKIA

The 1955 Universal 578 cc had a four-stroke twin-cylinder boxer engine, shaft final drive and a power of about 25 HP.

BÖHMERLAND

Böhmerland was active from 1924 to 1939. Of the relatively few models built by this company the most unusual was undoubtedly the Tourster, with a very long, rigid frame made up of thick tubes, spoked wheels of light alloy (a real novelty) and three seats, one behind the other. The petrol was contained in two cylinders, one on either side of the rear wheel, and there were two cases at the rear. It had a 600 cc single-cylinder engine with push rod valve gear and two gearboxes, one behind the other, giving a total of nine gear ratios controlled by two separate levers, operated by the rider and one of the passengers. It was nicknamed "the bike for eight" and could do 120 km/h (75 mph). It was sold under the name Böhmerland (Bohemia) in German-speaking regions and under the Czechie trademark in Slovakia.

CZ

CZ was founded at Strakonice in 1930. For the first few years they built mopeds and light motorbikes with 76 to 175 cc two-stroke engines. Then, in 1936, production was extended to include a 250 cc model and shortly before the war a handsome 500 cc two-stroke twin-cylinder with four gear ratios and a rigid plate frame, inspired by Zündapp, was launched. A few scooter prototypes were developed during the war, but never went into production. After the war CZ was nationalized and became part of the Jawa group. However, it retained some degree of independence in design and prepared various 125 to 150 cc lightweight models and a 175 cc scooter. CZ now makes 125 and 175 cc models, also with two-stroke single-cylinder engines.

◄ Böhmerland bikes were uncommonly long. The engine was a 600 cc four-stroke single-cylinder. The frame was of tubular steel and the wheels of cast aluminum alloy.

191

This 1971 175 cc CZ was a trail bike with an air-cooled two-stroke single-cylinder engine.

The 1970 Jawa California 350 was a road model with a two-stroke twin-cylinder engine.

For many years Jawa produced excellent off-road bikes like this 1970 350 single-cylinder.

JAWA

Around 1930 motorcycling was all the rage in Czechoslovakia; there were about thirty national brands and nearly three hundred foreign companies. Many companies built machines under license too, including a big arms manufacturer called Janeček, licensed to produce German Wanderer engines. From this union (and their two names) a new motorbike – the Jawa – was born in 1929.

The first model was a 500 cc machine with push rod valve gear, shaft drive, a plate-type duplex cradle frame and leaf-spring fork. It was not very popular because it was too expensive. The 175 cc of 1932, also with a plate metal frame but with a two-stroke engine built under license from the British company Villiers, was more successful; as was the Robot, with a 98 cc engine.

Until the outbreak of war Jawa's industry, which was becoming increasingly successful, was equally divided between two-stroke engines of small and medium displacement and four-stroke ones of higher displacement; the 350 cc four-stroke of 1933 with electric start and the 1935 500 cc supercharged twin-cylinder racing model were outstanding.

Apart from a brief experiment with a handsome 500 cc single-cylinder model with a double camshaft, Jawa's postwar production concentrated on two-stroke engines. In 1946 the company brought out a 250 cc with a telescopic fork, telescopic rear suspension and very elegant lines, which placed it at the forefront of world production. This was joined a couple of years later by a 350 cc twin-cylinder with the same general lines, and the company's production has been based on these two models – constantly updated and improved – ever since. Today, Jawa bikes are no longer progressive in technology and per-

The most popular Jawa road bike has for many years been the 350 cc model with a two-stroke twin-cylinder engine. This is the 1974 version.

formance, but they still constitute an excellent example – perhaps the only one now – of a simple, sturdy and reliable motorbike.

LAURIN & KLEMENT

In 1895 at Mladá Boleslav, a small town in Bohemia which was then part of the Austro-Hungarian Empire, the engineer Vaclav Laurin and bookseller Vaclav Klement decided to form a partnership and build bicycles, under the Slavia trademark. In 1898 they progressed to motorcycles, which were also sold under the Slavia trademark to begin with, the initials L & K being adopted a couple of years later. Unlike other

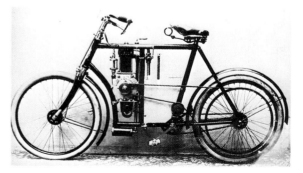

This is the 1900 Laurin & Klement, with a single-cylinder engine and side valves.

◄ The Jawa 350 is much used in Eastern bloc countries, for towing sidecars.

companies at the time, Laurin and Klement did not fit an engine to a bicycle frame; they did the opposite, designing the frame around the engine, to suit its requirements. People in Czechoslovakia thus claim that the L & K was the first true motorcycle in the world, and there is some justification for this.

Be that as it may, the L & K bikes worked extremely well and were soon very popular, a number of victories in sporting events contributing to their success. In 1911, for example, 300 machines a year were being produced and customers included the post offices of the United States and Mexico, which used them for urgent deliveries such as express letters.

The first model had a vertical single-cylinder engine of about 350 cc with an automatic inlet valve, a carburetor and ignition by an oscillating contact breaker built directly by the company, plus belt direct drive. In 1904 a V-twin was built which could do 85 km/h (53 mph), while in 1905 the company even produced a model with four cylinders in line, a clutch and chain drive.

In 1906 Laurin & Klement produced its first small car, after which cars were its main activity until it was taken over by the Skoda automobile company in 1925, and motorcycle construction was finally abandoned altogether.

DENMARK

NIMBUS

Throughout its career, from 1920 to 1957, this firm in Copenhagen devoted itself to a single model, but it was no ordinary model. It was in fact a 750 cc (later reduced to 500 cc) machine with four cylinders in line fitted longitudinally, an engine block like that of a car and shaft final drive. A most unusual vehicle even given the huge variety of motorcycles worldwide, and highly reliable, so that it was quite popular abroad too. Toward the end of the fifties it badly needed updating, but the manufacturers did not consider this worthwhile, preferring to stop production. Denmark thus lost her only motorcycle company.

SWEDEN

HUSQVARNA

This is one of the oldest companies, founded in 1903. It is named after the Swedish town where the head office is. It started production using engines of other brands like FN, Moto Rêve, etc. but became fully independent after World War I and distinguished itself for its high-technology road and racing bikes, especially the brilliant 550, 750 and 1000 cc V-twins. After World War II it was one of the first to specialize in motocross bikes, producing both 500 cc four-stroke (winners of five world titles) and 250 cc two-stroke (winners of four world titles) models. Despite stiff competition from abroad – above all by the Japanese – it has managed to remain on the crest

Detail of the four-cylinder engine of a 1928 Nimbus. The four cylinders were fitted longitudinally, in line, with opposed valves. Displacement 746 cc. Shaft final drive.

In the first half of the thirties, Husqvarna produced a racing bike driven by this beautiful 500 cc twin-cylinder engine. Push rod valve gear was used; the later versions delivered about 44 HP at 6700 rpm.

This is the 1978 Husqvarna MP 250, with a two-stroke single-cylinder engine and four-speed automatic transmission.

of the wave, still very much preferring the motocross sector, for which it produces bikes of all displacements and even boasts two "half-liter" models, one two-stroke and one four-stroke. At the beginning of 1986 it was acquired by the Italian company Cagiva, which is also keenly interested in the motocross sector, but for the time being production of its excellent machines continues unchanged.

The 1974 Husqvarna WR 250 had an air-cooled two-stroke single-cylinder engine.

BELGIUM

Belgium is a country which has always been keenly interested in motorcycling.

At the end of the last century, the Minerva auxiliary motor appeared. Designed to be fitted to bicycles, it soon became popular, large numbers being sold to many European countries. The company then went on to build complete motorbikes, but without managing to repeat the success of its "loose" engines.

Saroléa started up in 1898 and became famous throughout Europe, especially in the twenties, thanks to its excellent 350 and 500 cc single-cylinder sports and racing models with push rod valve gear. Its range of products in the years

leading up to World War II included a series of two-stroke single-cylinder machines (from 125 to 175 cc) and four-strokes, the most powerful of which was a 600 cc single-cylinder. After the war Saroléa merged with FN and built various models with two-stroke engines for displacements below 250 cc and with four-stroke engines for displacements above that. FN was one of the most important companies in the world for a long time and, like Saroléa, its head office was at Herstal. Already famous as a weapons manufacturer, FN decided to create a motorcycle division in 1901. Its first engines were 225 and 286 cc single-cylinders which were soon joined (in 1904) by 500 and 750 cc four-cylinder models. The motorbikes were air-cooled and had shaft drive, a system the company retained until 1923.

From 1924, when chain final drive was adopted, the company concentrated on models with 350 and 500 cc single-cylinder engines (both with side valves and push rod valve gear) and unit construction gearboxes. The most significant models included, before World War II, a 600 cc single-cylinder and a 1000 cc four-cylinder boxer produced for the Army, and after the war motorcycles with two-stroke engines up to 250 cc and with four-stroke engines in higher displacements. Their 500 cc single-cylinder machines were highly successful in motocross events in the fifties. FN stopped producing motorcycles in 1957.

Gillet was founded in 1919 and became particularly well known in the twenties for its two-stroke rotary-valve engines. Before World War II this company produced an interesting range of models with 350 and 500 cc four-stroke single-cylinder engines of its own design and a 1000 cc model with a MAG twin-cylinder engine. After the war Gillet built motorcycles with two-stroke engines in displacements from 100 to 250 cc, before closing down at the beginning of the sixties.

The FN 243 cc, produced in 1909, had a four-stroke single-cylinder engine and shaft final drive.

The FN 500 cc was unusual in having sprung handlebars. It was powered by a four-stroke single-cylinder engine with side valves and had a unit construction gearbox.

The engine of this 1938 Saroléa Supersport Type B was a 350 cc four-stroke single-cylinder with push rod valve gear, which delivered 14 HP. Four-speed gearbox.

INDEX

197

Picture Sources

The letters next to the page references indicate the position of the illustration on the page:
a = above; b = below; l = left; r = right; c = center.

Agrati: 116, 117, 119, 120

BMW: 160, 161

ERVIN: 166

Foto Rogge Archives: 138, 139b, 160al, 162cl, 162bl, 162bc, 162br, 164bl, 164br, 165a, 165cr, 171ar, 171al, 171bl, 188, 190, 191a, 194

Honda: 175

Kawasaki: 176, 177bc, 178a

Perelli: 123a, 124al, 126l, 128b, 129a, 130cb, 132c, 134b, 136b, 140, 141, 142, 143, 144, 145, 146a, 147a, 148al, 149, 150, 151, 152, 153, 154, 155, 156, 157, 159, 163, 164a, 167, 168, 169, 170, 171br, 173, 174, 177a, 179, 181, 185, 186, 189, 191b, 192, 193, 194l

Patrignani: 146b, 147b, 148br, 152l, 162cr, 165cl, 185ac, 185ar

Suzuki: 179b, 180

Willoughby: 123cr, 124r, 125, 126r, 127, 128a 129cb, 130a, 131, 132ab, 133, 134ac, 137, 139a

Yamaha: 182, 183